A COUNTRY OF CITIES

For my parents,

Who came from humble villages
And immersed me in the world's cities.

May they find peace on this, their final voyage.

You may ask yourself, what is that beautiful house?
You may ask yourself, where does that highway go to?
You may ask yourself, am I right, am I wrong?
You may say to yourself, my god, what have I done?

"ONCE IN A LIFETIME," TALKING HEADS

A COUNTRY OF CITIES: A MANIFESTO FOR AN URBAN AMERICA

VISHAAN CHAKRABARTI

Foreword by Norman Foster
Illustrations by SHoP Architects

Metropolis Books

CONTENTS

FOREWORD
Norman Foster

I am in Manhattan. I'm sitting in my eighth-floor apartment, drawing and looking out across Central Park. The phone rings—it's Vishaan. "I have something I want to show you," he says. "Let's have a coffee." Fifteen minutes later I take the elevator and then walk a couple of blocks to Madison Avenue. We're meeting at Sant Ambroeus—a neighborhood café and a perfect place to get together with friends. Vishaan is waiting for me. He's walked his son to school and taken the subway up from Union Square, where he lives. We order and Vishaan hands me a draft copy of this book. He asks if I will contribute a foreword. I know of his great commitment to the subject as an academic, with a body of work in the public realm as well as private practice, and so of course I immediately agree.

Now imagine if that scene had been played out in Detroit or Los Angeles, or any other sprawling American metropolis. We would both have jumped in our cars and headed for the freeway. One of us would doubtless have gotten stuck in traffic. Instead of fifteen minutes, it would have taken us an hour, with all the attendant frustrations.

One of the beauties of Manhattan is that it is a compact, dense, walkable city. It has thriving neighborhoods with a strong sense of community; it mixes living and working and has a messy vitality; it has an incredible park, as well as other smaller green spaces, and an extraordinary range of cultural and civic amenities close at hand; it has an excellent public transportation system; car ownership is very low; and it is natural to walk or take the subway, which is faster than driving.

It sounds attractive, doesn't it? So why are all cities not like that? The fact is that before the age of the automobile, most cities followed that pattern—the polar opposite of the relatively new car-dependent, zoned, and suburban metropolis one finds across much of the world today. Of course, we cannot turn back the clock, but we can set out development strategies to ensure that existing cities adapt to become more sustainable; and we can propose new urban models for the future, which learn from the best of the past. It has been said that if you wish to look far into the future, then you should first look far back in time.

Across the globe, an increasing proportion of the population is becoming urbanized. Currently, more than half of the world's population lives in towns and cities. By 2030, that proportion will have risen to two thirds. One result of this global population shift is the growth of megacities of unprecedented size. Significantly, the top six are all on the Pacific Rim, which the World Bank predicts will be the fastest-growing region in the world over the next five years. Look at that list of megacities and the immediate reaction is to note its diversity. Study it more closely, however, and you discover that cities around the world have common problems and can learn from one another.

We know that cities that sprawl are wasteful in terms of energy, land, and other resources. To put this into perspective, in industrialized societies, buildings and the transport of people and goods between them account for 70 percent of the total energy expended. Naturally, if you increase urban densities, one result will be shorter journeys, with fuel savings and carbon reductions. Compare Manhattan with Detroit and you find that the average Manhattan resident uses less than one fifth the amount of gasoline consumed by a Detroit citizen and a third of the electricity, even though the two cities have comparable climates. Other benefits also follow. For instance, recent data from the U.S. suggests that economic growth and job creation are stronger in city centers and poverty is rising faster in the suburbs. There is also a link between climbing gasoline prices and foreclosure rates in suburban communities.

Critics may denigrate such advocacy with the myth that higher urban densities lead to something poorer—literally and also in terms of quality of life. Examine the evidence, however, and you find the opposite is true. Macau and Monaco, for example, are among the densest communities on earth, yet their roots lie at opposite ends of the economic spectrum. Medium-density European cities such as Berlin, Copenhagen, and London typically offer a desirable lifestyle with higher property values. In most cases, proximity to a park or garden square is a major factor. Mayfair and Belgravia in London, for instance, pair with Hyde Park, just as the Upper East and West Sides of Manhattan relate to Central Park. The same applies in less affluent parts of cities. For me, the most desirable parts of Brooklyn, in New York, are on the borders of Prospect Park; and it is interesting to note that in the recent competition for a cultural district in West Kowloon, the people of Hong Kong voted for the solution that featured a new waterfront park.

Sustainability requires us to think holistically, and this is as true of a city's infrastructure—the "urban glue" that holds the city together—as it is of its architecture. I would go further and argue that the quality of a city's infrastructure impacts the quality of life more directly than does the quality of its individual buildings. Asian cities have been at the forefront in renewing their transportation infrastructure. Hong Kong, for instance, decided in the 1960s to invest in a mass-transit railway system. Today, that network is so comprehensive that it accounts for the majority of journeys—more than four million trips every weekday. Departure for the airport begins in the city center, when you board a luxurious train—the equivalent of the first-class cabin in a wide-body jet.

It is self-evident that if we are to create sustainable urban communities— not just in America, but across the globe—we have to take a number of essential steps. We have to build to higher densities in order to conserve land and reduce energy use; we must create neighborhoods that combine work-places with housing, and where transport connections, schools, parks, and other amenities are all within walking or cycling distance. Most important, we have to create inspirational urban environments where people want to live.

The contribution that design can make in this regard is profound and far-reaching. My own experience of numerous cities across six continents bears this out. But architects and planners can only ever be advocates. That is why *A Country of Cities* should be essential reading—not just for members of the many related professions engaged in urban design, but also for those in local and central government departments who shape planning policies and the politicians who enact them. Many of the environmental problems we face today are exacerbated by inappropriate policy decisions that were made in the past, often rooted in a lack of knowledge. Let us learn from those misjudgments and, with greater hindsight, pursue sustainable urban strategies for the future. With this book, Vishaan Chakrabarti shows us the way forward.

ACKNOWLEDGMENTS

All acknowledgments for this effort are eclipsed by the gratitude I have for my beloved wife, Maria Alataris, who through her support and encouragement gave me the confidence to believe I could write this book. Our son, Evan, ten, and our daughter, Avia, a young four, have stood by with grace (well, most of the time) as I missed this event or that game in order to juggle the demands of Columbia, SHoP, and the voracious appetite of this project, and for them I can only wish that they gain in the trade-off an appreciation for the analog virtues of books and cities in their increasingly digital worlds. And, finally, on the family front, I must thank their Energizer Bunny of a grandmother, Anna Alataris, who stayed with us through most of the summer of 2012 in large measure to give me the space to write.

Our family has now been extended to include my invaluable research associate, apprentice, and sidekick, Omar Toro-Vaca. A former student turned colleague, Omar has doggedly scrutinized every page of this book with me, confirming the verity of its passages and graphics, and has lifted my spirits with a laugh or a new brand of tequila whenever the gravity of the subject matter ensnared me. It is rare to encounter in someone so young such emotional intelligence, keen judgment, broad sense of social justice, and wide-ranging professional capability. When Omar is our mayor, governor, or senator, I hope he has the occasional moment for his old professor.

Working alongside Omar has been one of our employees at SHoP and also a former student, the immensely talented and prolific Ryan Lovett. Ryan tirelessly devoted himself to the graphic content of this volume, but instilled within each diagram much more than illustrative power. With strong analytical abilities to match his visual skills, Ryan has brought clarity to complex issues ranging from economics to environment and transportation to taxes. Beyond the data, however, readers will encounter images that verge on art. A poignant example of today's emerging hybrid professional, Ryan is a Swiss Army knife of the highest caliber. Similarly, the early stages of the book research would not have been possible without the efforts of Eli Ackerman, a former student whose fierce political convictions will serve him and all of us well.

To Norman Foster, one of the greatest living architects in the world, I owe a tremendous debt for contributing the foreword to this volume.

For over a decade, Norman has been a gracious friend, mentor, and role model in his tireless pursuit of design excellence and his abiding dedication to the global city and its sustainability. Through the lens of his work worldwide, I can contemplate no better figure to advise this nation as it seeks to urbanize.

None of our team's efforts would have been possible without the generous support of my fabulous partners at SHoP Architects: Gregg Pasquarelli, Kim Holden, Jon Mallie, and Bill, Chris, and Corie Sharples. From the outset, they did not flinch about embracing this book and its content, and without question both SHoP's architecture and analytical diagrams have served as tremendous personal inspiration. Ours is a firm dedicated not only to cities but also to the transformation of suburban typologies to urban form, and as such *A Country of Cities* adheres remarkably well to our core philosophy of urban practice whether we are designing an arena, a museum, a waterfront, a master plan, an office tower, or high-density affordable housing.

Similarly, my colleagues at Columbia University have been highly supportive, starting with the dean of the Graduate School of Architecture, Planning and Preservation (GSAPP), Mark Wigley, who first advised me to approach this project as a manifesto. In addition to Mark's continuous support, many GSAPP faculty have influenced my thinking through their work and camaraderie, particularly Gwendolyn Wright, Laurie Hawkinson, Galia Solomonoff, Michael Bell, and Reinhold Martin. Finally, my team at Columbia has been loyal through the chaos of it all, for which I thank Jessica Stockton, Jesse Keenan, Emily Griffen, and the indefatigable Linda LaBella.

I began *A Country of Cities* as a blog for the Architectural League of New York's groundbreaking website, Urban Omnibus. For this initial chance and inspiration, I must thank the League's executive director, Rosalie Genevro, Omnibus editor Cassim Shepard, and managing editor Varick Shute, as well as the many readers who commented, argued, disagreed, and spurred me on. Cassim in particular pushed me to write more, and for this I am in his debt. It is through his urging, and a well-timed introduction from Pamela Puchalski, that I met my publisher and friend, Diana Murphy of Metropolis Books. Few publishers could do justice to a project so simultaneously driven by text and graphics, but Diana and her colleagues took the leap fearlessly. Diana and I felt it obvious that the only person with whom we could entrust the look and feel of this book was the great Michael Bierut of Pentagram, with whom we both had collaborated in the past. I am grateful as well to Michael's very able team member Britt Cobb.

The work of these and many other colleagues made this book what it is, but few friends had a greater impact than architect, writer, and historian James Sanders, who after reviewing my initial outline suggested revisions to reflect more of my own thoughts and experiences. Genie Birch at the University of Pennsylvania; David M. Childs of Skidmore, Owings & Merrill; Gene Kohn of Kohn Pedersen Fox; Arthur Cohen of LaPlaca Cohen; my friend Tom Campanella at the University of North Carolina at Chapel Hill; and Risa Heller of Risa Heller Communications have all been wise and encouraging. There are too many past professors to thank as inspirations, but Gary Hack, Roy Strickland, and the late Lois Craig from my studies at MIT, as well as Stanley Saitowitz, Tom Chastain, and Kathleen James-Chakraborty from my time at the University of California at Berkeley, all stand out as intellectual friends, design instructors, and mentors. From Kevin Lynch to Allan Jacobs, I owe so much to the urban legends of both institutions, and can only hope this book in its small way pays homage to their enormous legacy.

I must also acknowledge the seemingly forgotten states of Alaska and Hawaii, which certainly factor into my vision for a more urban America. They have often been excluded from the diagrams in this book because of formatting limitations, but their people and cities were in my thoughts.

In closing, I must express my appreciation to Dan Doctoroff, former New York City deputy mayor, and Amanda Burden, chair of the New York City Planning Commission, under whom I learned so much about effective city building. My grandfather advised that I always play chess with players better than myself, and on the vast chessboard of New York City, none could be better teachers than the formidable pair of Dan and Amanda.

CAN WE UNITE?

A COUNTRY OF COUNTRIES: OF HIGHWAYS, HOUSES, AND HEDGES

The United States today is a country divided, a country of countries. Gridlocked by bitter partisanship, economic decline, environmental degradation, and growing social inequity, our nation is stuck in traffic with little visible in the rearview mirror or on the road ahead. When we ask how did we get here, or how do we move forward, do we consider the subway not taken? When we ask how we lift ourselves up, do we consider the elevator not used? While the same tired debates define our political rhetoric, do we consider whether our profligate use of land is the primary culprit behind our vexing national malaise?

As I illustrate throughout these pages, our reckless subsidization of suburban sprawl is arguably the leading cause of our most pressing challenges, from foreclosures, to unemployment, to unfunded schools, to spiraling health-care costs, to climate change, to oil wars. Yet this overarching issue never surfaces in the national discourse. In election after election, our presidential candidates rarely utter the words "city" or "suburb" in their speeches, as if the way in which Americans live is irrelevant to the state of the nation.

For politicians of any stripe, questioning the American lifestyle and the taxpayer dollars that underwrite it would represent unthinkable risk and would likely require expertise well outside of their grasp. Most elected officials originate from the legal profession and rarely consider questions of *where* Americans work and live as topics worthy of debate.[1] Despite all the changes politicians promise, reforming our sprawling, gluttonous lifestyle is never among them. To the contrary, the policies advanced by both parties continue to fuel a country of highways, houses, and hedges.

LOW VOTER TURNOUT

In 2012, only 4 in 10 people living in America voted in the presidential election.
Those who did were split almost evenly along Democratic and Republican party lines.

RAMPANT LAND CONSUMPTION

Land development has quadrupled since 1945, increasing at about twice the rate of population growth.

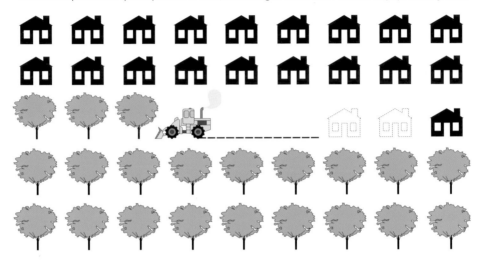

AMERICANS ARE UNDER WATER

Nearly 11 million Americans hold mortgages with outstanding balances that are greater than
the value of their homes.

A Country of Cities contemplates a renewed nation, a country of trains, towers, and trees. By removing the legal, economic, and moralizing incentives for sprawl—most of which are rooted in misguided and outdated public policy—we can realize a more prosperous, more sustainable, and more equitable nation. Throughout this text, I unapologetically advocate for this alternate path and reach the unavoidable, data-driven conclusion that cities, once put on a level playing field with suburbs in terms of federal, state, and municipal government policy, would be the silver bullet for many of the ills confronting our nation and planet.

A Country of Cities is not a survey of urban design and planning initiatives intended to further the agenda of like-minded urbanites. In it, I hope to expose the larger social and political forces that are holding the country's progress hostage regardless of ideological allegiances, and with particular concern for mounting evidence regarding the declining competitiveness of America's socioeconomic structure.[2] Rather than debating the existence of challenges such as stagnating wages, increasing inequity, failing public health, or a deteriorating environment, I instead assume that such problems have infected the very structure of the nation and propose a measured and proven structural cure: cities.

For the sake of clarity, I define a "city" as a place that can provide significant ridership for rapid mass transit such as a subway network, which typically requires a density range above 30 housing units per acre.[3] Such concentrations of population can be found across the United States, from St. Louis to Chicago, to Seattle, to Miami. This definition is not intended to belittle places of lesser density; it simply asserts that while villages, towns, and suburbs may exhibit some of the same valuable characteristics as much denser environments, they cannot be scaled to accommodate the millions that big cities with metros can so effectively house. Ironically, some might call a transit-based definition of a city elitist, but it is confounding and somewhat comical to think that subways as an organizing force for human habitation could be construed as elitist in a nation dominated by Escalades and Yukons.

In the pages that follow, I use the terms "city" and "hyperdensity" interchangeably to indicate densities greater than or equal to 30 housing units per acre. This transit-based criterion is critical for differentiating our big and real cities from the kind of easy urbanism being perpetrated by so much of the architecture and planning professions today. Such efforts may create slightly more compact places served by an expensive and barely used trolley, but where most residents still have to drive to get a quart of milk, and often do so in a light truck disguised as a car. This distinction between promoting truly transit-based hyperdensity versus density of any

One acre of land is 90% of a typical football field.

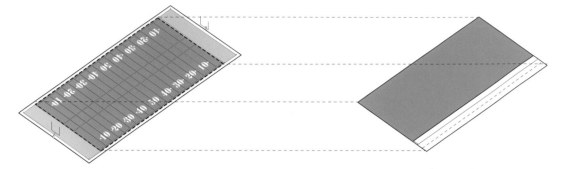

DENSITY CAN TAKE MANY FORMS WITH VARYING QUALITIES

30 DWELLING UNITS PER ACRE AS LOW-RISE APARTMENTS

Horizontality has a limited ability to accommodate open-space uses on the ground plane.

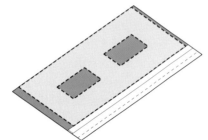

30 DWELLING UNITS PER ACRE AS MID-RISE APARTMENTS

Verticality allows for greater open-space uses on the ground plane.

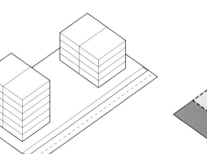

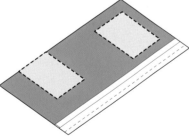

30 DWELLING UNITS PER ACRE AS HIGH-RISE APARTMENTS

More height allows for the maximization of open-space uses on the ground plane and the vertical intensification of amenities in the tower.

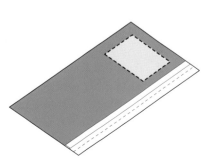

sort is an essential distinguishing factor between this book and the abundance of "urbanist" literature available today.

Most so-called urbanists, out of fear of backlash, conservative myopia, or both, tend to ignore big cities for more politically palatable and less socially diverse microfantasies of "new," "walkable," "regional," or "retrofitted" urbanism. In such microfantasies, the strengths of small-town America—which does share some of the strengths of big-city America in terms of density, community, sustainability, and walkability—are romantically grafted onto the car-dependent landscape of the American suburb, a romance that attempts to force the suburbs into a "both-and" condition with small towns, to borrow the terminology of architect Robert Venturi. Yet, on closer inspection, such grafting actually creates a "neither-nor" condition, a tormented love child of small-town and big-city America that is neither walkable nor drivable, more mutant than hybrid, more bastard than breakthrough.

The crisis of our profligate land use cannot be answered by the fashionable callings of most urban planners and scholars today, be they the stylistic neo-conservative ponderings of new urbanism, the overemphasis on community control at all costs, or even the admirable but trendy wonders of bicycles, electric cars, and locavorism. Rather, we must understand this as a national density crisis resolvable only through holistic policy reforms, many of which are suggested in the latter half of this volume.

Instead of attempting to retool failing suburbs, and while remaining respectful of small towns across this great nation, I focus throughout this text almost entirely on the economic and environmental engines of this country that hide in plain sight: our big cities, be they Charlotte, Houston, Portland, Atlanta, Chicago, Nashville, Los Angeles, or New York. Our society is in a crisis in terms of the economy, the environment, and income inequity: this is no time for making small plans, adjusting life at the margins, or retro-fitting failure. Our national landscape is broken and must be fixed using all the tools of the Swiss Army knife, not just the tweezers.

It is important to note that my assertions stand on the shoulders of many, particularly those outside of the urbanism professions. A host of scholars from different points along the political spectrum, including economists, environmentalists, and public-health experts, have made a variety of findings supporting the central premise that American cities offer a cure for many of our most urgent problems. One of the primary goals of *A Country of Cities*, however, is to integrate these findings from various disciplines into a comprehensive and approachable argument for the advantages of urban living writ large, an argument that equally challenges both the left and the right wing of our political system to consider, embrace, and promote market-driven urban growth in the United States.

While the sa
debates def
political rhe
consider wh
profligate us
is the primar
behind our v
national mal

me tired
ne our
toric, do we
ether our
se of land
y culprit
exing
aise?

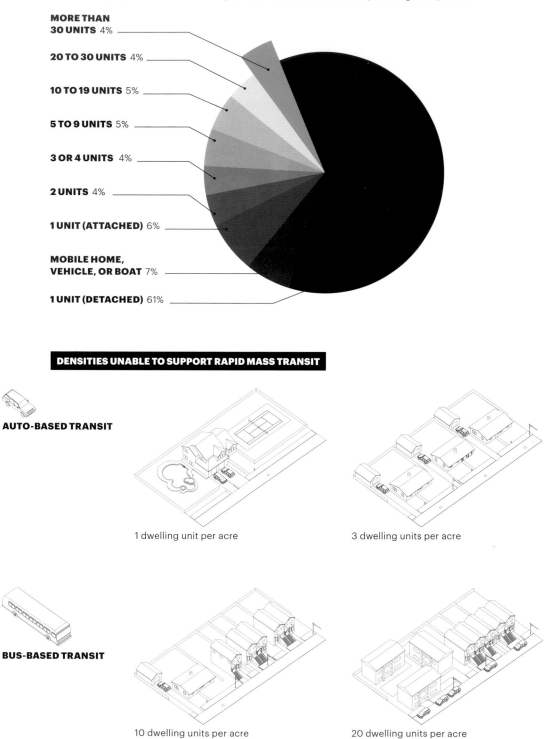

AT WHAT DENSITIES DO AMERICANS LIVE?

The vast majority of Americans are living in very low densities, defined by dwelling units per acre.

**MORE THAN
30 UNITS** 4%

20 TO 30 UNITS 4%

10 TO 19 UNITS 5%

5 TO 9 UNITS 5%

3 OR 4 UNITS 4%

2 UNITS 4%

1 UNIT (ATTACHED) 6%

**MOBILE HOME,
VEHICLE, OR BOAT** 7%

1 UNIT (DETACHED) 61%

DENSITIES UNABLE TO SUPPORT RAPID MASS TRANSIT

AUTO-BASED TRANSIT

1 dwelling unit per acre

3 dwelling units per acre

BUS-BASED TRANSIT

10 dwelling units per acre

20 dwelling units per acre

Free choice is a critical foundation of our society. For this reason, *A Country of Cities* contemplates a nation in which most Americans would *choose* to live in density above 30 units per acre—not due to sanctimony or regulations, but due to the better quality of life people would experience at these densities, a condition that we will explore in detail in the forthcoming pages. This hyperdensification of the already developed areas of the United States would, in turn, trigger the increased land values needed to help fund the transit, school, and other improvements that such density would necessitate. Certainly, many Americans would choose to live in small, rural towns away from big cities in such a model. However, exurbs on the outskirts of cities reachable only by highways would gradually atrophy due to the removal of the incentives that sustain them. Suburbs connected to large cities by regional rail would become much denser around their train stations, creating a wider regional urban boundary that would represent a new form of a transit-based, multi-centered American city similar to contemporary London. Single-family homes would continue to exist in this framework, but without subsidization, most people would instead gravitate toward cities.

Hyperdensification is an approach that, if used ambitiously, could serve as the catalyst for a new era of progressive and prosperous stewardship, not only for our nation but also for economies that are transforming worldwide and looking to the United States for leadership. Just as the gated communities of growing cities worldwide echo our own suburban enclaves, a hyperdense America could provide an economically and environmentally sustainable model for a rapidly developing world to embrace.

Given the ambitious reach of this proposal, I have written *A Country of Cities* as a manifesto. Clearly, it is not within our immediate future for most Americans to desire life at such high densities. But it is important to remember that the suburbs barely existed at the turn of the nineteenth century; they were spurred over decades by the sweeping ideas of men like Garden City proponent Ebenezer Howard, automobile titan Henry Ford, and urban renewal czar Robert Moses. We must now adopt a new paradigm in a new century for a new set of conditions, a paradigm that would reverse our declining economics, environment, and social equity and be as all encompassing as the earlier visions that drove us into this calamitous ditch. This new paradigm imagines a United States where government policy would place cities and suburbs on a level playing field and where Americans, in response, would embrace urban life for greater economic opportunity, for deeper environmental wisdom, and for a more just society—goals that are at the core of our founding as a nation and embodied in our Declaration of Independence. In short, people would seek out cities to fulfill their dreams of life, liberty, and the pursuit of happiness.

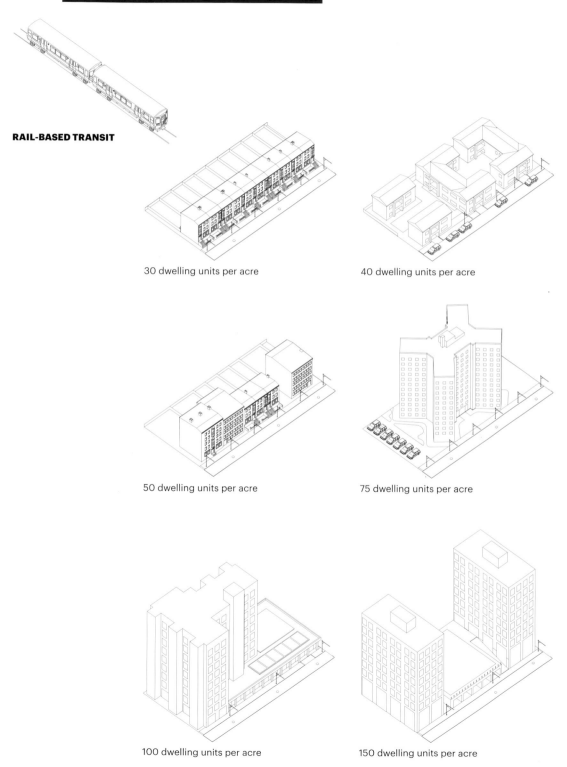

DENSITIES ABLE TO SUPPORT RAPID MASS TRANSIT

RAIL-BASED TRANSIT

30 dwelling units per acre

40 dwelling units per acre

50 dwelling units per acre

75 dwelling units per acre

100 dwelling units per acre

150 dwelling units per acre

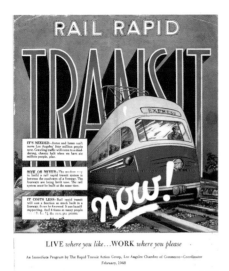

LIVE *where you like*…WORK *where you please*

An Immediate Program by The Rapid Transit Action Group, Los Angeles Chamber of Commerce—Coordinator
February, 1948

RAPID RAIL TRANSIT NOW!

Mass-transit advocacy in the mid-twentieth century attempted to galvanize political support for new cable-car projects in downtown Los Angeles.

As a society, we would need to overcome a series of barriers to arrive at this new urban frontier, but none so formidable as the substantial anti-urban cultural biases we would have to uproot as a nation. Anti-urbanism is not necessarily endemic to Americans or our history—to the contrary, much of the nineteenth century bore witness to new manufacturing processes that engendered new products and favored the juxtaposition of labor, capital, and resources. This inherently urban way of life was in sharp contrast to rural living throughout the United States at the time, and the need to cluster, along with the invention of steam-powered engines, elevators, and structural steel, enabled the creation of cities. Pro-urban policies grew out of pro-American policies as a result of the War of 1812 and the push to make the country less dependent on imports. The policies that built the urban juggernauts of the Industrial Revolution focused on the expansion of transportation, the harnessing of energy, and the improvement of industrial processes.[4]

But a number of well-documented factors that originated in the 1920s, gained momentum after World War II, and reached their apex in the 1970s caused America to sour on its cities. With roots dating back to 1922, the infamous National City Lines cartel formed by corporations including General Motors, Firestone, and Standard Oil led to the elimination of many of the electric streetcar routes across the country, including those in Los Angeles.[5] While the automobile allowed for the suburbanization of the San Fernando Valley, and funds from expansive development bolstered redevelopment in L.A.'s central business district, little could be done after 1946 to resist the momentum behind low-density residential development outside the city's boundaries. In 1948, an attempt to reposition downtown as a major retail destination with a program called "Rail Rapid Transit Now!" failed to gain enough votes for approval by the city council, despite having the support of business leaders and San Fernando Valley developers alike.[6]

A decade earlier, as part of President Franklin D. Roosevelt's New Deal, the National Housing Act of 1934 created the Federal Housing Administration and the Federal Savings and Loan Insurance Corporation to stem the tide

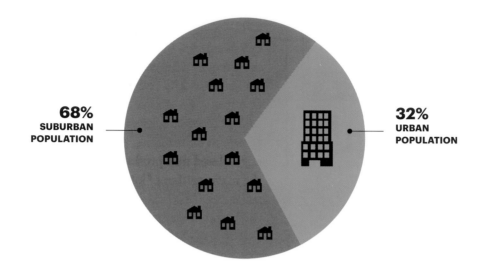

68%
SUBURBAN
POPULATION

32%
URBAN
POPULATION

AMERICANS LIVING IN SUBURBS, 1910–2010

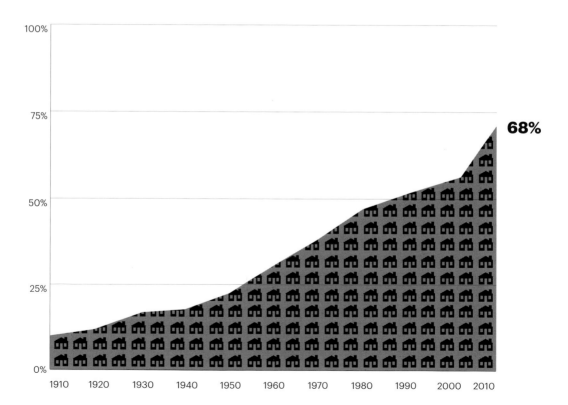

68%

100%

75%

50%

25%

0%

1910   1920   1930   1940   1950   1960   1970   1980   1990   2000   2010

of foreclosures resulting from the Great Depression and to make housing and mortgages more affordable. As a result, more people could afford down payments and interest on mortgages and the market for single-family homes became much larger than it would have been had it not been manipulated.

After World War II, government subsidies again poured into the market-place with the passage of the Federal Highway Act of 1956 and intense lobbying by the National Association of Realtors.[7] Further enabling home-ownership through the expansion of roadways into, out of, and between cities, the law's unprecedented level of funding for highway construction resulted in an otherwise impossible level of suburban development. In the summer of 1956, while Elvis soared to popularity with three number-one hit singles, racial tensions flared nationwide. Skepticism about cities and public safety began to grow, and by April 1958, the country reached the depths of a recession—Detroit, for example, hit 20 percent unemployment.[8] The cold war fed the impetus to disperse the population, and in 1962, the Cuban Missile Crisis solidified fears that communism could prevail over capitalism if the Soviets continued to target American cities.

Extraordinary as it was, the Civil Rights Act of 1964 only exacerbated the anxieties of the many Americans who fled cities in record numbers, leaving the urban cores of the United States largely devoid of the tax base that local businesses and residents provide.[9] As city services declined due to dwindling municipal budgets, and nuclear tensions rose, middle-class whites—and blacks with means—fled for the suburbs. There, selective housing policies ensured that only certain Americans would populate new housing subdivisions and nearby schools; African-Americans were often redlined in many communities, impeding their access to mortgages. The poorer residents who remained in the inner city provided an insufficient tax base, especially for places like New York and Chicago, where crime grew as businesses and jobs decamped, causing local governments to plummet into debt. The Detroit riots of 1967, and the social unrest of 1968 alongside President Lyndon B. Johnson's expansion of U.S. involvement in Vietnam, reflected a period of deepened mistrust in the federal government.

By 1973, Watergate provided the proverbial nail in the coffin for most Americans whose faith in Washington was already declining. Beyond the political scandal, the economy had performed poorly, with persistent high inflation, during President Richard M. Nixon's first term. Though prospects improved with the end of the Vietnam War, the ensuing oil crisis directly affected pocketbooks throughout the country, especially for people reliant on gas-guzzling cars and cities now caught in a vicious downward spiral. By 1975, New York City's finances hit bottom, and when the city sought rescue funds from President Gerald Ford, his public refusal in a speech was

TODAY: THE AMERICAN SCHEME

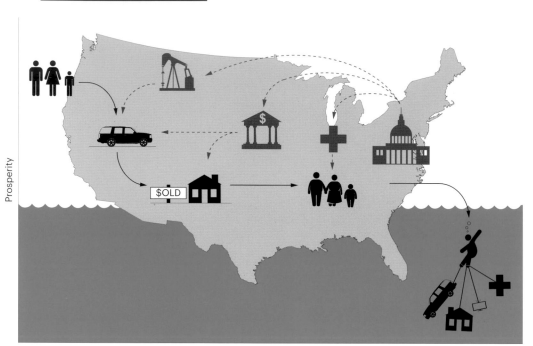

TOMORROW: THE AMERICAN DREAM

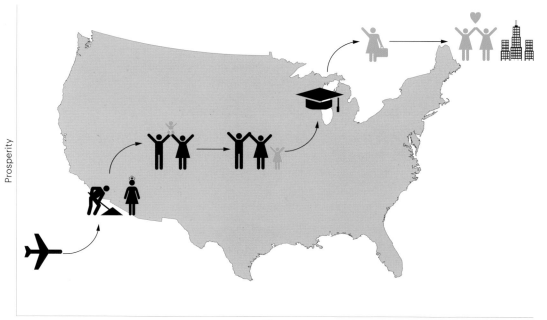

reported by the *New York Daily News* under the famous headline (and mis-quotation): "Ford to City: Drop Dead."[10] Ford eventually led efforts to secure aid for New York from congress, but his initial denial did as much to galvanize New York's business leaders to rescue the city as it did to bolster the anti-urban sentiment that had pervaded much of the century.[11]

The suburbs, therefore, are not a mere reflection of the way people want to live, or even a reflection of true market forces, but a synthetic consequence of history. The suburbs are largely a creation of "big government," an explicit, policy-driven, subsidized scheme that has guided how we live, work, and play. Over the last century, this has created the most consumption-based economy the planet has known—that is, until the music stopped: the twenty-first century debuted in America with an epic collapse of the housing market (particularly the single-family housing market), the rapid acceleration of climate change, and the largest division between rich and poor in the postwar era.[12]

And it is on this last point, of growing social inequity, that we must ask what, if anything, this American Scheme of suburbia has to do with the American Dream of opportunity, a dream that so many of us cherish. While many origins of the concept have been proposed, it is most often ascribed to historian James Truslow Adams, who in 1931 wrote of the American Dream:

> It is not a dream of motor cars and high wages merely, but a dream of social order in which each man and each woman shall be able to attain to the fullest stature of which they are innately capable, and be recognized by others for what they are, regardless of the fortuitous circumstances of birth or position.[13]

It is notable that this definition of the American Dream contains no reference to single-family homeownership, unlike what would ultimately become President George W. Bush's "ownership society." By contrast, President Barack Obama has spoken of the American Dream as an aspiration of equal opportunity regardless of how or where one resides. To be sure, cities left to their own devices do not ensure equitable outcomes—evidence of income inequity can be found across the spectrum of American communities, and sometimes more so in our largest cities. But one of the key questions we must address is whether opportunities for lower-income Americans and immigrants could be greater in cities than elsewhere if they were designed for this purpose. It is this effort—toward building opportunity—that is the key to the American Dream, not some scheme pulling us toward lawn mowers, traffic jams, and snow shovels. This important distinction is what sets apart the true and steadfast American Dream from an American Scheme now in free fall.

The suburbs
largely a cre
"big governn
an explicit,
driven, subs
scheme tha
guided how
work, and p

are

ation of

nent,"

policy-

idized

has

we live,

ay.

A conflation of the American Dream
and the American Scheme was fostered
in our culture by the television and film
industries, which came of age simultaneously
with the federal programs that fueled
suburbanization. It is critical to understand
the consistency with which, whether inten-
tionally or unintentionally, popular culture
and its imagery has reinforced government
policy during the twentieth century, par-
ticularly given that we live in a democracy. People often believe what they see
and, in turn, vote on their beliefs. Moving pictures—with cinema popular
since its inception and television a staple of the American household—became
the primary arbiter of culture and consumption for our society in the decades
following World War II.

With the baby boom, Americans were barraged with footage heavily
biased toward the house, the car, and the requisite appliances. It is remarkable
to consider the anti-urban movies produced in the brief but critical period
of 1945 to 1950. The 1948 film *Mr. Blandings Builds His Dream House* stars
Cary Grant as a New York advertising executive trying to break free of city
life by buying a suburban fixer-upper that turns into a money pit. (Contrast
this with his work from just a decade earlier: *Holiday, Bringing Up Baby*,
and *Topper* all star Grant as an urbanite to the core and, in some cases,
visibly uncomfortable in the countryside.) Even the Manhattan-based 1947
Christmas movie, *Miracle on 34th Street*, features a young heroine pining for
a suburban home, a wish that, of course, the Macy's department store Santa
ultimately grants. The previous year gave us the most enduring Christmas
classic of all, Frank Capra's *It's a Wonderful Life*. The film's protagonist,
George Bailey, yearns to travel, see cities, and build infrastructure, but must
learn the hard way—and only with the help of divine intervention—that city
life is corrupting and immoral. With young women becoming prostitutes
soon after they arrive in the city, the film stops just short of invoking Sodom
and Gomorrah to convey its relentless moralizing.[14]

Decades would pass before movies or television shows would depict any
form of suburban dystopia. It is not until the emergence of the extraordinary
1975 cult classic *The Stepford Wives*, released in a time of social upheaval,
that Hollywood presents to mainstream Americans a contrarian view of
suburban life. Only recent films such as *The Ice Storm* and *American Beauty*
hold a candle to the satire of Stepford's mind-bending lifestyle, with its
uniquely searing feminist critique of the suburb's impact on women.

By contrast, the film most commonly beloved among architects, the 1982 epic *Blade Runner*, depicts the city as dystopia, with poverty below, wealth above, and a menacing prognostication of American cities becoming more Asian in the most damning sense. Ultimately, for all of its compelling visual power, Ridley Scott's classic is an Anglican cautionary tale that warns against Los Angeles becoming a Tokyo or Hong Kong, complete with the stereotype that, should we let down our guard, we will become urban automatons, or "replicants." Ironically, as we will see in the pages that follow, it is precisely from the great cities of Asia that Los Angeles, under the leadership of Mayor Antonio Villaraigosa, is finally adapting the means to become more economically and environmentally sound.

It is not until the 1980s that the anti-urban bias in American film and television begins to markedly shift. With the globalization of capital and the consequent shift in the economics of leading cities the world over, certain cities like New York take on a different cultural meaning as places of opportunity.[15] In this period, films like *Working Girl* and *The Secret of My Success* and television shows like *The Cosby Show* appear, offering an optimistic but simplistic vision of urban prosperity, with only a few films, including *Do the Right Thing*, providing a critique of the uneven access to this new urban opportunity.

Into the nineties, as urban crime fell, contemporary movies and television began to show a wider range of both urban and suburban settings, with new cultural signals regarding the potential merits of city life. Although federal energy and housing agencies continued to promulgate suburbia with modifications of the CAFE standard that reclassified SUVs and minivans from trucks to cars, Americans during this period began to return to cities in response to the employment opportunities, energy prices, and social life associated with denser areas.[16]

IDYLLIC SUBURBIA IN MOVIES

Between 1945 and 1950, Hollywood aggrandized the suburbs.
1 *It's a Wonderful Life*, 1946
2 *Miracle on 34th Street*, 1947
3 *Mr. Blandings Builds His Dream House*, 1948

A 2012 *Wall Street Journal* article indicated that American cities are now growing faster than their suburban counterparts for the first time since the 1920s.[17] Another article published a year later by MSNBC summarized the reasons for the change in growth patterns and attributed the phenomenon to factors that may or may not be temporary: the slump in the economy (temporary), the inability of young people to afford down payments for mortgages (temporary), and a preference to live in places that don't require driving everywhere (not temporary).[18] In his book *The Great Inversion*, Alan Ehrenhalt writes extensively about this trend and its causes, highlighting national case studies of urban rediscovery and labeling this shift "demographic inversion."[19]

While this "inversion" is irrefutable and, some would argue, welcome, few examine the potential long-term benefits of this trend—particularly if government rather than promoting suburbanization instead encouraged urbanism, or at least gave it an even chance. The necessary changes would include modifying or curtailing the vast array of federal policies that currently subsidize suburban America, including: phasing out the federal home mortgage interest deduction (MID); ceasing the backing by Fannie Mae and Freddie Mac of large mortgages that otherwise would not be underwritten by the private market; removing subsidies for the oil industry; reclassifying SUVs and minivans as light trucks; allocating federal transportation dollars by population, and distributing those dollars fairly across all modes of transportation, including rail and mass transit, instead of disproportionately funding highways and runways; streamlining the National Environmental Protection Act (NEPA) to drastically reduce the red tape associated with urban development and building large-scale infrastructure; and, finally, pricing fuel to reflect what economists call the "negative externalities," or the actual price of gas if the societal costs of pollution and congestion were included (many economists put this price at $10 or more per gallon).[20]

Blade Runner, 1982

As we will see in the pages that follow, such policy reforms would dramatically improve our economy, our environment, and our chances for equal opportunity. Achieving consensus for these changes, however, would be a tremendous challenge, and would require a recasting of the political spectrum as we know it. People are accustomed to their subsidies, particularly those in the middle class, who tend to believe they are not subsidized at all.[21] The uproar over eliminating the home-mortgage deduction would light up the split screen alongside the "get your government hands off my Medicare" sentiment. But increasingly, politicians need to get honest with their constituents. The MID is enormously expensive in a deficit-laden era; it unfairly subsidizes large homeowners, who are typically suburban, over renters, who are typically urban; and in a mobile economy, it incentivizes people unwisely to not only take on unaffordable mortgages but also tether themselves to homes that hinder mobility should their jobs move from one part of the country to another, an argument forcefully put forward by economist Richard Florida and others.[22]

Such tectonic policy reform would require fundamental changes to the status quo of each political party. Anti-urbanism is not just a conservative stance—many liberals also fail to understand the power of cities to transform our economy, better our environment, and increase social opportunity. Most self-designated environmentalists are dead wrong in their emphasis on individual feel-good actions like putting solar panels on McMansions. More professionalized environmental organizations tend to focus on burdensome regulatory requirements that often impede infrastructure and sound urban development by requiring, for instance, complex and expensive environmental impact statements, which can delay or destroy projects. And while some extreme conservatives like former Speaker Newt Gingrich and the Tea Party consider an urban agenda a takeover of the American Dream—not to mention a United Nations plot to overthrow the U.S. government—most mainstream conservatives understand the economic power of healthy American cities.[23]

Even a "severe" conservative like former Governor Mitt Romney was for smart growth before he was against it.[24]

The bipartisan nature of anti-urbanism goes back much further in our history, lurking with Henry David Thoreau, deep in the American mindset. The idea of sub-dividing America into a one-mile-square grid was, after all, conceived by the liberal Thomas Jefferson, who was a lifelong skeptic about the concentration of power in cities. Ingrained in our very Constitution is the geographic dispersal of power, a balance against the supposed tyrannies of a truly representative democracy, in which population density would guide federal policy and resources unfettered by the special interests of the hinterland. Democrats are equally guilty of embracing anti-urban policies, reflecting in large measure a constituency steeped in the belief that sprawl is superior to tall.

Consider one last cinematic example that illustrates this point, a "progressive" children's film directed at young hearts and minds to engage them in issues of environmental sustainability. In *Bob the Builder: Bob's Big Plan* (2005), the most renowned builder in America today takes on the supposed ugliness of urbanization. For those unfamiliar with Bob's character, he is an American everyman with deep environmental convictions and lots of gas-guzzling trucks. He lives in a progressive community of single-family homes in the American heartland, where he preaches his refrain, "Reduce, Reuse, Recycle." In *Bob's Big Plan*, our hero is working in town when he runs across the local architect, a mustached gentleman with a bespoke, crested, double-breasted blazer and a fancy office plastered with elite degrees. The architect explains that there is a competition for Sunflower Valley, an area nearby, and shows Bob his proposed design, a model of a gleaming city of skyscrapers. Bob leaves the architect's office unsettled, remembering his childhood playing in Sunflower Valley. That night, he has a nightmare of skyscrapers and limousines destroying the unspoiled landscape, causing animals to flee and sunflowers to die, only to be replaced by synthetic flowers. Bob awakes with a jerk, realizing that he, too, must enter the competition. He furiously begins to build his own model, but instead of skyscrapers he proposes a scattering of a few small "green" houses, equipped with solar panels and windmills, all at a density of about four acres per house and unreachable by anything but automobile. Bob wins the competition, of course. The architect congratulates Bob and admits to the error in his urban ways. Bob wins the right to build

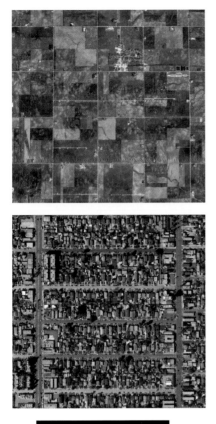

THE JEFFERSONIAN GRID

The Jeffersonian grid has guided rural and suburban development patterns in America since its inception, in the early nineteenth century.

his vision of Sunflower Valley, and the progressive mayor of his liberal town awards him with . . . a brand new gas guzzler for his fleet!

Missing from this quaint tale, which says so much about our lingering cultural biases, are the disastrous economic and environmental consequences of Bob's eco-suburban scheme. His Sunflower Valley is nothing more than a green version of Levittown, replete with the liberal vision of solar panels and electric cars to redress the sins of the past. But the ugly carbon-footprint implications of this vision cannot be glossed over with technology as so many seem to be hoping—a world of seven billion people living at the density of a city stands a chance, but that same world at the density of Bob's suburban vision would be crushed by the weight of its own resource demands. In fact, if all seven billion lived at the density of townhouses instead of single-family homes, but nowhere close to the density of big American cities, the entire planet's population would fit in the state of Texas surrounded by nothing but nature and agriculture.[25] I make this point not to propose we all move to Texas, but rather to illustrate that climate change demands solutions that diminish our carbon footprint en masse, with reductions in land and resource usage on a per capita basis.

This is among the most critical factors in understanding the merits of transit-based hyperdensity at a global level. Societies worldwide are growing wealthier, with the middle-class burgeoning in places including China, India, Brazil, Turkey, Russia, Vietnam, Nigeria, and Lebanon. In his book *The Post-American World*, Fareed Zakaria outlines what he calls the "rise of the rest," indicating that while global prosperity is a good thing, the resource constraints presented by more than two billion people becoming middle-class are daunting and, most likely, our most pressing international challenge.[26] If those two billion souls attempt the same profligate suburban lifestyle so many American's cherish, even Bob's "green" version of it, the planet will careen toward disaster.

Beyond the environment, however, Bob's vision for Sunflower Valley is demonstrably less economically productive than denser parts of America. I examine this topic in the first of three chapters that form the initial section of this book, "Why Cities Are Good." These chapters bring together literature that empirically and objectively indicates why cities are performing better than their suburban counterparts in terms of three critically important metrics—the economy, the environment, and public wellness. In section two, "How to Build Good Cities," I propose methods and policies, drawing on public- and private-sector techniques from across the nation, for creating prosperous, sustainable, and joyous urban environments. I have also structured this section in three chapters: on building sound urban development, on constructing the infrastructure to support that development, and on making new urban development affordable and accessible to all.

BOB'S BIG PLAN

The local architect proposes a city.

Bob's nightmare inspires Bob's eco-suburb counterproposal.

Bob wins a gas guzzler for his eco-suburb proposal!

The conclusion imagines a "Country of Cities," conjuring the implications of a fully realized, truly urban America—a place characterized by cities, small towns, agriculture, nature, and little else—and considers how such a landscape would perform, prosper, and perpetuate itself. In it, I ask the reader to consider that a largely urban country spurred by policy reform, in contrast to our sprawling reality, would unite to become economically stronger, environmentally sounder, internationally safer, physically healthier, socially more fair, experientially more livable, and globally envied and emulated.

This is a polemical vision, a manifesto, put forth with an understanding that the gap between our reality today and a Country of Cities is vast. Even readers who agree with this vision will, for good reason, be skeptical of its likelihood. However, we arrived at our current national landscape not by accident or by pure market forces, but rather by design . . . a poor, inadequate, and anachronistic design that manifested itself within one rapid century and could cease to exist just as rapidly. A remarkable, explicit agenda set suburbanization in motion, and the demands of a new epoch call for a different paradigm that is just as explicit and far-reaching. For the sake of future generations, we must take this new urban path to a more prosperous, more sustainable, and more equitable America and, by extension, create the model for a joyful global lifestyle capable of supporting the 10 billion souls projected to walk this planet at the turn of the next century.

HOUSEHOLD SIZE VS. HOME SIZE

While newly constructed homes have nearly doubled in size since 1960, the total number of people per house has steadily decreased. Larger, more inefficient homes are now occupied by fewer people.

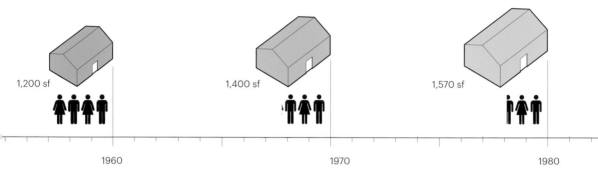

1,200 sf

1,400 sf

1,570 sf

1960

1970

1980

HOUSING STOCK AND POPULATION GROWTH

In the United States, the number of housing units has increased at a greater rate than the population. This means we use more energy, resources, and land to house Americans today.

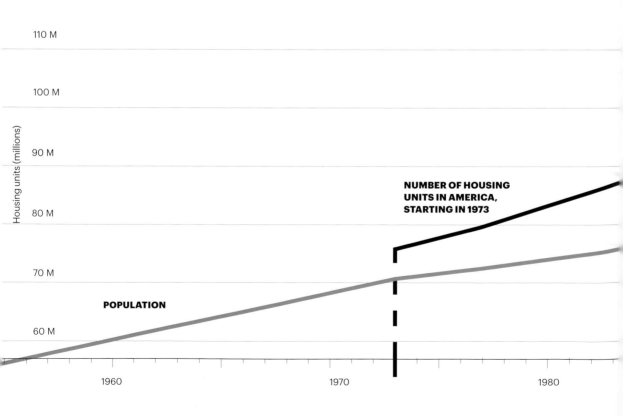

110 M

100 M

90 M

80 M

70 M

60 M

Housing units (millions)

NUMBER OF HOUSING UNITS IN AMERICA, STARTING IN 1973

POPULATION

1960

1970

1980

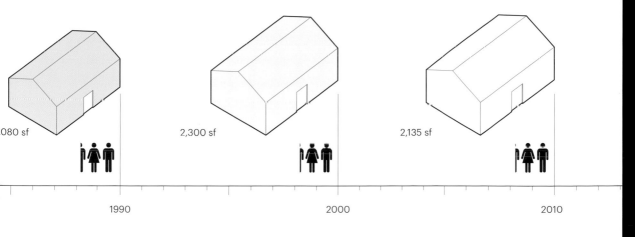

080 sf

2,300 sf

2,135 sf

1990

2000

2010

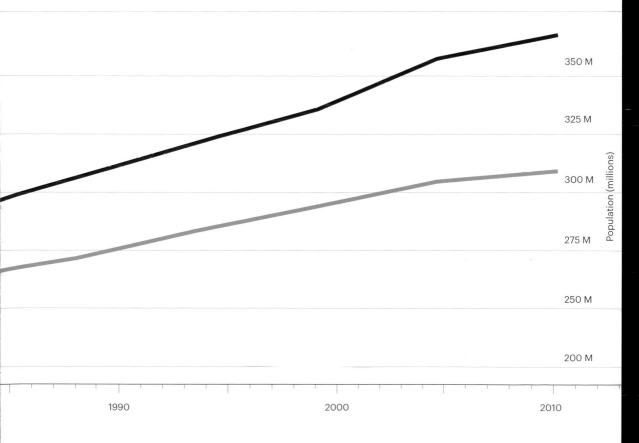

350 M

325 M

300 M

275 M

250 M

200 M

Population (millions)

1990

2000

2010

DEVELOPMENT ON PLANET EARTH

Humans directly influence 83% of the earth's land area.

THE WORLD'S POPULATION COULD FIT IN TEXAS

At a density of approximately 25 dwelling units per acre, the entire population of the world could fit in the state of Texas, leaving the remainder of the planet for nature and agriculture. As improbable as this scenario is, it illustrates the vastness of our planet's land area and the power of density to promote more efficient land use.

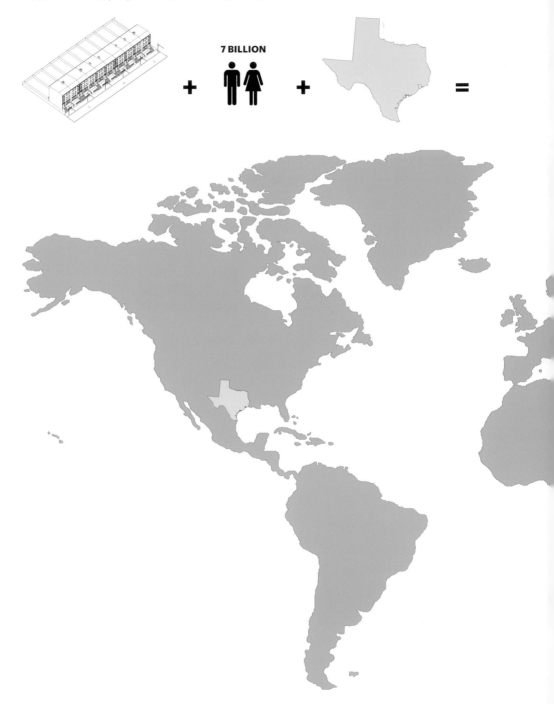

7 BILLION

+ ☗ ☗ + ⬡ =

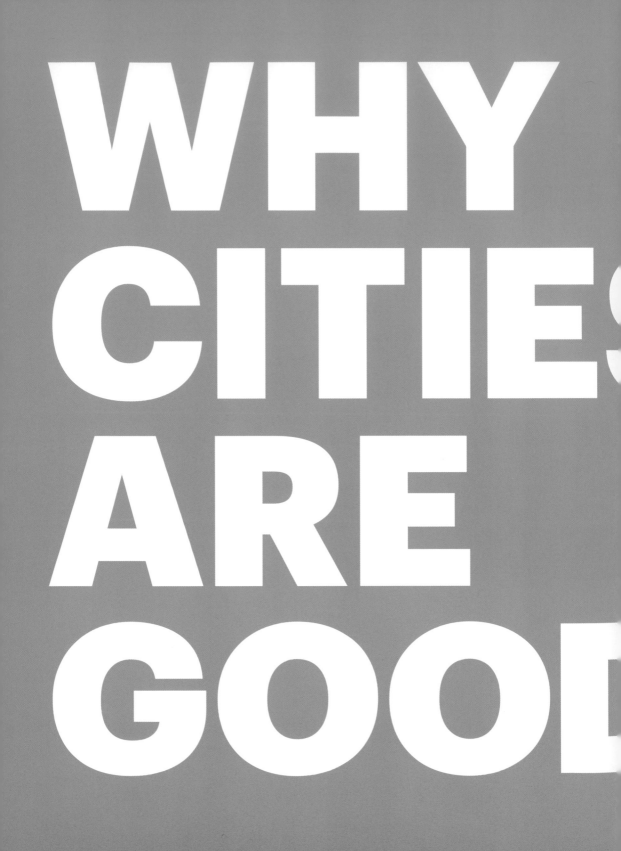

WHY
CITIES
ARE
GOOD

JANE JACOBS, ECONOMIC EXPANSIONIST

"If I were to be remembered as a really important thinker of the century, the most important thing I've contributed is my discussion of what makes economic expansion happen."[1]

CITIES, PROSPERITY, AND GLOBALIZATION

In today's globalized economy, dense urban environments have demonstrably greater capacity than urban sprawl to deliver widespread economic prosperity. Prosperity—defined by success in work, economic stability, and transference of wealth from one generation to another—is a shared aspiration in many countries, including the United States. Not only do city planning professionals have an interest in more efficient land use and denser development patterns; so do the millions of people who want new economic opportunities, upward income mobility, and the long-term financial stability that is increasingly commonplace in successful cities today.

While extolling the economic advantages of cities has become fashionable recently, it was in 1984 that writer Jane Jacobs championed the notion that cities are the fountainhead for the wealth of nations. Ironically, while Jacobs is a hero among community activists for her grassroots ability to fight power, she wanted her primary legacy to be her belief in the economic expansion of cities and, specifically, her theory of "import replacement." Central to this concept, she argued, is the notion that all cities imported goods and services but over time came to manufacture these goods and services internally, thus replacing import reliance with internal economic growth. Once a city could produce these goods and services, it would export them to other cities, which would eventually learn to produce and export these same goods and services themselves, and so on in a virtuous cycle. Decades ahead of its time, Jacobs's theory sheds light on precisely what is happening in the technology industries today, in which the ability to produce goods and services that originated in Silicon Valley has regenerated worldwide, from Bangalore to Brooklyn, Houston to Haifa.

More recent work by scholars including economists Edward Glaeser, Gerald Carlino, Ryan Avent, and Matt Yglesias forms an exciting new body

JANE JACOBS'S THEORY OF IMPORT REPLACEMENT IN CITIES

Cities, initially importers, in turn become capable of producing the imported goods and services themselves. Eventually, they are able to export their own goods, services, and expertise to other cities, thus perpetuating the virtuous cycle.

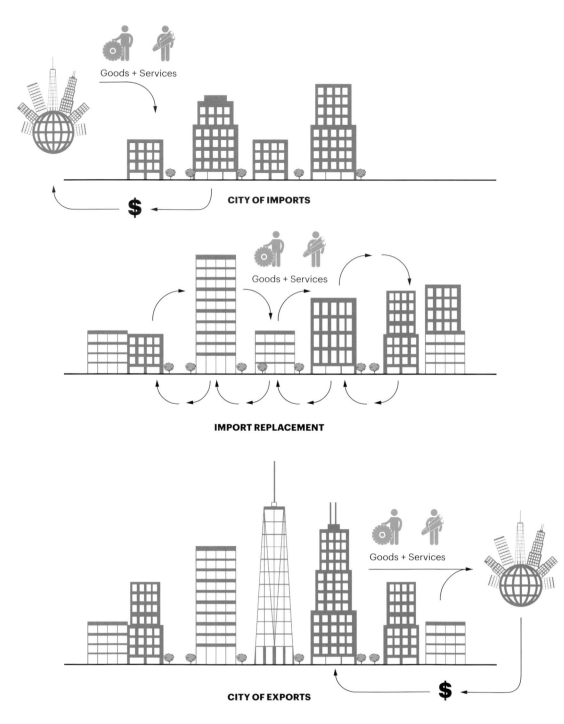

Goods + Services

CITY OF IMPORTS

Goods + Services

IMPORT REPLACEMENT

Goods + Services

CITY OF EXPORTS

of research that builds on Jacobs's ideas and makes an overwhelming case for the economic advantages of cities, which today are exhibiting lower unemployment, fewer foreclosures, and fewer of the problems associated with economic distress than in many suburbs and exurbs. In "U.S. Metro Economies," the 2012 United States Conference of Mayors reported that 3 percent of the nation's land mass generates 85 percent of its gross domestic product (GDP), a finding that confirms and expands research conducted earlier this decade. It is astonishing to understand that such a small percentage of the United States—essentially, its cities—generates the vast majority of its economic output.[2]

The effects of density on economic growth and stability are part of a significant and lasting phenomenon in cities today. For instance, in his cluster theory, Harvard business professor Michael Porter states that amassing talent and skills in dense urban centers contributes to economic growth at a pace that is likely greater than the sum of otherwise individual efforts.[3] Glaeser, in his human capital theory, looks at similar effects through the lens of skill levels and the propensity for higher-skilled people to migrate toward and settle in cities.[4] Richard Florida argues in his creative-capital theory that a subset of highly skilled professionals who drive creative industries not only earn more and contribute to economic growth but also can have a significant impact on reversing the decline of once prominent cities by reinvigorating their urban cores, attracting both investment and development funds.[5] The research of Carlino and others indicates "that patent intensity— the per capita invention rate—is positively related to the density of employment in the highly urbanized portion of [metropolitan areas]." Avent's research shows that when urban density doubles, productivity increases in a range between 6 and 28 percent.[6] Taken together, these studies make it crystal clear that when cities realize the benefits of agglomeration, heightened economic activity resulting in greater prosperity and innovation occurs again and again.

These findings support the positions presented throughout this book, and they advocate that the United States build on the inherent competitive advantages of its dense cities. Young people are already flocking to cities for their economic opportunities and freer lifestyles. And if urban affordability, public safety, and schools continue to improve, they will most likely choose to remain in cities to raise their families. Similarly, immigrants historically gravitate to cities to climb the rungs of the economic ladder and, like young people, are critical to urban productivity. However, many cities today remain unaffordable for both groups, which is often a consequence of overly regulated housing markets.

3% of the land in the U.S.

90% of the GDP
86.2% of the jobs in the U.S.

90% OF OUR GDP AND **86%** OF OUR JOBS
ARE GENERATED IN OUR METROPOLITAN AREAS.

In his book *The Gated City,* Avent recommends a relaxation of policies that limit density and prevent cities from welcoming these inward migrations. Even dense places need the growth required to ensure affordability and keep pace with cities worldwide. In line with other research, Avent exposes zoning regulations, historic designations, and building-height limits as factors that suppress housing supply in our already dense cities. He sees the combination of these distortions as a catalyst in driving people out of urban environments and away from the heightened potential for prosperity they, and we, might otherwise encounter:

> Our thriving cities fall short of their potential because we constantly rein them in, and we rein them in because we worry that urban growth will be unpleasant. The residents of America's productive cities fear change in their neighborhoods and fight growth. In doing so, they make their cities more expensive and less accessible to people with middle incomes. Those middle-income workers move elsewhere, reducing their own earning power and the economy's potential in the process.[7]

In his seminal book, *The Triumph of Cities,* Glaeser exhaustively makes the case for why cities are "our greatest invention." In his view, human capital is at the forefront of why cities thrive, and to remain economically viable and therefore competitive, they must retain and nurture talent. Glaeser proposes that cities must either grow talent by having numerous great schools (Boston), by attracting talent with superior amenities (Portland, Oregon), or offering some mixture of affordability, good education, and livability (Austin).

Yglesias's work proposes that, in theory, "proximity to prosperous people is itself, prosperity-inducing—especially in an economy where people mostly sell services to one another."[8] Yglesias argues that in practice, however, the cost of proximity to many of the country's most productive urban cores has prohibitively elevated barriers to entry, in both the housing and business markets, simply because rents are "too damn high." If prosperity does fuel prosperity for others, it must do so in a way that enhances the earning power of all citizens on the socioeconomic ladder, while also creating the conditions that allow for everyone to live together. There is little benefit to having a city in which the poor serve the rich, while the middle class drives in to work and back home to the suburbs to spend its money and pay its taxes.

Many urban economists have produced studies confirming that our service economy cities are the nation's essential economic engines, but have found that these same cities have become too expensive because of the limited supply of spaces for people and business to inhabit. While this in many cases is a consequence of over-regulating new development, it is also true that we

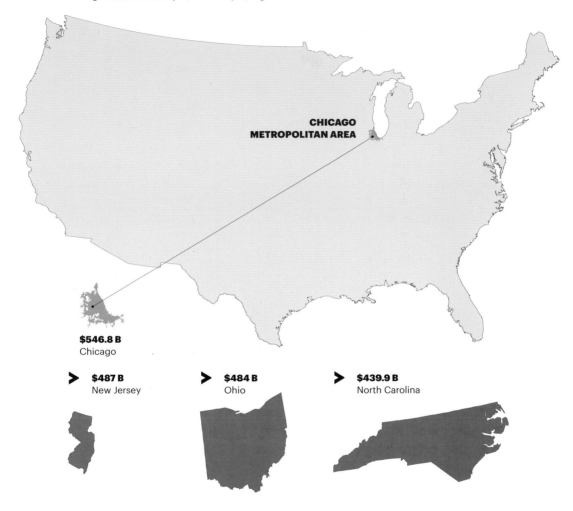

AMERICAN CITIES ARE MORE PRODUCTIVE THAN THE VAST MAJORITY OF STATES

Chicago's economic output, for example, is greater than that of 42 states in the U.S.

CHICAGO METROPOLITAN AREA

$546.8 B
Chicago

> $487 B
New Jersey

> $484 B
Ohio

> $439.9 B
North Carolina

AS WELL AS EACH OF THESE 39 STATES

Alabama	$173.1 B	Indiana	$278.1 B	Mississippi	$97.8 B	Rhode Island	$50.1 B
Alaska	$51.4 B	Iowa	$149 B	Missouri	$249.5 B	South Carolina	$165 B
Arizona	$258.4 B	Kansas	$130.9 B	Montana	$38 B	South Dakota	$40.1 B
Arkansas	$105.8 B	Kentucky	$164.8 B	Nebraska	$94.2 B	Tennessee	$266.5 B
Colorado	$264.3 B	Louisiana	$247.7 B	Nevada	$130.4 B	Utah	$124.5 B
Connecticut	$230.1 B	Maine	$51.6 B	New Hampshire	$63 B	Vermont	$25.9 B
Delaware	$65.8 B	Maryland	$301.1 B	New Mexico	$79.4 B	Washington	$355.1 B
Georgia	$418 B	Massachusetts	$391.8 B	North Dakota	$40.3 B	West Virginia	$66.8 B
Hawaii	$67 B	Michigan	$385.2 B	Oklahoma	$155 B	Wisconsin	$254.8 B
Idaho	$57.9 B	Minnesota	$281.7 B	Oregon	$194.7 B	Wyoming	$37.6 B

$546.8 BILLION
ANNUAL ECONOMIC OUTPUT OF THE CHICAGO METROPOLITAN AREA

need to better utilize our existing urban building stock. In some instances, municipalities have preserved industrial neighborhoods as retail and tourist destinations, including festival marketplaces, but such efforts have limited economic impact without a more urbane mix of cultural and professional uses.

More interestingly, pioneering artists for decades have steadily converted derelict manufacturing buildings into live-work lofts. Entrepreneurs have been redeveloping similar buildings for the businesses of the twenty-first century. Information technology companies now tend to desire non-traditional work environments that bear little resemblance to the offices of *Mad Men* Manhattan. Many technology companies want to be located near hip, amenity rich, mixed-use neighborhoods where their employees can live and socialize without long commutes. Biotechnology and other industries often favor proximity to major universities and medical centers, and this has generated a new focus for urban economic development officials on the "eds and meds."

In addition to changing the way they use urban space, technology companies have changed the way the economy now functions. The dot-com era led to a number of successes and failures, but its most pronounced physical impact was to make the world a smaller place in which to do business. With expansive access to the Internet and the explosive growth of e-commerce came the need for increased levels of customer service, which proved expensive to operate in many of the cities where goods and services were being consumed. As has been well documented, the rise of the Internet contributed to the acceleration of globalization as businesses increasingly relied on overseas manufacturing and the outsourcing of service jobs to cut costs. This, in turn, stimulated the economies of countries like India and Indonesia, as call centers proliferated in many of their urban centers. An educated, English speaking, and enthusiastic population could easily perform jobs at a fraction of American labor costs. As wealth and prosperity increased for these nations and their businesses, so did opportunities to move up the economic ladder for billions worldwide. The rise of consumerism in these countries has led to the liberalization of their economies, and as their populations looked to America for lifestyle cues, many have sought life in suburbs complete with time wasted in traffic jams. This condition has become emblematic of burgeoning economies across the globe.

While it is conventional among academics and journalists to point out that the world's population is urbanizing, data suggests the world is primarily suburbanizing.[9] Other nations are, to their and the world's detriment, adopting the inefficient and unsustainable development model for which America is, decades later, starting to pay the price. Housing, feeding, and transporting the world's growing population will deplete and destroy

DENSITY AND PRODUCTIVITY

The work of Ryan Avent shows that as job density doubles, productivity rises between 6% and 28%.

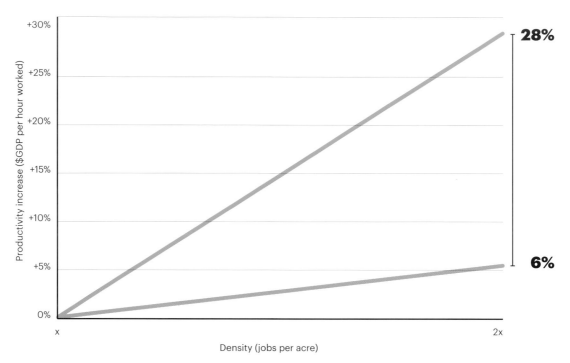

Productivity increase ($GDP per hour worked)

Density (jobs per acre)

JOB DENSITY AND PER CAPITA INNOVATION RATE

The work of Carlino, Chatterjee, and Hunt shows that a city with twice the employment density
(jobs per square mile) of another city will exhibit a patent intensity (patents per capita) that is 20% higher.

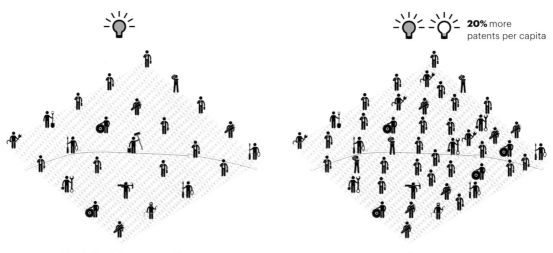

20% more patents per capita

City "A" x jobs per sq. mile

City "B" 2x jobs per sq.mile

the earth's resources if everyone adopts the same inefficient, unhealthy, and unsustainable living habits of much of the United States. Commentator Fareed Zakaria lucidly points out that the problems we confront are less "the products of failure than the products of success," in which the increasing prosperity and growth of the middle class worldwide, while wonderful in terms of poverty alleviation, raises significant questions regarding the availability of natural resources. Urban development represents the best path forward for physically accommodating a growing and hopefully prosperous world.

The differences between urban development and suburban development, however, are as economic as they are physical. As Saskia Sassen writes in her book *The Global City*, suburban life relies primarily on the investment of capital, while urban life and the process of gentrification rely more heavily on the investment of labor.[10] Although building cities and the infrastructure to support them has high capital costs, cities provide a much higher level of demand in the labor market and a more varied array of options in the housing market; this explains why individuals at any level of the economic ladder are more likely to find economic opportunity in cities.

Historically, the longest period of shared prosperity in America ranged from the 1940s to the 1970s. This era ended in large part due to global economic changes that the United States itself initiated through outsourcing, coupled with a well-documented deterioration of the nation's public education system. In real dollar terms, widespread prosperity has declined steadily since, part of a larger trend of economic globalization that has led to more opportunities for the striving, hard-working lower and middle classes abroad than for our own population.[11]

The economies of entire nations have changed with the rapid expansion of a newly powerful middle-class concentrated largely in cities. The arrival of thousands of new inhabitants has created intense pressures on cities throughout the Eastern and Southern Hemispheres. China, Brazil, and India have led the charge in building new cities and suburbs, and the demands of their growing middle-classes in hyperdense megacities such as Shanghai, São Paulo, and Mumbai have accelerated the global consumption of natural resources, manufactured byproducts, and general consumer goods to unprecedented levels.

Economic growth in countries that were once perceived to be "third world" triggered homeownership that typically relied on large down payments and low levels of personal debt. In contrast, at the outset of this century, "first world" nations with highly industrialized economies led by the United States further expanded access to mortgage lending despite a decline in real wages. The "ownership society" promoted by President George W. Bush's administration was bolstered largely by market deregulation and subprime

JOB DENSITY AND PROXIMITY TO OTHER ACTIVITIES

EXURBAN SQUARE MILE OUTSIDE OF CHICAGO

Office building houses 19 jobs per acre.
Location offers access to parking and some
activities and services within one mile.

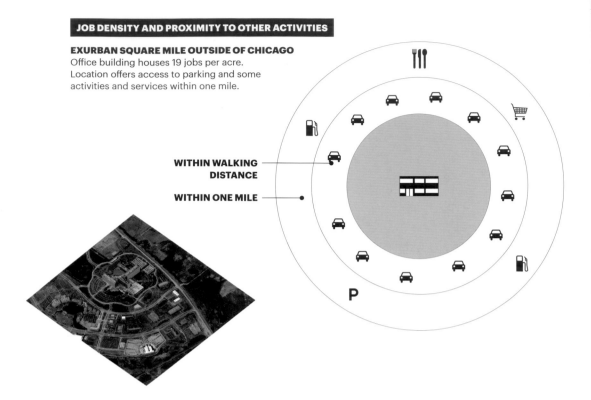

WITHIN WALKING DISTANCE

WITHIN ONE MILE

URBAN SQUARE MILE WITHIN CHICAGO

Office building houses 932 jobs per acre.
Location offers a number of other activities,
services, and mass transit within walking distance.

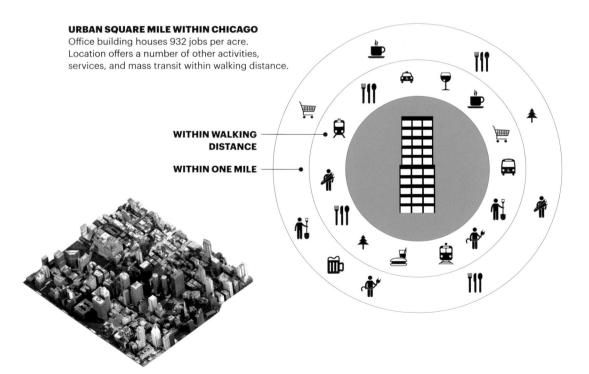

WITHIN WALKING DISTANCE

WITHIN ONE MILE

loans, which led to speculative lending and the eventual collapse of the global credit markets.

But the phenomenon of excess was not limited to the United States or to the expansion of homeownership in suburban settings alone. As many new financing mechanisms appeared in the housing marketplace of the 1990s and 2000s as did variations on the concept of the traditional American home. One could buy or custom-build McMansions as well as benefit from government programs that subsidized tractor sheds and horse barns.[12] Overseas, many countries, including those unfortunately labeled by the media and the financial industry as "PIIGS" (Portugal, Italy, Ireland, Greece, and Spain), contributed to the global expansion of reckless credit.[13] The sudden acceleration of homeownership, along with speculative lending and indiscriminate public and private spending worldwide, led to the precarious finances of government at all levels, of global banking giants, and of the Euro itself. Exported far beyond its shores, the Bush Administration's ideology encouraged homeownership globally as the prevalent form of building equity and securing wealth, and people across America and Western Europe borrowed (and were happily lent) sums of money that too few had the resources to fully support without good jobs and rising incomes.[14]

Whether in Europe or the United States, prosperity is increasingly tied to job security, as personal savings decline, principal-protected interest rates plummet, pension and retirement benefits atrophy, and stock and bond markets entail substantial risk. As a result, people have been encouraged, largely through government subsidies, to use the purchase of a house as a means to secure wealth and draw down equity despite the fact that both the wealth and the equity have proven illusory.

A growing population and dwindling natural resources call for a new global economy as the way to a more prosperous future for all. A new emphasis on human resources (that is, human capital, as Sassen discusses) and more effective production systems (such as automation) will likely supplant the capitalization of natural resources and mass production that propelled our economy through much of the nineteenth and twentieth centuries. As education becomes more important and opportunities to make a living through hard labor and physical skills diminish, those who have less access to education will become less employable and income gaps will widen even further.[15] This is not to say that manufacturing will cease in the United States, but it clearly will no longer be the primary source of employment and wealth creation for our population, a realization that has far-reaching implications for the physical form the nation should take as an advanced service economy.

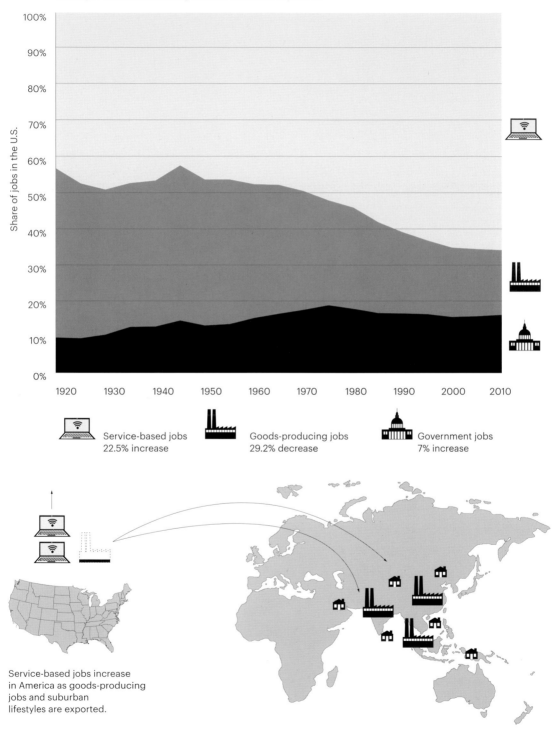

AMERICA'S WORKFORCE HAS CHANGED OVER TIME

Manufacturing and construction jobs have largely been replaced with service economy jobs, although some manufacturing remains viable and important.

Share of jobs in the U.S.

100%
90%
80%
70%
60%
50%
40%
30%
20%
10%
0%

1920   1930   1940   1950   1960   1970   1980   1990   2000   2010

Service-based jobs
22.5% increase

Goods-producing jobs
29.2% decrease

Government jobs
7% increase

Service-based jobs increase in America as goods-producing jobs and suburban lifestyles are exported.

Two choices emerge: We can continue down the path we have been on since the latter decades of the twentieth century, with reduced or stagnant incomes for most Americans. Or we can pursue strategies for economic development that put people first in this young and transformative century. We must create environments that foster prosperity by building on the successes of our cities, which by far represent our most productive domestic environments in terms of service-economy jobs and even occasional resurgences in specialized manufacturing jobs.[16]

To densify cities is to also build the infrastructure that supports them, and this is central to a discussion of prosperity. "Thus, to discuss the financing of infrastructure is to discuss many connections between public infrastructure and private prosperity, between revenue bases and the ability to finance public infrastructure, between a government's capital budget and its operating expenditures, between federal aid programs and state and local capital financing."[17] We cannot correct the nation's course without policy reform that supports infrastructure and existing urban areas, and thereby bolsters businesses. As Edward Rendell, former governor of Pennsylvania, and Kenneth Lewis, chairman and CEO of Bank of America, explain in the foreword to *Retooling for Growth*, revitalizing and repopulating America's older industrial areas is critical to achieving sustainable economic growth, and strengthening older industrial areas makes good economic sense because of the vast infrastructure and resources already in place.[18] Given the globalized economy in which we now live, urban infrastructure is the key to our competitiveness and our prosperity.

Because even our faltering cities are bastions of opportunity, laden with all of the investments we have already made to date, there is little reason to let them further decline in favor of sprawl. As Jacobs points out:

> The region of an economically declining city does not revert to its former, largely rural condition. For a long time it retains its characteristic of being a mixed and intricate economy, but the region's economic life slowly grows thinner and backward, too. The regional fabric develops holes and tatters as it were. Young people who leave settlements within the region for city jobs tend to bypass the region's own city or cities and go instead, to distant cities if work there is open to them.[19]

Rather than give up on our failing manufacturing cities, we should understand how places like Pittsburgh have begun to transform for our new era. This is not to make light of the enormous challenges faced by our most distressed manufacturing cities. A major example is Detroit, which, as Glaeser explains, declined in large part because of "the process of suburbanizing

While it is
conventio
point out
world's po
is urbaniz
world is p
suburban

nal to
hat the
pulation
ng, the
rimarily
zing.

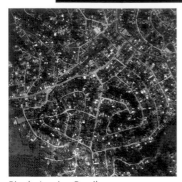

Rio de Janeiro, Brazil

Dubai, United Arab Emirates

Shanghai, China

Berlin, Germany

Paris, France

Toronto, Canada

Moscow, Russia

Bangalore, India

Sydney, Australia

Cairo, Egypt

Johannesburg, South Africa

Jakarta, Indonesia

manufacturing," which triggered the location of factories such as River Rouge outside of the city core, forcing workers to drive to work and removing managers from an innovative, collaborative, urban environment.[20] It was the very invention of cars and trucks that helped create the boundless, low-density growth of Detroit. And in addition to the diffusion of goods and services generated by this expansiveness, the city has since struggled to cope with changes in the global economy, with the market mandate to innovate, and with the governmental policies that have historically favored its suburbs over its downtown. Nonetheless, in terms of urban dysfunction, Detroit today stands as more exception than rule, and while every measure should be taken to transform it, it can no longer be used as a cautionary tale against urbanism, given that our major cities have otherwise proven their economic significance.

Big, dense, modern cities around the world have also become economic powers, and are capable of competing directly with U.S. cities for talented residents and important companies. While a few nations have become prosperous by emulating the American suburban model, the most successful global economic engines have succeeded by doing the opposite. That is, the extent to which nations can provide incentives for their growing middle classes to stay in dense urban centers and away from gated compounds on city outskirts will likely contribute to their sustained success. And to the extent that we can learn from the prosperity of city-states such as Hong Kong and Singapore—the more we come to understand cities that can govern themselves through home rule, breaking loose from the shackles of rural and suburban special interests that constrain their politics and resource allocations—the more successful cities will be. Here in the United States, for example, such a move toward urban home rule would mean concentrating resources for diffuse and failing school systems, systems that have significantly harmed our economy. Urban home rule would similarly allow investments in inner-city transit infrastructure that would serve much larger percentages of our population. If we strengthened home rule in our cities so that they were free from state legislatures to govern and invest resources as they saw fit, we would likely see a tremendous and sustained surge in our national economy given the track record of prosperity that cities have already established. For this reason alone, the United States should adopt policies that unleash our thriving urban economies. But beyond our self-interest, we should also do so to become an exemplar for other modernizing societies that have adopted sprawl in a manner that, like our own, could lead to disastrous environmental consequences.

The Federal Reserve reported that the total amount of mortgage debt owed in the U.S. is almost as much as our entire annual GDP. Single-family homes make up the vast majority of that debt.

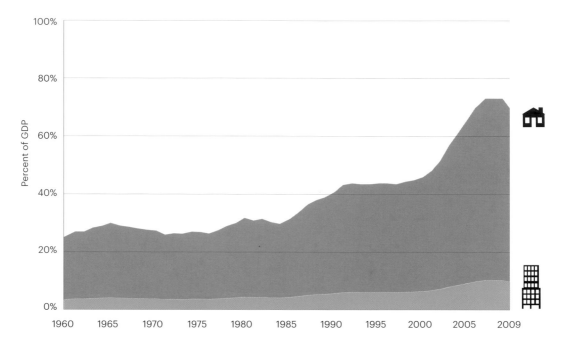

NON-PERFORMING HOME MORTGAGE LOANS, 2002–10

Increased mortgage debt contributed to the global financial crisis.

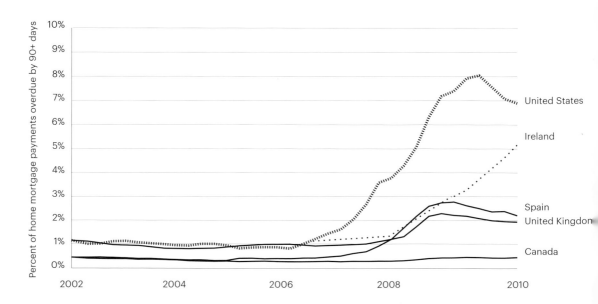

REAL HOUSE PRICES

Housing prices soared in the years leading up to the Great Recession. When the housing bubble burst, it ushered in the global financial crisis, causing the number non-performing home loans to rise sharply worldwide.

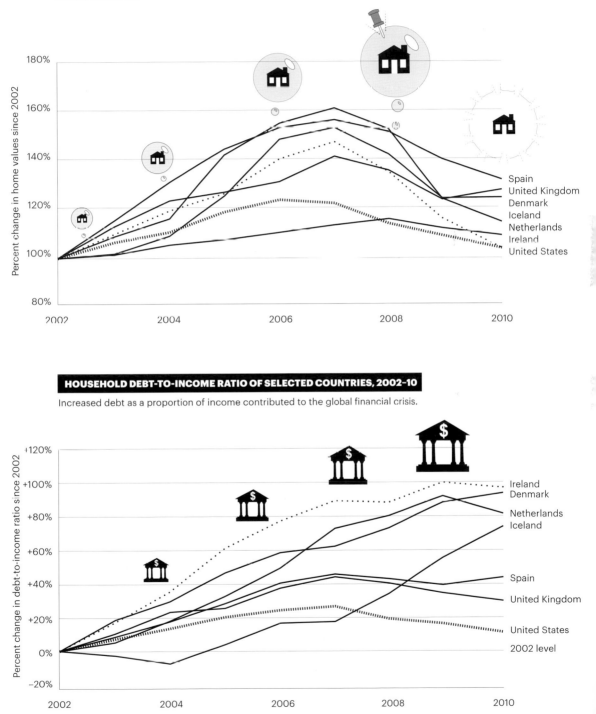

Percent change in home values since 2002

180%
160%
140%
120%
100%
80%

2002   2004   2006   2008   2010

Spain
United Kingdom
Denmark
Iceland
Netherlands
Ireland
United States

HOUSEHOLD DEBT-TO-INCOME RATIO OF SELECTED COUNTRIES, 2002–10

Increased debt as a proportion of income contributed to the global financial crisis.

Percent change in debt-to-income ratio since 2002

+120%
+100%
+80%
+60%
+40%
+20%
0%
−20%

2002   2004   2006   2008   2010

Ireland
Denmark
Netherlands
Iceland
Spain
United Kingdom
United States
2002 level

AMERICAN MODEL VS. CITY-STATE MODEL

AMERICAN MODEL: LOS ANGELES

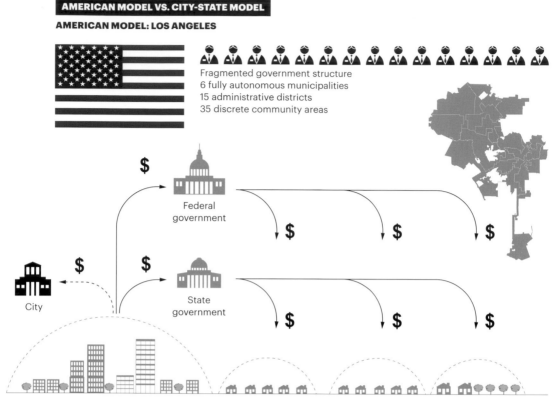

Fragmented government structure
6 fully autonomous municipalities
15 administrative districts
35 discrete community areas

$

Federal government

$ $ $

$ $

City

State government

$ $ $

Tax revenues generated within higher-density areas are sent to local, state, and federal governments. These are redistributed to suburban areas.

AMERICAN MODEL: Los Angeles is an even blanket of height-restricted, low-density sprawl.

CITY-STATE MODEL: HONG KONG

Centralized government structure

City-state
government

Tax revenues are reinvested within the city, where two thirds of the land is a protected wildlife preserve.

CITY-STATE MODEL: Hong Kong is a hyperdense city surrounded by protected forestlands.

THIS IS NOT SUSTAINABILITY

Sustainability is decidedly not Henry David Thoreau's misanthropic vision of a virgin forest occupied by one person.

CITIES, SUSTAINABILITY, AND RESILIENCE

As crucial as the concept may be, "sustainability" has become an over-marketed, hackneyed, and largely misunderstood term as it relates to urbanism. I define sustainability as the aspiration that human activity be made compatible with the long-term health and safety of the natural environment, which, in turn, would ensure the longevity of our own species. Sustainability is decidedly not Henry David Thoreau's misanthropic vision of a virgin forest occupied by one person. In the contemporary context, it is not about camping, or visiting eco-resorts in areas that should remain untouched, or living in "green" McMansions in the wilderness. To the contrary, sustainability is about running toward people, not away from them. It is about embracing all of humanity in order to leave most of the natural world just that—natural. Put in the simplest possible terms, if you love nature, don't live in it. Cities represent the best chance of realizing this aspiration of global sustainability in a rapidly growing world.

There is an alternative to the human self-loathing embedded in so much of environmentalism today: the rare belief that worldwide population growth and sustainability can be mutually compatible.[1] While efforts to stem the rate of population growth are admirable, and through the implementation of economist Jeff Sachs's extraordinary Millennium Development Goals we can and should reduce population growth rates, it remains clear that a world of 10 billion or more is inevitable by the year 2100.

Should environmentalists explicitly or tacitly focus on this growth as the primary problem, they do so at their own peril. Curtailing population growth is certainly one method to reduce resource usage, but who decides who gets to procreate and at what rate? Humanity's history with such judgments is nothing short of bleak, with everything from genocide to forced sterilization representing the most terrifying moments in our collective past. Of course, as Sachs advises, we should actively promote birth control, prosperity, women's education, public health, and all other measures that ethically reduce the rate of population growth. But again, we must have an

GLOBAL CONSUMPTION VS. AMERICAN CONSUMPTION RATES

We must avoid depleting our natural resources.

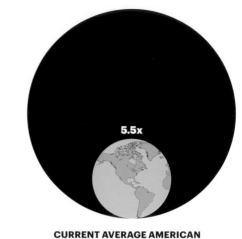

PLANET EARTH
There is only one.

CURRENT AVERAGE GLOBAL CONSUMPTION RATE
Requires 30% more land and resources than there are on earth.

CURRENT AVERAGE AMERICAN CONSUMPTION RATE
Requires 550% more land and resources than there are on earth.

WORLD POPULATION, 1750 PROJECTED TO 2100

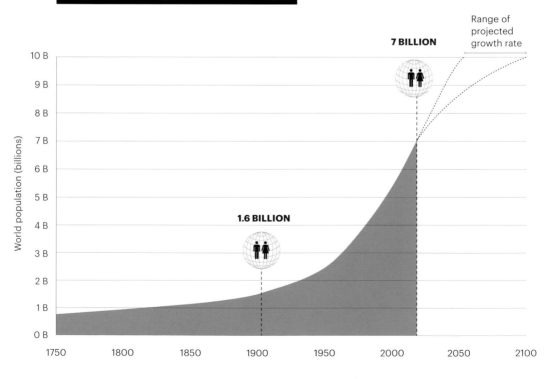

environmental strategy that works with the reality of billions reaching the middle class worldwide in this century.

As human consumption continues to increase the world over, it is now abundantly clear that we use more natural resources than the world can replenish. We are, in our current state, collectively unsustainable. We must address resource usage at a global scale, and we must do so with a full embrace of every baby born. Individual feel-good actions have limited impact at a larger scale. We face a planetary environmental crisis, and must stop believing that solely through our individual choices will we solve this existential threat to current and future generations.

Sustainability, therefore, is not about the negligible benefits of the latest hybrid SUV, fluorescent light bulb, organic floor cleaner, or any of the other technological panaceas that attempt to absolve our gluttonous use of land and resources. Technology will not save us from ourselves, nor will the continual purchase of more stuff, however "green" it may be.

Addressing climate change at a global level will require a dramatic adjustment of our lifestyles—particularly those of the middle and upper classes. But Americans will never adopt en masse dictums that are punitive, self-righteous, and costly. Instead, these adjustments in lifestyle need to lead us to demonstrably more prosperous and joyful lives. For example, the Obama Administration has pushed to increase the fuel efficiency of cars, which certainly will result in lower carbon emissions, improved air-quality, and better health. Coupled with living at higher densities and mass transit, however, people would also drive far fewer miles per year, which would double down on the environmental benefits of more efficient cars. This would in turn increase productivity, enable people to walk for local errands, and free up substantial personal time for friends, family, and other pursuits.

As David Owen describes so eloquently in his book *Green Metropolis,* cities are embodiments of sustainability despite beliefs to the contrary. Whether one considers New York, Paris, or Tokyo, hyperdensity linked to infrastructure consistently lowers carbon footprints per person, creates walkable neighborhoods, and builds enjoyable lifestyles. In looking at cities, many environmentalists point out that they are heat islands and intense users of energy. This is true, but it misses the central point that whatever amount of energy cities may consume, they do so far less on a *per capita* basis. This is precisely why accepting the size of our growing population is essential to effective environmentalism—reductions in carbon footprint matter only if extended over large swaths of our population.

If you love
don't live i

nature,
n it.

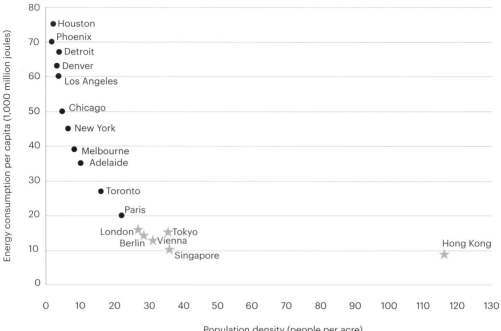

POPULATION DENSITY AND ENERGY CONSUMPTION IN SELECTED METROPOLITAN AREAS

Higher-density areas use less energy per capita.

Energy consumption per capita (1,000 million joules)

- Houston
- Phoenix
- Detroit
- Denver
- Los Angeles
- Chicago
- New York
- Melbourne
- Adelaide
- Toronto
- Paris
- London
- Berlin
- Vienna
- Tokyo
- Singapore
- Hong Kong

Population density (people per acre)

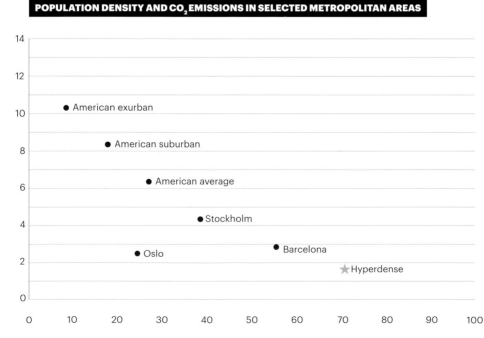

POPULATION DENSITY AND CO$_2$ EMISSIONS IN SELECTED METROPOLITAN AREAS

Total CO$_2$ emissions per capita (tonnes)

- American exurban
- American suburban
- American average
- Stockholm
- Oslo
- Barcelona
- Hyperdense

Population density (people per acre)

Adopting a truly urban lifestyle is clearly the "greenest" and most sustainable choice one can make.[2] Urban residents use far fewer natural resources per person than their suburban counterparts. This is not because city dwellers are environmental angels; to the contrary, most have little realization that they are such valiant stewards of the environment. A widower takes the bus to his doctor because it is simpler, safer, and cheaper than driving. An executive takes the subway to work because in a big city it is her fastest option. A father and daughter walk to the playground because it is easy and they probably will run into friends. An upper-middle-class family pays millions for a condo because it is how they want to live in today's new urban race to keep up with the Joneses, Kims, Patels, and Castellanos. (This is why housing the wealthy in luxury urban condos, balanced by the construction of affordable housing for the less affluent, is better for the environment than encouraging rich people to move to 15,000-square-foot McMansions with five-car garages in the suburbs.)

City dwellers, regardless of income level, have a lower carbon footprint than their suburban counterparts primarily because they walk and use mass transit for their daily commutes, and because they live and work in smaller quarters that heat and cool one another partly through party-wall construction. In essence, because urbanites share transportation and land in closer proximity, they use far fewer resources per person and destroy far less wilderness than would be required to house everyone in cul-de-sacs of single-family houses. Because of this proximity, they can also take advantage of all of the shared services that cities offer, from playgrounds to vast public parks and waterfronts, all of which collectively use far less irrigation and consume less energy to maintain than a lawn owned by each individual household.

In fact, America's densest cities—and not houses scattered in the woods—produce the lowest greenhouse-gas emissions per capita. Most interesting, and of the most telling consequence to true environmentalists, is that this has proved to be true without self-righteous movements or "eat your spinach" mandates. Since most urbanites are green without trying, a baseline of sustainability clearly can be achieved in cities without new products, technologies, or "holier than thou" sacrifices. However, we should not settle for this baseline. Cities may be inherently sustainable, but far more can and must be done to lower their carbon footprints, and many cities are taking action, with impressively scalable results. Cities as diverse as Chicago, Seattle, New York, and Fort Lauderdale have adopted dramatic plans to lower their carbon emissions and address the fact that buildings are among the largest contributors to greenhouse gases. Chicago's Climate Action Plan, for example, is based upon five strategies:

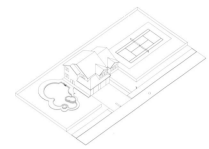

Annual carbon emissions
per household

EXURBAN AVERAGE
0.7 to 1 dwelling units per acre
26.5 jobs per acre

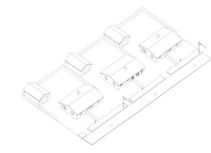

Annual carbon
emissions per household

SUBURBAN AVERAGE
3 to 4 dwelling units per acre
72 jobs per acre

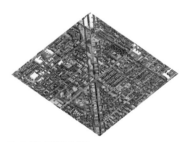
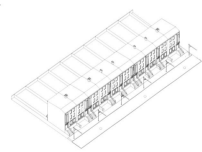

Annual carbon
emissions per household

URBAN AVERAGE
30+ dwelling units per acre
268 jobs per acre

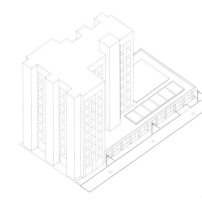

Annual carbon
emissions per household

CARLESS URBAN AVERAGE
60+ dwelling units per acre
1,049 jobs per acre

1   Improve the energy efficiency of buildings.
2   Increase access to clean and renewable energy sources.
3   Improve transportation options.
4   Reduce waste and industrial pollution.
5   Adapt to the new circumstances of climate change.[3]

Together, these strategies form a comprehensive plan that other cities can use to periodically evaluate their performance with respect to the environment, and to make policy decisions focused on realizing medium- and long-term goals regardless of the short-term political cycles that tend to redefine local government's priorities every few years.

There is a significant "green urbanism" movement afoot, both in academic circles and on the political agendas of some of the more progressive governments here and abroad. Green urbanism attempts to take a more active role in shaping communities and the lifestyles of their inhabitants. Timothy Beatley, an urban sustainability expert from the United States who writes about, among other things, the virtues of European cities, points out that "the amount of land consumed by urban growth far exceeds the rate of population growth" in American cities.[4]

Today, numerous aspects of contemporary Western culture continue to spread around the globe despite their proven negative impacts on the environment. In addition to sprawling land use are emissions-causing technologies so helpful in increasing our productivity that they have become hard to live without. One prominent example is air-conditioning, which significantly improves workspaces in climates where humidity and heat otherwise hinder productivity. A series of articles in the *New York Times* chronicled the world's complex and growing need for air-conditioning as well as the challenges to limiting such dependency.[5] This is particularly pressing because so much of the urban growth worldwide is occurring in hot and humid climates in cities such as Singapore, Mumbai, and Dubai. Research associated with this challenge will be paramount, particularly in terms of designing new buildings in extreme climates that can keep occupants cool with less environmental impact. For instance, in their Masdar project, outside of Abu Dhabi, architects Foster + Partners attempt to create a comfortable, zero-carbon-emissions environment by adapting cooling techniques associated with traditional Arabic architecture, such as screening and shading, rather than going the more typical route of adopting international standards of floor-to-ceiling glass and air-conditioning.

The work of architect William McDonough and chemist Michael Braungart approaches sustainability from the perspective of this type of research, design, and industry; they argue that such a place-based

AVERAGE DISTANCES TRAVELED BY CAR FOR SELECTED ACTIVITIES

0.7%
of all car trips are for vacation

29.4%
of all car trips are for work

69.9%
of all car trips are for daily activities
other than work or for vacation

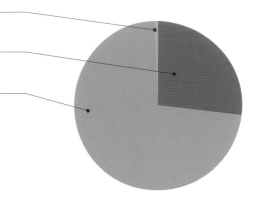

Shopping

Personal errands

Recreation

School/church

Medical

Commute to/from work

Friends/relatives

Work-related trips

Vacation

| 0 | 5 | 10 | 15 | 20 | 25 | 30 | 35 |

Trip length (miles)

consciousness of the environment is a driving factor of good design. Their groundbreaking book, *Cradle to Cradle*, has a simple thesis, which advocates "remaking the way we make things." This approach can be especially powerful if urban designers can create forms of human habitation that better match the inherent challenges of nature rather than simply grafting Western city-building techniques onto a project regardless of the local climate. As the authors state, "Human industry has been in full swing for little over a century, yet it has brought about a decline in almost every ecosystem on the planet. Nature doesn't have a design problem. People do."[6]

Peter Newman and Jeffrey Kenworthy's book, *Sustainability and Cities: Overcoming Automobile Dependence*, focuses on a critical element in the process of suburbanization and the design of our environments. That Americans love cars is no surprise—after all, what's not to love? The first automobile patent granted in the United States dates back to 1789, and subsequent developments, such as Henry Ford's assembly production line, eventually revolutionized the world. Automobiles represent the freedom of the open road, and in a land as vast and beautiful as the United States, the call of that open road is almost definitional for most Americans. This is more than some cultural artifact that can be tossed aside; it is part of our national soul. But it is critical to not confuse the tranquility of driving across our great landscape with the tension of two-hour traffic jams on the outskirts of our cities. Belief in the sustainability of mass transit and urbanization does not deny the great American sojourn—on the contrary, it enables it by leaving the roads open for pleasure, not for commuting. Driving across the country is a joy; driving to work is folly.[7]

Though revolutionary for progress in the twentieth century, cars today fail to meet the transportation needs of a rapidly urbanizing global population of several billions. Newman and Kenworthy point out that our sprawling cities finally face land constraints, and distances from exurbs to jobs are no longer acceptable or practical. There are two primary sustainability challenges in this world—oil depletion and greenhouse-gas effects—and most Americans are finally coming into contact with at least the first challenge due to the increased cost of driving. The average price of a gallon of gasoline in July 2008 exceeded $4.10 and dropped to a four-year historic low of just above $1.65 in December of that year, which is commonly thought of as the depth of the global recession.[8] But it has taken only three years to climb

DRIVING COULD BE FUN AGAIN

Mad Men's protagonist Donald Draper driving a convertible on the open road in Los Angeles

Driving ac
the count
driving to
is folly.

cross
ry is a joy;
work

AVERAGE ANNUAL RETAIL PRICE OF GASOLINE, 1929–2011

The average national price of gasoline is increasingly volatile. Prices are in 2011 dollars.

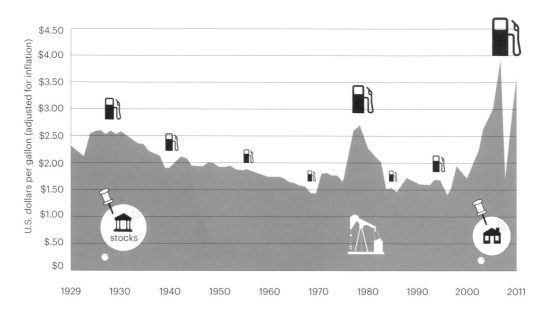

TOTAL VEHICLE MILES TRAVELED BY ALL AMERICANS YEARLY, 1987–2011

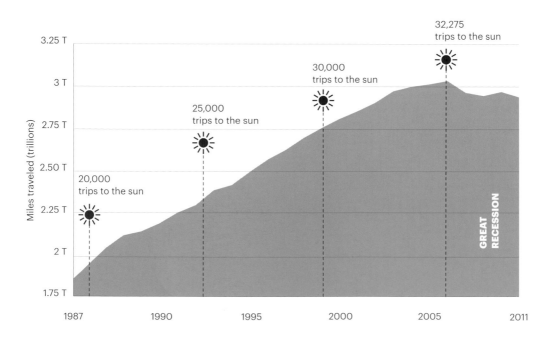

back to pre-recession prices, even while the world economy continues to sputter. Prosperous times can lead to revolutionary advances in technology, but they can just as well lead to the artificial sustenance of technologies that no longer serve our needs as a society. The global magnitude of this reality cannot be understated, given the prosperity that is now reaching billions. Traffic jams have become the hallmark of the world's burgeoning economies, with mobility at a standstill and pollution from sprawling urban areas at an all-time high.

As a consequence of these factors worldwide, and as Newman and Kenworthy discuss, environmentalism has evolved from a grassroots movement to a matter of increasing international political concern. This significant shift happened gradually but was formalized in 1992 with the adoption of Agenda 21 by 178 governments including the United States at the United Nations Conference on Environment and Development (UNCED), in Rio de Janeiro. The authors of Agenda 21 laid out 27 core principles, the eighth of which says: "To achieve sustainable development and a higher quality of life for all people, States should reduce and eliminate unsustainable patterns of production and consumption."[9]

While the United States is not legally bound to adopt the provisions of Agenda 21, many local governments have used it in planning smart growth and transportation initiatives, as well as in limiting the development of rural land. In spite of voluntary adoption, some perceive Agenda 21 as a threat to property rights. In the 2012 election cycle, it provided fodder for the Tea Party and presidential candidates vying for the GOP's nomination who oppose any kind of link between international development goals and those of local governments here in America.[10] And yet principle two makes clear that Agenda 21 recognizes national sovereignty in decision-making:

THE TEA PARTY AND AGENDA 21

Tea Party propaganda is intended to spread fear that the federal government and global organizations such as the United Nations have outsized influence over the decisions of everyday Americans.

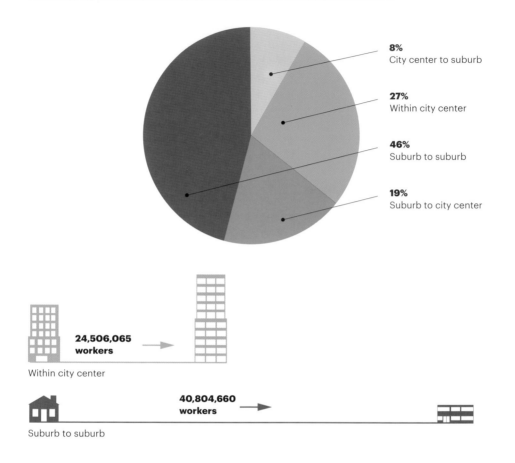

8%
City center to suburb

27%
Within city center

46%
Suburb to suburb

19%
Suburb to city center

24,506,065 workers

Within city center

40,804,660 workers

Suburb to suburb

AMERICAN COMMUTER MASS-TRANSIT RIDERSHIP

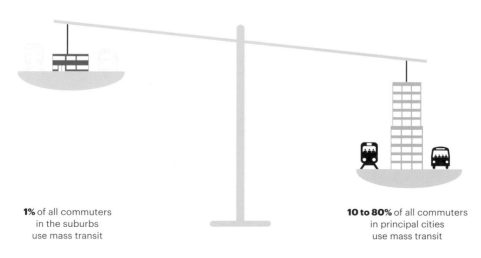

1% of all commuters
in the suburbs
use mass transit

10 to 80% of all commuters
in principal cities
use mass transit

States have, in accordance with the Charter of the United Nations and the principles of international law, the sovereign right to exploit their own resources pursuant to their own environmental and developmental policies, and the responsibility to ensure that activities within their jurisdiction or control do not cause damage to the environment of other States or of areas beyond the limits of national jurisdiction.[11]

The misguided perception that global interests could someday dictate how Americans develop land and set transportation policy to further connect the country causes some Americans to be wary of losing not only their personal property but also their ability to drive as freely and as cheaply as possible thanks to government-subsidized roads, vehicles, and gasoline. Yet the notion that smart growth threatens American sovereignty is cynical at best and delusional at worst. *Our* culture, and often our cultural confusion, drives the global climate-change crisis, and *we* must lead the world out of it. America uses more energy and emits more pollutants per capita than any other major nation. It is our solemn obligation to address this issue, and to address it at a global scale.

An Inconvenient Truth, former vice president Al Gore's companion book to the award-winning documentary of the same title, catalogues the damage we perpetrate on the environment, as well as the areas where hope remains for correcting the course of global warming and environmental degradation. Arguing for a clean-energy future and the opportunities it offers us as a society, he writes:

> There's something even more precious to be gained if we do the right thing. The climate crisis also offers us the chance to experience what very few generations in history have had the privilege of knowing: *a generational mission*; the exhilaration of a compelling *moral purpose*; a shared and unifying *cause*; the thrill of being forced by circumstances to put aside the pettiness and conflict that so often stifle the restless human need for transcendence; *the opportunity to rise*.[12]

By illustrating the environmental impacts of common practices in forestry, mining, irrigation, and urban sprawl, Gore's survey of the world's most environmentally damaging practices, in tandem with his knowledge of the politics surrounding climate change, has created direct access to the findings of countless scientists.

Making data about climate change accessible is a critical step in coalescing the world's growing population in a campaign to save the planet, and Gore's Climate Change Reality Project has enlisted five million people in the

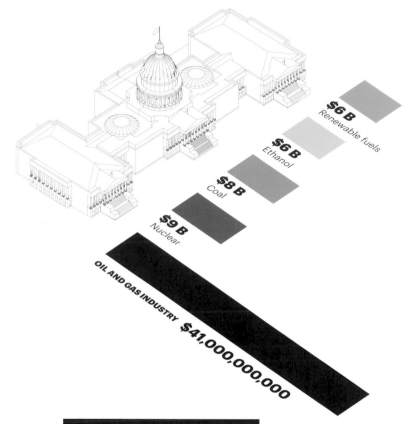

ANNUAL FEDERAL ENERGY SUBSIDIES

$6 B
Renewable fuels

$6 B
Ethanol

$8 B
Coal

$9 B
Nuclear

OIL AND GAS INDUSTRY $41,000,000,000

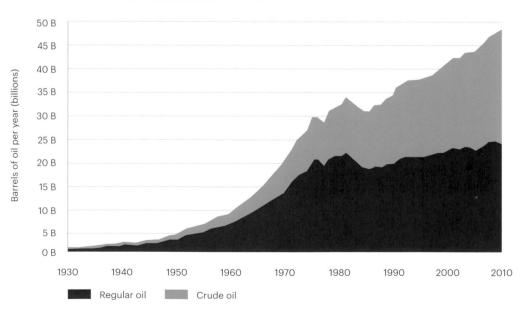

GLOBAL OIL PRODUCTION, 1930–2010

Barrels of oil per year (billions)

50 B
45 B
40 B
35 B
30 B
25 B
20 B
15 B
10 B
5 B
0 B

1930   1940   1950   1960   1970   1980   1990   2000   2010

■ Regular oil   ■ Crude oil

effort "to reveal the complete truth about the climate crisis in a way that ignites the moral courage in each of us."[13] This kind of grassroots approach is decidedly different than trying to affect climate change by running for president of the United States. But, in many ways, this strategy may prove more effective for Gore because it has generated the kind of boundless movement that crosses political borders and ideological divides in favor of sharing information. Even if none of Gore's efforts to stall global warming comes to fruition in tangible policy reforms, he will at least have succeeded in coalescing a new generation of activists, thinkers, and leaders in a conversation about the future of our local communities as well as our global environment. Most important, and largely thanks to Vice President Gore, most Americans today believe that climate change is real and caused by human activity.[14]

Given the tremendous implications of an unsustainable future, we must finally acknowledge and accept that catastrophic climate change may well be upon us. Environmentalist Bill McKibben's *Rolling Stone* article, "Global Warming's Terrifying New Math," makes it plain that the scientific data that substantiates climate change is no longer opaque or contestable. We are living in an era of global warming, acidifying oceans, and unprecedented glacier melt that will have severe and lasting implications for our energy bills, our food crops, and our weather, just to name a few of the realities. As McKibben reports, 20 years after the creation of Agenda 21, not a thing was accomplished at the most recent global summit, in 2012, which also took place in Rio. With President Obama focused on a recession at home, and few items of any consequence on the agenda, the summit dissolved with little done to chart a plan of action for the world to continue moving forward in a collective effort to address the threats of climate change.

Nonetheless, in the same article, McKibben argues that the summit was a milestone of sorts because it coincided with a mathematical understanding of climate change that can be easily explained with three numbers. The first is 2 degrees Celsius, or the maximum number of degrees by which the planet can afford to get warmer without dire consequence. The second is 565 gigatons, or the budgeted number of carbon-dioxide emissions scientists believe can still be pumped into the atmosphere without raising the temperature more than 2 degrees Celsius. And the third is 2,795 gigatons, which represents the amount of carbon contained in the world's proven oil and gas reserves. In short, our existing but untapped carbon resources will easily allow us, if we keep using them, to elevate the world's temperature far beyond 2 degrees Celsius.[15] The case is clear: We must find and adopt all measures to consume less carbon, and cities are the most obvious means of doing this at mass scale while still allowing people to prosper and enjoy life.

GLOBAL WARMING AND SEA LEVEL RISE

According to Bill McKibben, the world's oil and gas reserves are sufficient to destroy civilization.

There are 2,795 gigatons of carbon in known global oil and gas reserves.

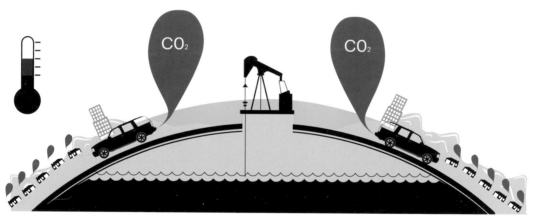

If more than 565 gigatons of carbon are released into the atmosphere,

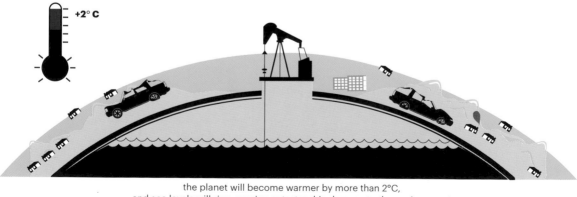

the planet will become warmer by more than 2°C,
and sea levels will rise, causing catastrophic damage to the environment.

The role of municipal governments in advancing sustainable policies that protect and enhance the lives of their constituents is of paramount importance in moving from federal inaction to urban action. The tightening of public budgets also mandates a more sustainable approach to allocating revenues and to reducing resource consumption. Governments concerned with sustainability are adopting new programs that reduce expenses, such as more efficient trash collection, extension of local transit routes, and the replacement of municipal fleets with more efficient vehicles. The costs associated with these new technologies may well pay for themselves, and in some cases even if they don't, they may be worth sacrifices in other areas.

Regardless of their sustainability, however, cities are vulnerable sets of materials and systems. They are subject to the natural disasters that have become more frequent and threatening in the past few years; they are also subject to manmade dangers such as terrorism, war, and economic divestment. New Orleans presents a particularly vivid example of a city whose resilience has been tested by both kinds of threat. Hurricane Katrina was a natural disaster of significant magnitude in its own right, but the disintegration of much of the city's social fabric in its aftermath was as much the fault of the local government and institutions as it was the storm. Furthermore, a number of manmade problems, including infrastructure that channeled waters into the Lower Ninth Ward, greatly exacerbated the natural disaster.[16]

Similarly, Hurricanes Irene and Sandy challenged much of the northeastern United States in an unprecedented one-two punch spaced apart by only a year, indicating the potential for a new normal in which storms anticipated every hundred or five hundred years may be coming with far more frequency and ferocity. The resulting damage indicated the need for a variety of measures to protect everything from the nation's financial district to mass transit infrastructure to coastal and inland communities heretofore considered safe from hurricanes. It is particularly telling that in the aftermath of Sandy, higher-density neighborhoods and centralized infrastructure such as underground power and mass transit generally fared better than lower-density areas with small houses, elevated power lines, and automobile dependency that led to gas lines not seen since the oil crisis of the 1970s.

We must recognize that climate change is upon us, and protection from its most adverse effects must be a top priority, especially in concentrated population centers and coastal cities. Indeed, from natural disasters to terrorist attacks, cities appear to be outsized objects of vulnerability. Just as some scholars suggest the threat of terrorism can only grow, the threat of severe weather associated with climate change appears to be accelerating. But when one looks at ancient as well as modern history, as Professors Larry Vale and Tom Campanella do in their book *The Resilient City*,

LOWER MANHATTAN POST-9/11

After the terrorist attacks of September 11, 2001, federal policymakers and local government leaders, in coordination with private developers, set out to build a vibrant mixed-use neighborhood with 24-hour services, parks, and a variety of new commercial and residential buildings supported by rapid mass transit.

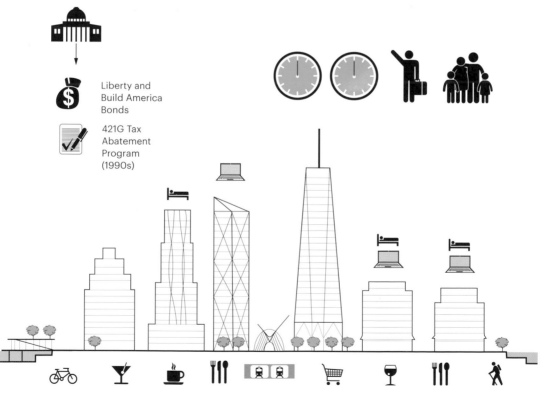

Liberty and Build America Bonds

421G Tax Abatement Program (1990s)

one sees that cities have proven remarkably durable in the face of disasters both natural and manmade, from Rome to Chicago to Nagasaki.

In New York after 9/11, many reputable thinkers from economists to biologists predicted the end of the skyscraper and even the end of Lower Manhattan. Their suggestions seem preposterous now—but this is not to suggest it is easy to cope with destruction. Cities must make investments and adjustments to fend off and bounce back from inevitable threats. For many waterfront cities, dramatic interventions ranging from manmade wetlands to sea gates may be necessary to cope with storm surges and rising sea levels as have occurred in London and Rotterdam, interventions that will undoubtedly be costly and may require creative public-private partnership mechanisms to fund.[17] By contrast, we should rethink the wisdom of oceanfront homes on barrier beaches, sandbars that primarily function to protect the mainland if their dunes have not been destroyed by housing construction. Such development is made possible by private insurance policies that are backed by the federal government, yet another form of subsidy for low-density areas that we should reconsider.

Unlike the clear vulnerabilities of sprawl, the resilience of cities is often underappreciated. New York after 9/11 and several California cities that were struck by earthquakes or fires in the latter half of the twentieth century are prominent examples of American cities that, with the right mix of private- and public-sector coordination, have grown stronger and more sustainable than before. In time, and with the right mix of strategic pro-growth policies, American cities can withstand the challenges of climate change. Perhaps more important, these same cities feature inherent environmental benefits that when amplified can lead us to a safer and more sustainable world for generations to come.

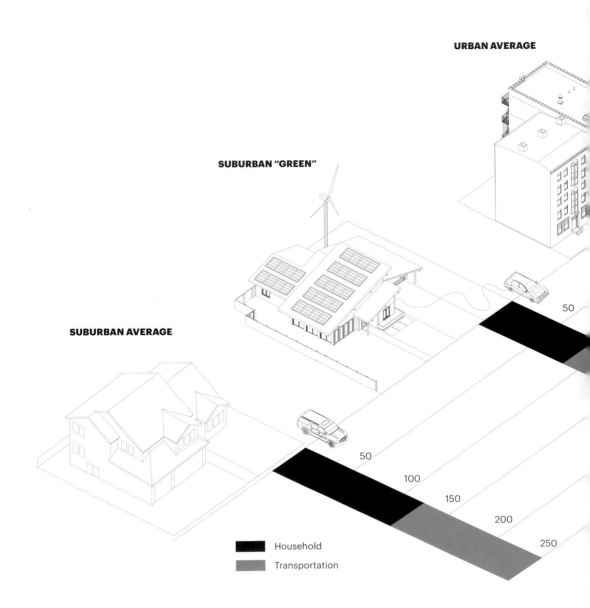

URBAN AVERAGE

SUBURBAN "GREEN"

SUBURBAN AVERAGE

50

50

100

150

200

250

Household

Transportation

URBAN "GREEN"

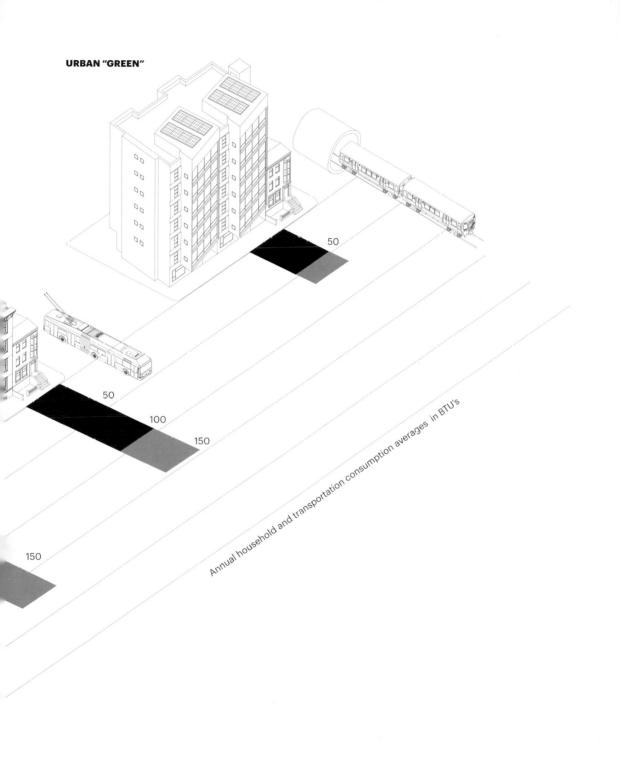

50

50

100

150

Annual household and transportation consumption averages in BTU's

150

HYPERDENSITY LEAVES NATURE NATURAL

With or without new green technologies, suburban and exurban development is less sustainable than compact cities.

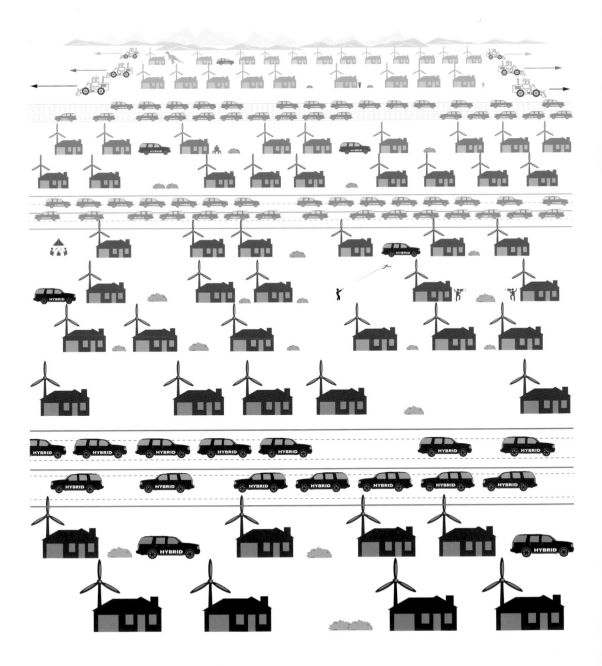

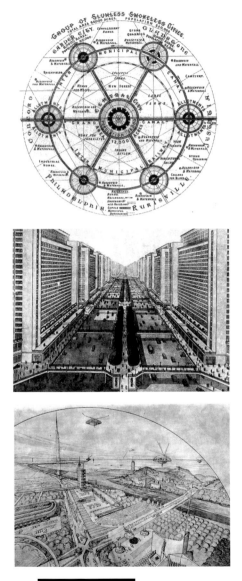

TAMING THE CITY

1 Ebenezer Howard, Garden City, 1898
2 Le Corbusier, Ville Radieuse, 1924
3 Frank Lloyd Wright, Broadacre City, 1932–58

CITIES, HEALTH, AND JOY

Historically, cities have been considered a scourge to public health and happiness. During numerous pandemics that killed millions worldwide, people who lived cheek by jowl in urban areas were most vulnerable to widespread contagion. The soot and grime in cities during the Industrial Revolution resulted in tuberculosis and other lung diseases. Dense concentrations of humanity living with inadequate sewage systems caused numerous waterborne diseases such as cholera. The social mixing that accompanies close quarters, combined with easy access to prostitution and drugs, made cities hotbeds for sexually transmitted diseases, substance abuse, and needle sharing. Violent crime has, for centuries, diminished urban public health in terms of murders, rapes, and assaults.

Taken together, such physically harmful conditions were considered by many to have triggered or exacerbated the mental health problems associated with cities, such as stress and urban isolation. One need only turn to the paintings of cities through the 1800s and 1900s to see a stream of depictions of alienation and unhappiness, sensations that are perhaps best embodied in Edward Munch's haunting image, *The Scream*.

Throughout the nineteenth and twentieth centuries, the physical, cultural, and mental ailments associated with urbanity have been primary arguments for suburbanization. Ebenezer Howard's vision to segregate residents from industrial areas into Garden Cities, the parkways of Robert Moses, and even the suburbanizing city plans of great modernist architects such as Le Corbusier's Ville Radieuse or Frank Lloyd Wright's Broadacre City were proposed based on the need to escape "the urban jungle" in pursuit of healthier environs.

With World War II and the advent of weapons of mass destruction, the public health vulnerabilities of cities reached a drastic new scale. Technological "advancements" created a new and very real threat, in which thousands or even millions could be killed in a single, targeted strike. The unthinkable decimation of Hiroshima and Nagasaki, as well as the less destructive but no less socially impactful bombings of London and Dresden, seared the images of burning cities into society's collective imagination. As mentioned in the introduction, President Dwight D. Eisenhower's

The National Highway Defense Act of 1956 set the stage for a national highway system that is now more than 450,000 miles long (including state and local highways).

Federal Highway Act was primarily a cold-war defensive measure, providing a means to not only disperse and protect the U.S. population but also provide infrastructure—complete with appropriate bridge clearances—to transport intercontinental ballistic missiles.[1]

PRESIDENT EISENHOWER

Eisenhower and his advisors discuss the National Highway Defense Act in 1956.

While Eisenhower's freeway overpasses were raised to keep our middle class safe, the parkway bridges of Robert Moses were lowered to keep our middle class white.[2] There is no question that in the postwar United States, a fear of race, as well as the arms race, drove the public health and safety concerns that fueled suburbanization. Racial segregation, at its heart, was based on the gruesome misconception that social homogeneity led to a healthier, safer environment for white middle-class families.

It is astonishing to consider how much has changed in only a few short decades. Many Americans today cherish diversity primarily because they see it as enriching their and their children's social well-being. And as a whole, the United States is far more diverse than it was in the mid-twentieth century. People from scores of countries and cultures now seek out this diversity, in neighbors, classmates, partners, and spouses, because it expands their minds and their knowledge of the world, which leads to greater happiness.

Consequently, we must consider the public health implications of cities not only in terms of medical metrics such as lifespan and freedom from physical ailments, but also in terms of metrics that represent public happiness and joy. Today, we know that physical health and mental happiness are inextricably linked, and, as a result, we must understand how the design of our communities impacts both. This knowledge is critical to meet the essential goal of creating a happier and healthier populace: designing healthier communities may significantly lower physical- and mental-health-care costs nationwide, costs that today threaten our nation's economic stability.

Increasingly, it is clear that on both counts—health and joy—American cities are reversing long historical trends, both real and perceived, that associated urbanity with illness and unhappiness. While some of the world's poorest cities continue to house vulnerable populations without access to clean water, waste management, and health care, most American cities today are significantly further ahead in terms of such systems. We are, for the most part, an advanced service economy that no longer generates the levels of dirt and pollution associated with the industrial city. And while threats remain, they are nowhere near as widespread as what the nation confronted decades ago, when the cold war made population dispersal seem prudent. Moreover, urban crime rates have fallen dramatically across the country. To wit, most of what historically concerned middle-class Americans about the health and safety of city life has all but dissipated with the dawn of this new century.

Compared to the largely overdramatized health threats of urban pandemics, gang warfare, and dirty bombs, we are in reality confronted with much more significant and widespread public health challenges that have arisen from the sedentary, automobile-oriented lifestyles that dominate the nation today. With an ageing population and skyrocketing health care costs, we must address these challenges if we are to achieve increased public health and happiness.

In 2003, researchers Barbara A. McCann and Reid Ewing published an exhaustive study of 200,000 inhabitants of 448 U.S. counties. Those living in counties with sprawling built environments were found to be more likely to suffer from obesity than those living in cities. For every 50-point increase in the degree of sprawl, the odds of a county resident being obese rose by 10

COMMUTING DISTANCE AFFECTS LEVELS OF PHYSICAL ACTIVITY

Over a seven-year period, a major study conducted by Dr. Christine Hoehner charted levels of physical activity among 4,300 people who live and work in the metropolitan areas of Dallas, Fort Worth, and Austin, Texas. Those who traveled farther to get to work were less likely to exercise the recommended 30 minutes per week.

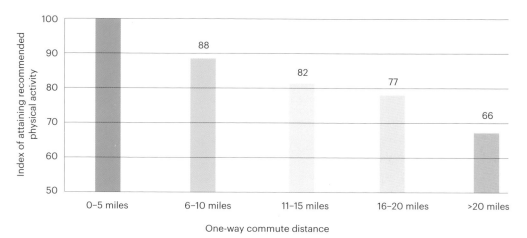

COMMUTING DISTANCE AFFECTS PREVALENCE OF OBESITY

The work of Dr. Hoehner published in the *American Journal of Preventive Medicine* recorded that the prevalence of obesity increases when people have longer commuting distances.

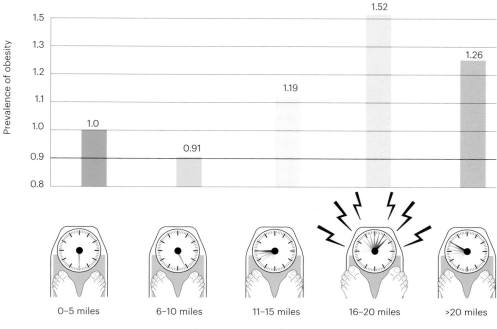

percent.[3] More recent medical studies link hypertension and high blood pressure to driving and, particularly, to sitting in traffic jams, which can cause stress, muscular pain, and road rage.[4]

Dense cities encourage public health simply because they engender a culture of beneficial habits, such as walking and bicycling, and because they provide people better access to more numerous healthcare options. This is not just anecdotal, wishful thinking. Life expectancies in America's densest cities, which include areas with poor air quality, are significantly longer than in areas thought to be more "natural."[5] In fact, studies have shown traffic accidents to be the number one cause of childhood fatalities worldwide, beating HIV, malaria, and other diseases for this horrifying title.[6]

Americans who live in hyperdense cities are healthier than their suburban counterparts not only because they have more opportunities to walk but also because they tend to spend less time commuting. This time saved can add tremendously to one's quality of life, as it can be used for recreation, relaxation, and social interaction. These essential activities are often invaluable to the joy of life, making one happier and more productive.

Freeing up time spent in traffic jams pays even greater dividends when that time is spent with family members, a partner, or contributing to one's community. Today, many American families live frustratingly complex lives, often characterized by two parents who work, children who need to be shuttled from one activity to the next, and an array of social, cultural, educational, and religious endeavors that require navigating a dispersed network including office parks, schools, places of worship, nursing homes, community centers, and playing fields. While this world of activities can be rich, rewarding, and fundamental to our happiness, traversing its geography can be unpleasant, especially for a single parent. Ask most suburban parents about the daily grind of school drop-offs, grocery shopping, ballet recitals, and play dates, and the most common laments tend to center wittingly or unwittingly around the automobile and its failings, such as growing congestion, the cost to fill up the minivan, or the "spare tire" forming around junior's waist. While all parenting is stressful, urban child-rearing is largely free of the specific issues associated with driving such as vehicular costs and childhood obesity.

And such complaints represent only the problems that can be measured. More immeasurable is the opportunity cost of the time lost to traffic jams, a cost that in a busy world isolates us from each other and frays our social fabric. A 2011 Swedish study associates significantly higher divorce rates with commuting, and a recent American study found an increasing number of couples living in long-distance marriages because one of them had to relocate for work.[7] More and more, research points to the correlation

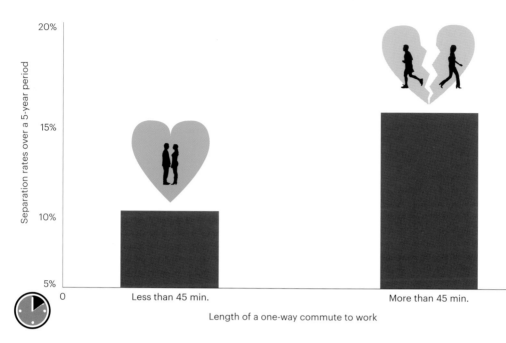

ROMANCE AND COMMUTING TIME

Long commutes put unnecessary strain on relationships. In a 10-year study of over 2 million Swedish couples, those with commute times of over 45 minutes each way experienced a 5% higher rate of separation or divorce than those who had shorter commutes.

Separation rates over a 5-year period

20%

15%

10%

5%

0

Less than 45 min.

More than 45 min.

Length of a one-way commute to work

between sprawling environments and economic hardship, which naturally leads to more familial stress.

Compound this with the advent of smart phones and tablets, and one has a full picture of a disassociated culture in which the means of interaction between partner and partner, or parent and child, are increasingly limited and virtual. This, in turn, has led to a new national health issue that compounds the known problems of drunken and teen car use: texting while driving now causes thousands of annual traffic deaths and injuries.[8] While the media abounds with stories about the dangers of this practice, few journalists seem to consider why people continue to do it. Driving, particularly in congested areas, is boring and unproductive. So, alone and stuck in our cars, we turn to our devices in search of productivity, entertainment, or some other mode of happiness to compensate for staring out the windshield at the next car's bumper.

The boredom of driving in hours of traffic can be compounded by the isolation some may encounter when they finally pull into their driveways. I am by no means asserting that suburbs are boring, which is a gross stereotype that indiscriminately lumps together lifeless exurbs with more vibrant, increasingly diverse communities. But however socially diverse suburbs have become, the physical consequence of single-family homes is by definition an array of houses, lawns, and fences designed to separate people. Look at a suburban street on a typical day and the most common sight is a landscape devoid of human beings. Many people will tell you that privacy and serenity are the very qualities that attract them to their homes and communities, and their right to pursue a quieter suburban life is inalienable and should not be impugned. Solitude, however, does come at a price. Lower density by its nature leads to fewer social interactions, and for a stay-at home parent or a senior living alone this may result in unhealthy isolation.

Seinfeld, Friends, and *Sex and the City* portrayed American urban life in a positive light.

By contrast, people seeking more social contact are increasingly choosing cities. Urban housing demand, including multi-family housing, clearly represents a shift in people's desires for a different, less isolating lifestyle.[9] In addition, the allure of the social life of the city has been elevated by popular culture. The arrival in the 1990s of a new breed of "urban sitcom" including *Seinfeld*, *Friends*, and *Sex and the City* transformed the image of urban living in America, indicating to the entire country that perhaps cities may be more about fun than fear, albeit for a lily-white set of young elites with seemingly undemanding jobs.[10]

Homogenous though those images have been, the significance of positive urban imagery showing the happiness engendered by city living should not be understated. As we transitioned to a service economy, ended a cold war, moved toward budget surpluses, and were troubled by nothing more significant than the dalliances of our president, many Americans partied like it was 1999, and decidedly did so in our cities.

For young people, cities have historically represented economic opportunity, but, arguably, the turn of the century witnessed the attractiveness of cities expand well beyond the potential to find jobs. Cities were

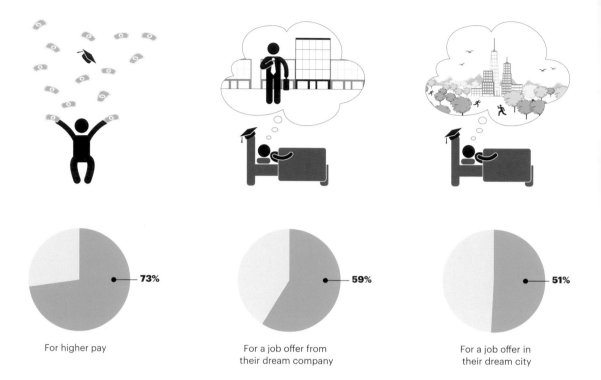

CITIES APPEAL TO YOUNG PROFESSIONALS

According to the 2012 Adecco Graduation Survey, most recent college graduates would relocate to cities for the right opportunity.

73%

For higher pay

59%

For a job offer from
their dream company

51%

For a job offer in
their dream city

no longer a place for recent college graduates to simply grab the first rung of the economic ladder, only to escape to the suburbs once they had climbed a little higher. Suddenly, for a much wider spectrum of American youth beyond the usual urban hipsters, cities held the potential to find not only jobs but also culture, excitement, and their own personal dalliances. Despite the Great Recession's impact on the job market—and perhaps because cities are the main centers of job growth—a 2012 survey by the staffing and recruiting agency Adecco shows that 73 percent of recent graduates would relocate to a city for higher pay; 59 percent for a job offer from their dream company; and 51 percent for a job offer in their dream city.[11]

Similarly, many older Americans are seeking the economic opportunity and day-to-day ease of metropolitan life. Many empty-nesters and retirees choose to shed the expenses associated with large houses, lawns, car maintenance, and commuting. They primarily sell their houses and move to apartments because it makes sense financially, but they also want to be closer to activities and services, including medical care, whose importance to them will only increase with time. Cities offer indispensable networks for ageing in place (that is, ageing in one's own home for as long as possible), and as life expectancies continue to rise for Americans, so does the desire for a full and healthy urban life.[12]

People old and young often live in cities by themselves or, at least, outside of nuclear family structures, an experience that can be a "scream" in the positive sense, the opposite of Munch's existential wail. Groundbreaking work by the sociologist Eric Klinenburg found that within the social and cultural capacity of cities, independent singles find a range of enjoyment, with companionship when they need it and solitude when they don't. Interesting new models of naturally occurring retirement communities, or NORCs, are emerging in cities, with a mix of young and old supporting each other in large apartment buildings or apartment complexes, where easy intergenerational exchange is possible.[13]

In addition to the needs of young, single professionals and retirees, there are those of families with children. Through the postwar era, due to many of the threats to health and safety supposedly endemic to cities that we have discussed, American middle-class families sought the refuge of suburban life. Slowly Americans are re-examining this set of choices as well, and many are opting to raise their children in cities. Seeing the reductions in crime and the consequent safety of more-affordable fringe neighborhoods, the availability of active parks, and the betterment of some school systems, parents have begun to embrace the possibility of less time driving and more time with their children. Children in turn are embracing the cultural diversity, the shared spaces, and the ever-changing landscapes of city sidewalks.

So, cities in general—and again in a marked shift away from the stereotype of being centers of hostile, greedy people—increasingly are sources of happiness for their residents. Edward Glaeser, in *Triumph of the City*, states: "Across countries, reported life satisfaction rises with the share of the population that lives in cities, even when controlling for the countries' income and education."[14]

Nonetheless, cities still have significant health and social problems, and only through sound planning and policies can local governments ensure the health and well being of their residents. Long-embedded disparities in the ways cities developed over time still contribute to economic and social inequities today; they exacerbate community health problems and create a larger share of crime in disadvantaged neighborhoods. It is well documented that obesity, childhood asthma, and diabetes disproportionately affect poor, inner-city areas that are characterized by nearby highways, noxious municipal facilities, deteriorating housing conditions, inadequate health education, and limited access to medical care.

Most of wha
middle-clas
about the he
safety of cit
all but dissip
with the daw
new century

concerned
s Americans
alth and
 life has
ated
n of the

CRIME IN AMERICA: CITIES VS. SUBURBS

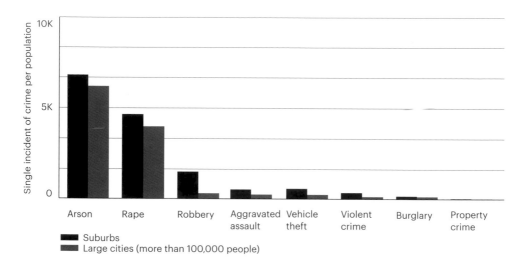

Single incident of crime per population

10K

5K

0

Arson Rape Robbery Aggravated Vehicle Violent Burglary Property
                       assault   theft   crime   crime

■ Suburbs
■ Large cities (more than 100,000 people)

NATIONAL HOMICIDE RATES PER 100,000 RESIDENTS

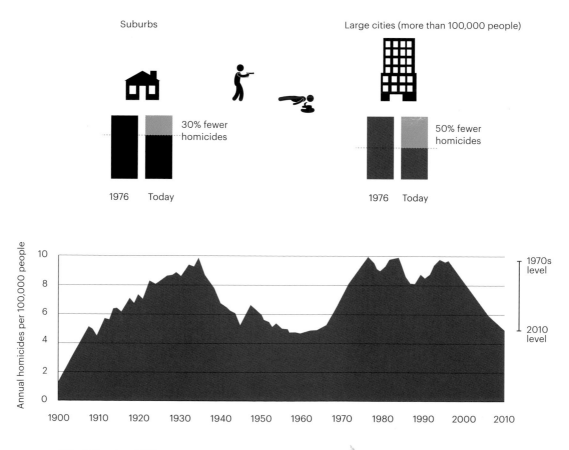

Suburbs

30% fewer homicides

1976   Today

Large cities (more than 100,000 people)

50% fewer homicides

1976   Today

Annual homicides per 100,000 people

10

8

6

4

2

0

1900 1910 1920 1930 1940 1950 1960 1970 1980 1990 2000 2010

1970s level

2010 level

Taken together, these are serious problems that affect a large proportion of people in even the most successful of American cities. Add in factors such as literacy, race, and teenage pregnancy rates, and our country's persistent inequities become obvious. The silver lining is that cities are better equipped to deal with these disparities than suburbs, where the same lack of opportunity can lead to the precipitous decline of entire towns through disinvestment, declining property values, increased crime, physical degradation of housing stock, and spiraling vacancy rates. Successful cities, by contrast, can turn around less-healthy areas through a series of measures, be they more equitable siting requirements for noxious municipal facilities, investment in parks and education, community policing, the use of congestion pricing, or the adoption of zero-emission fleet vehicles, such as taxis and buses. Examples of these measures have been effective in some of the world's poorer nations, including Brazil and India, and generally have a much greater impact in cities where large-scale changes can be implemented at once through centralized reforms rather than piecemeal actions.

Urban communities nationwide are adopting policies that build health and culture. Whether it's community gardening, farming on a larger scale, tree planting, or the maintenance and upkeep of our public spaces and parks, individuals who are actively involved in their neighborhoods are part of a new movement that is striving to redefine the way we live in cities.

Much has been written and broadcast about the value of new urban public spaces, including Los Angeles's Grand Park, Chicago's Bloomingdale Trail, and Dallas's Klyde Warren Park, which decks over Woodall Rodgers Freeway in an effort to

NEW URBAN PARKS

Urban parks have long played an important role in providing quality open space for recreation. A new breed of parks builds on this legacy by activating central business districts and creating links between diverse communities.

1 Frank Gehry, Millennium Park, Chicago, 2004
2 Nelson Byrd Woltz, Citygarden, St. Louis, 2009
3 The Office of James Burnett, Klyde Warren Park, Dallas, 2009

SHoP Architects, East River Waterfront Esplanade, 2011

SHoP Architects, East River Waterfront Pier 15, 2012

SHoP Architects, East River Waterfront Pier 15, 2012

knit a new high-rise, mixed-use development into the downtown cultural district.[15] These are just a few examples of a nationwide push to create public parks, realize waterfront redevelopment projects, and encourage the adaptive reuse of obsolete infrastructure. Such projects capitalize on the popularity of cities and build public connections between neighborhoods and new cultural institutions. A recent wave of philanthropic investment in cultural buildings, such as Frank Gehry's Disney Concert Hall in Los Angeles and Norman Foster's Winspear Opera House in Dallas, is adding dramatic new venues for the enjoyment of city life. Cities can take the opportunities presented by the construction of these new destinations to rethink entire neighborhoods and sectors. Through the combination of public space improvements, better infrastructure, and the market-calibrated increase of development capacity, cities can achieve the kind of hyperdensity that is economically capable of supporting parks, arts venues, and affordable housing in mixed-income buildings.

Also of critical importance are the sustained use and maintenance of these new public places. No matter how successful their opening season, the work of continuously programming spaces and making them an integral part of a neighborhood continues well into the future. New parks must have sustainable funding sources that ensure they will remain well lit, clean, safe places for recreation regardless of the economic profile of the neighborhood.

Parks, public spaces, and cultural buildings play a critical role in enhancing the joy of traversing a city on foot. Similarly, when it is successful, public art has a positive impact on its surroundings because it enhances one's experience of the public sphere, it creates focal points, meeting places, and educational opportunities that enhance the civic realm, and contributes to our joyous experience of streets and sidewalks, gardens and parks. ArtPlace, a consortium of national foundations, banks, and government agencies, is one of many national organizations focused on expanding the role of art and cultural programming in cities to accelerate creative place-making across the United States.

Progressive mayors around the country and the world are making strategic investments to infuse their cities with the culture and recreation that promote a healthy and happy population. A prominent example is Enrique Peñalosa, the former mayor of Bogotá, Colombia, who is largely credited with returning the streets to order and safety by curtailing the use of private automobiles, reclaiming public spaces throughout the city, encouraging mass transit and cycling, improving parks, and creating megalibraries in poor neighborhoods.

As American mayors and civic leaders seek inspiration from such international examples, they should also note success stories in our own cities, where a quest for health and happiness is motivating many people to move

into diverse communities. For instance, Seattle's public library by Rem Koolhaas is a stunning confluence of design excellence, public leadership, and local involvement. Yet livable, enjoyable neighborhoods with a variety of amenities, resources, and activities require hyperdensity. The intense proximity of urban parks; neighborhood theaters; local bars, restaurants, recreation centers, and gyms; and a variety of shops is critical to a pedestrian's everyday experience—as Jane Jacobs so clearly illustrated 50 years ago.

American cities have come a long way from the smoke, soot, crime, squalor, and health risks of the industrial age. Polluted skies and acid waterways have had a significant negative impact on people and the nature that surrounds them, but government intervention enacted under President Nixon has done a good job of curtailing rampant pollution and must continue to do so. Yet while U.S. environmental policies have accomplished much in terms of improving the air and water quality of cities over the past few decades, national housing and transit policies have simultaneously encouraged a sprawling, unwalkable landscape that has diminished the health and well-being of too many Americans. In section two, we will look at how the right set of policies in terms of building hyperdensity, infrastructure, and social equity can reverse this trend, providing more Americans with not only an urban way of life, but one that is fundamentally healthier and more joyous than our current, perilous state.

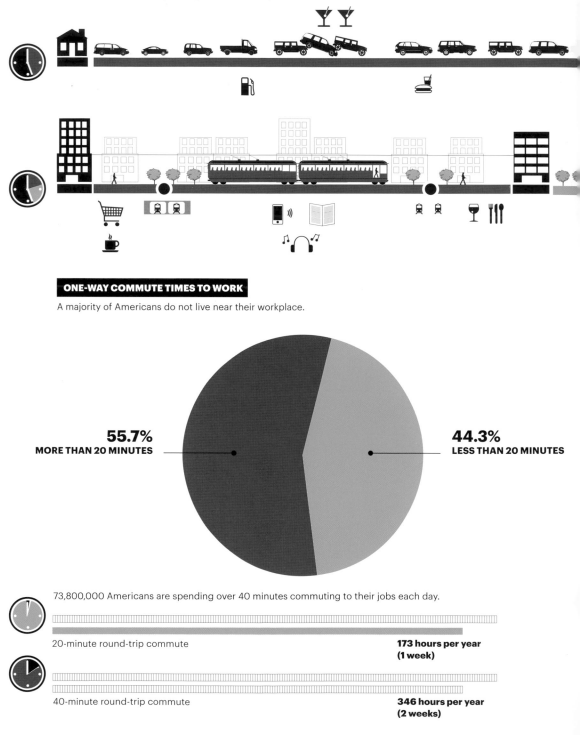

THE ADVANTAGES OF MASS TRANSIT AND WALKABILITY

Compared to commuting by car in traffic, using mass transit between dense, walkable neighborhoods can be filled with positive experiences. Shorter commutes free up time for other activities, like spending time with family.

ONE-WAY COMMUTE TIMES TO WORK

A majority of Americans do not live near their workplace.

55.7%
MORE THAN 20 MINUTES

44.3%
LESS THAN 20 MINUTES

73,800,000 Americans are spending over 40 minutes commuting to their jobs each day.

20-minute round-trip commute

**173 hours per year
(1 week)**

40-minute round-trip commute

**346 hours per year
(2 weeks)**

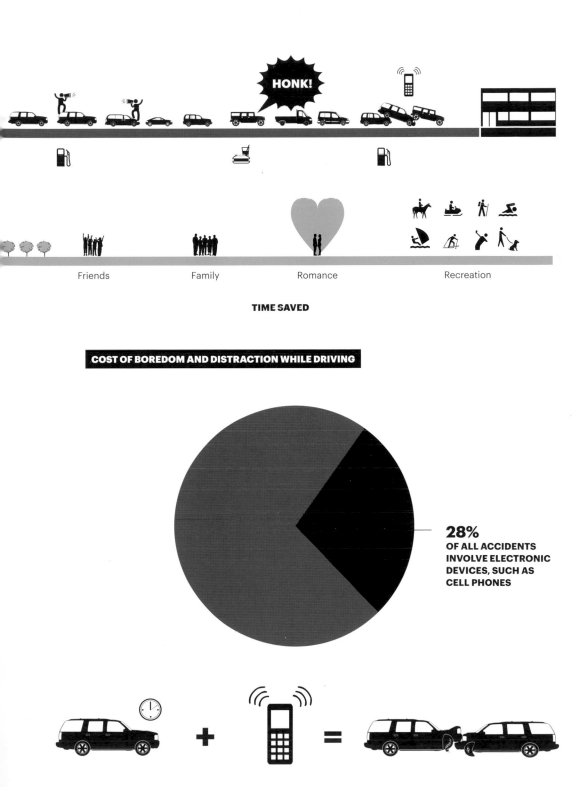

HONK!

Friends   Family   Romance   Recreation

TIME SAVED

COST OF BOREDOM AND DISTRACTION WHILE DRIVING

28%
OF ALL ACCIDENTS INVOLVE ELECTRONIC DEVICES, SUCH AS CELL PHONES

A WALKABLE CITY OF CULTURE AND DIVERSITY

Parks

Pedestrian- and
bike-friendly streets

Local mass transit

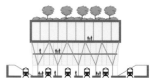

Regional mass transit

Cultural institutions   Museums, hospitals, and schools   Mixed-income affordable housing

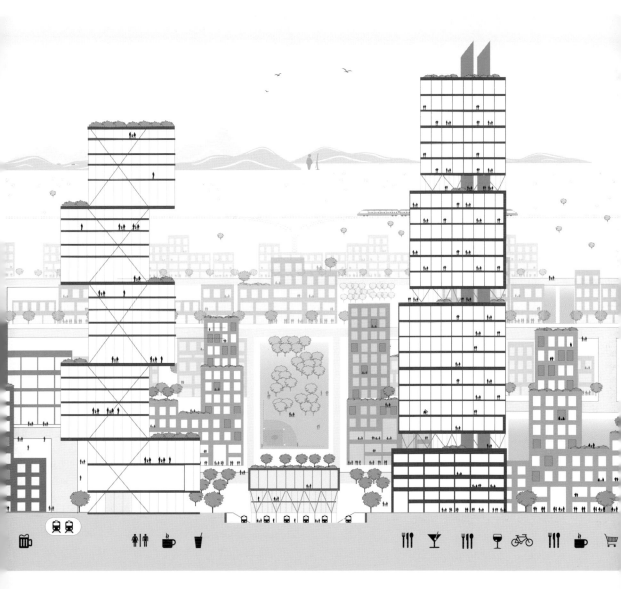

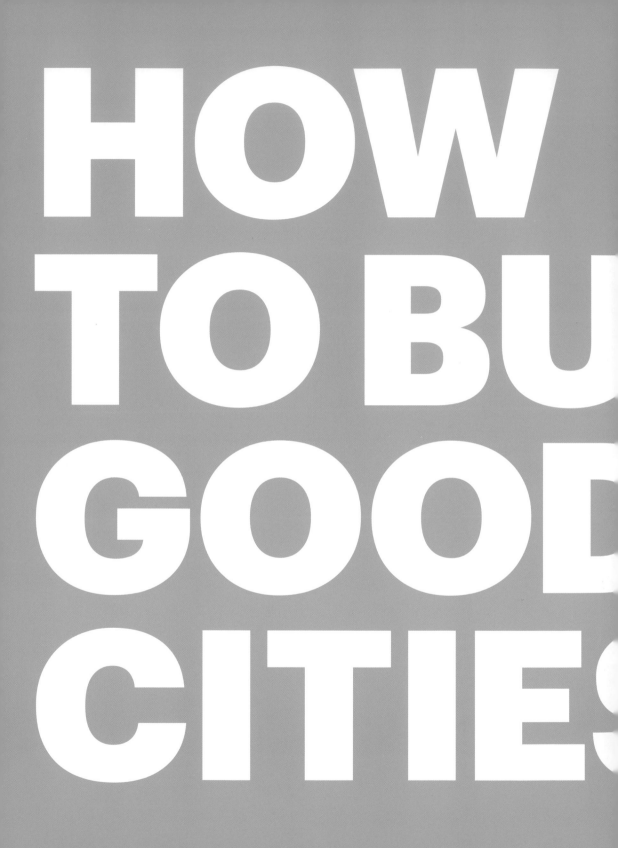

1 A typical high-rise sector in Hong Kong
2 Traffic congestion in São Paolo

BUILDING HYPERDENSITY AND CIVIC DELIGHT

Because hyperdensity—defined as density sufficient to support subways—contributes to the prosperity, sustainability, and health of cities, the densification of our built and social environments will in no small part determine our strength as a nation.[1] As we determined in section one, compared to most forms of human habitation, dense cities are the most efficient economic engines, are the most environmentally sustainable, and are the most likely to encourage joyful and healthy lifestyles. So, how do we build delightful cities that make us more prosperous, ecological, fit, and equitable? This chapter lays out the factors that impede hyperdensity in our cities today, and the conditions necessary to create hyperdense environments in the future, including great design, responsible preservation, and sound urban planning. Chapter five examines the infrastructure needed to make hyperdensity livable. Chapter six explores the means to make hyperdensity affordable for all in order to advance equal opportunity.

Sound, new urban development is the lynchpin of the hyperdense environment. Yet public advocacy for high-density urban development is extraordinarily low, primarily because its merits are misunderstood. Even among those who appreciate the benefits of cities, an enormous amount of confusion remains about how best to build density, which in turn has led to widespread impediments to creating prosperous, sustainable, and opportunity-laden urban development. This is largely because the rationale for hyperdensity is often lost on those who should be its biggest advocates: America's so-called urbanists—broadly defined as urban planners, architects engaged in city building, and urban theorists—paradoxically tend to be enthralled with density yet enraged by real-estate development. In fact, it is a common trope in most schools of architecture and urban planning today to believe that density is good but development is bad.

HOW TECHNOLOGY AFFECTS BUILDING HEIGHTS

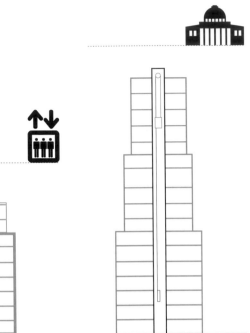

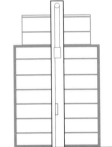

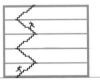

BEFORE ELEVATORS
Comfortable walk-up distance determines five-story height limit for buildings.

1853, AFTER ELEVATORS
Advances in elevator technology and structural design allow for high-rise construction.

PRESENT
Current municipal height restrictions and market conditions limit development.

TOOLS OF URBAN PLANNING

Dense development has historically been derided for creating a lack of light and air, but municipal zoning rules can ensure that new buildings provide better living conditions.

BEFORE BUILDING-BULK CONTROLS
Buildings were often set too close to one another to allow for adequate light and fresh air.

BUILDING-BULK CONTROLS
Municipal zoning rules provide for better light and air through easements, setbacks, and sky exposure planes.

UPWARD TO HOME!

HIGH in an apartment and away from the buzz and bustle of a busy city, two happy-faced children watch eagerly from the window for the familiar figure of daddy. Now they see him and they can hardly wait until an elevator speeds him upward to home.

Soon they'll pounce upon him with the lusty enthusiasm of youth. And he'll be showered with questions by the score. He'll have to answer to them for being ten minutes late. And he'll probably say a traffic jam held him up.

He'll never blame the elevators for making him late . . . not in this building. For the building owners have secured the services of the maker, Otis Elevator Company, to maintain them . . . to inspect them regularly and adjust all working parts . . . to replace a worn part before it causes trouble . . . to attend to the cables, the motors, the brakes . . . to keep the entire installation running smoothly.

To give constant, uniform service, an elevator, like any other fine machine, must receive regular inspection and expert care. That is why Otis Elevator Company, maker of the finest elevators known today, keeps a large staff of highly trained elevator mechanics who do nothing but care for elevators. These men are stationed in squads all over the country, where they can be of most service to building owners. These men know an elevator . . . know it from top to bottom. Their services may be secured at the Otis office in your city.

Before you sign another lease for an apartment home or office quarters, first inquire if the elevators are cared for by Otis. This point is important.

OTIS ELEVATOR COMPANY

UPWARD TO HOME!

In the 1930's, the Otis Elevator Company advertised elevators much like other household commodities:

"High in an apartment and away from the buzz and bustle of the city, two happy-faced children watch eagerly from the window for the familiar figure of daddy. Now they see him and they can hardly wait until an elevator speeds him upward to home."

Instead, most urbanists consider European capitals such as Paris and Barcelona as the exemplars of "good density." And, indeed, with city centers that support mass transit and walkable neighborhoods built at more than 80 units per acre—as is the case in Paris—these downtowns do represent some of the most densely built environments in the world.[2] Since they achieve these densities without, as some would say, ugly skyscrapers built by ugly developers, these cities represent the meritorious urbanity, commonly known as "low rise, high density," that the design and planning fields champion.

However, these fields tacitly or explicitly consider the growing hyperdense cities of Asia as embodiments of "bad density." They generally deride places such as Tokyo, Hong Kong, and Singapore as being too congested and characterless, the products of mindless real-estate development, inept urban planning, and, of course, impoverished (read, non-Western) civic culture. Implicit in such parochialism is that only Western civilization can—and will—continue to produce superior urbanism, indicating a willful contempt for the fact that many Asian cities are outpacing European capitals not only economically but also in terms of cultural production, mass transit, environmentalism, racial integration, and other key metrics.[3] It is unrealistic and irresponsible for any true urbanist to embrace European capitals as models for future development when they are among the most segregated urban centers on earth and have increasingly unstable finances characterized by debt-driven *grands projets*.

Cities such as New York, Chicago, and Toronto fall somewhere in the middle of the spectrum between beloved and bemoaned urbanism; praised for their picturesque brownstone neighborhoods, criticized for areas where skyscrapers have been allowed to thrive. In fact, Toronto blogs and newspapers have questioned whether that city's new towers will usher in new urban ghettos.[4] Brownstone Brooklyn, we are told, is sustainable, community-based, and charming. Midtown and Lower Manhattan, by contrast, are often

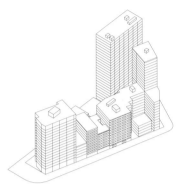

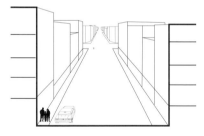

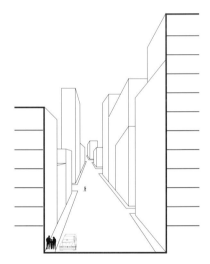

Barcelona, Spain
120 units per acre

Tokyo, Japan
175 units per acre

derided as the immoral land of "the 1 percent," despite the fact that those two business districts generate the majority of the tax dollars that fund the extraordinary array of social goods throughout New York City that most progressives care about, including schools, parks, and affordable housing.

Missing from these simplistic judgments about good and bad urbanism is an understanding of the origins of the low-rise, high-density environments, not to mention an appreciation for the rationale that will necessitate high-rise, high-density environments in the future. The majority of the historic buildings in Paris, Barcelona, and Brownstone Brooklyn were built by the private sector—yes, by real-estate interests and wealthy businessmen. To be sure, as with any great city, grand public parks, lovely streetscapes, efficient transit systems, and dignified foreground buildings frame these charming places. But the much-lauded "good density" in such cities is the building stock itself, which was actually built by powerful development interests and typically fueled by unsavory capital, such as the spoils of colonialism or labor exploitation, and enabled by top-down government. The dripping ornamental wonders of Paris's Fifth Arrondissement or the stately mansions of Kensington are no less the manifestations of ill-gotten gains than the luxury Manhattan condos that house today's wealthy and powerful. Yet these older environments now, remarkably, merit the acceptance of progressives through the patina of history.

Furthermore, it was not the rigors of urban planning but the limits of technology that kept these dense environments low-rise, often to the detriment of their residents. Cities built low-rise buildings because elevators and structural steel did not yet exist, not because of regulations mandating street-walls, cornices, or streetscapes. As a consequence, and despite their visual charms, many European capitals were notorious for their vulnerability to epidemics, fire, and squalor. Much of the historic housing stock of low-rise, high-density New York is known for its lack of light and air and, before hipsters invaded it, was inhabited by the tenement dwellers who comprised Jacob Riis's "other half."[5]

It is indisputable that technology—the elevator, structural steel, and the subway—ushered in a different and fundamentally better way of life for billions. Consider, given the death tolls of pandemics in history, the devastation that the H1N1 virus would have brought to Hong Kong if the majority of its residents lived in low-density brownstones. Consider the light and air that residents in high-rise housing enjoy compared to their counterparts who lived in tenements; in parts of Europe, some people prefer towers to quaint town centers because, though centuries have passed, they still associate low-rise urbanism with the bubonic plague.[6] When the well-off live in low-rise, high-density housing, they inhabit wider, more light-filled structures, while

SKYSCRAPERS AND GDP IN EUROPE

Where skyscrapers are permitted in city centers, per capita GDP tends to be higher.

Per capita GDP

- $100 K
- $75 K
- $50 K
- $25 K
- $0

$102,940 — Frankfurt
$73,370 — London
$57,030 — Paris
$55,380 — Rome
$35,975 — Barcelona
$28,500 — Berlin

City center where skyscrapers are allowed

City center where most skyscrapers are prohibited

their poorer counterparts are relegated to small, lightless, low-rise boxes. For many urbanists, if this means the cityscape can be tower free, this is a worthwhile trade-off despite the depressing implications for the poor.

In addition to housing, the global economy demands that we embrace large buildings for many modern office functions, yet most planning professionals remain fixated on smaller-scale development. They tend to ignore that limitations on height have held back the Parisian economy in comparison to the forward-looking redevelopment of London, both at Canary Wharf and within its city center, which is now marked by a series of glistening and respectful new towers by Norman Foster, Richard Rogers, and Renzo Piano. There is, in fact, a marked correlation between those European cities that have allowed skyscrapers and those that have successful, urban-led economies.[7]

We cannot expect big American cities to reach their potential when the very professions that purport to defend and perpetuate urbanism recoil at the presence of towers. Left rudderless by the experts, we are forced to inhabit the bleak consequences of a poorly regulated marketplace, analogous to a population that must operate on its own cancers due to the confused surgeons who keep cutting away at the healthy tissue. Expanding cities at their edges, even in ways deemed "smart" by planners, is by no means what we need to do. To the contrary, efforts to "densify suburbia" tend to backfire, creating places like Bethesda, Maryland, mutated environments that exhibit

London allows skyscrapers, resulting in a variegated, hyperdense environment of high and low buildings.

the worst of both worlds, neither urban nor rural, and typified by growing and endless traffic jams despite the presence of token mass transit and a Main Street riddled with chain stores.

As a result, people often think "development" and rightfully believe it means congestion and traffic snarls. Indeed, if the word conjures images of a bucolic Main Street being transformed into a big-box commercial strip or an office park, they are justified in having that fear. For decades, growing U.S. cities have gained density not through strengthened downtowns—through hyperdensity—but through sprawling borders and, consequently, metropolitan regions have become less efficient and bigger consumers of our resources. In the process, cities have also lost a cohesive order, hierarchy, and structure that made them marvels of communal living dating back to ancient Xi'an and Athens.

For their part, urban residents also tend to balk when they hear "development" because they fear any change to their neighborhoods. Every development proposal has come to be construed as a Robert Moses highway project in disguise, a wolf in sheep's clothing designed to displace people and tear apart the fabric of a neighborhood. Cities today continuously bear witness to residents channeling Jane Jacobs to fight dense, mixed-use, transit-based projects that any true Jacobs acolyte should support. The lessons of Jacobs seem to have translated into the process of fighting rather than the substance she espoused, despite the fact that the large-scale urban renewal projects she fought are all but impossible today. Public policy has caught up to a point where environmental and social concerns are just as important as cost and feasibility, and litigation risk now drives major projects far more than the unilateral temperament of any one all-powerful development czar. And in many cases, the pendulum has swung in the other direction: regulatory policy and environmental disclosure requirements can be so stringent as to impede the kind of sound, compact development that is in our collective best interest, despite the predictable NIMBY concerns.

By contrast, consider the growing national support for urban light rail, improved subway service, and expanded bus routes.[8] City residents tend to support the mass transit networks that hyperdensity requires but none of the development that would make these improvements financeable and sustainable—namely, tall buildings containing affordable housing along transit lines, in communities with shared open spaces, schools, and social

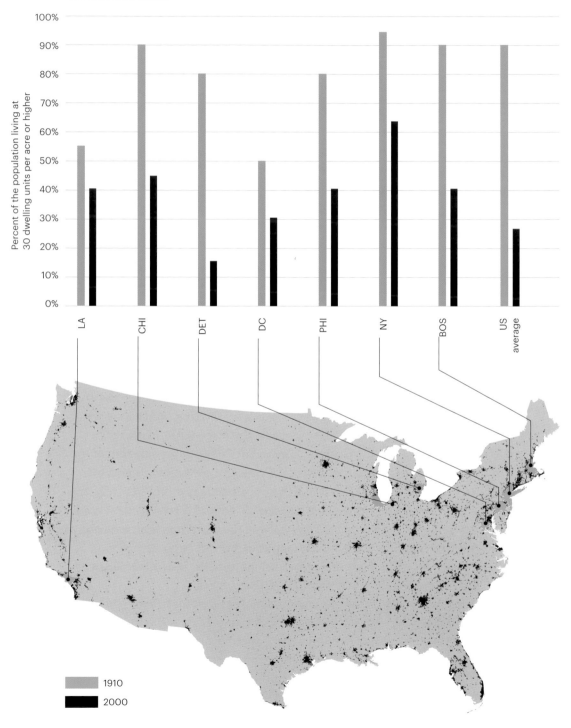

LOSS OF DENSITY ACROSS METROPOLITAN REGIONS IN AMERICA, 1910–2000

Americans are increasingly supportive of building new mass transit. Yet after a century of decentralization and sprawl, nearly all American cities lack the density to support new, rail-based mass transit.

Percent of the population living at
30 dwelling units per acre or higher

LA CHI DET DC PHI NY BOS US average

1910
2000

services. And so we are witnessing misguided investments in urban mass transit, particularly light rail, where there is insufficient density to provide ridership for the system, which results in economic and environmental inefficiencies as well as cries of government waste from transit opponents.

Hyperdense development is not synonymous with the destruction of a neighborhood's fabric or its "character," as it is now often called. New York City balanced the two in West Chelsea and Hudson Yards, newly planned neighborhoods that represent Manhattan's development frontier. In Nashville, developers and designers with Market Street Enterprises have built a beautiful new neighborhood in an underdeveloped part of the city's core called the Gulch. It features mixed-use, dense development that improved the neighborhood by enhancing the quality of housing options for its residents. Instead of neighbors killing a new development because it meant more people and more traffic, they supported the construction of the first LEED Certified neighborhood in the South, producing a compact and sustainable community based on the unique identity of the Music City.[9]

In addition to the benefits of vertical residential neighborhoods, the way people work today demands a range of spaces, from mid-rise manufacturing and commercial buildings to high-technology skyscrapers, building types that low-rise neighborhoods alone cannot supply. The buzz phrase of the office development world today is "collaborative space," which is often characterized by large column-free expanses that would be impossible without steel or concrete construction. Light and views are at a premium, with natural daylight considered key to increasing worker productivity and lowering the energy demands of artificial lighting. While not always the case, providing access to light and views typically means building tall.

It is important to note, however, that the notion of central business districts comprised solely of office towers is losing ground, and the impact of decades of city planning focused on "mixed-use development" is bearing significant fruit. The concept of a commercial downtown with little housing or retail—a place that typically goes quiet at night—is increasingly rare. Across the country, urban cores that successfully mix living, working, and play have gained remarkable popularity. Even in large cities like New York, decisions by technology companies such as Google to locate in emerging neighborhoods; the resurgence of Lower Manhattan after 9/11; the realization of sports and entertainment venues like Brooklyn's new Barclays Center; and the development of new areas on Manhattan's West Side have turned the tables on the traditional office market. As a result, the commercial district near Grand Central Terminal, for example, is now competing with these vibrant new mixed-use precincts featuring more amenities and nightlife. In response to these concerns, New York's Department of City Planning

DENSIFIED SUBURBIA: THE WORST OF BOTH WORLDS

Automobile-centric density and underutilized mass transit create the worst of both suburban and urban neighborhoods.

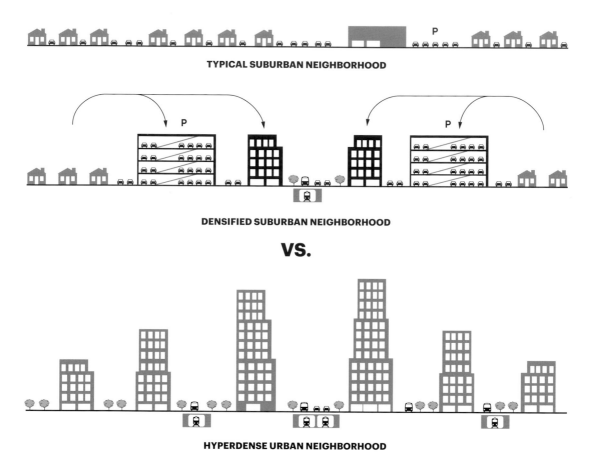

TYPICAL SUBURBAN NEIGHBORHOOD

DENSIFIED SUBURBAN NEIGHBORHOOD

VS.

HYPERDENSE URBAN NEIGHBORHOOD

BETHESDA, MARYLAND

Bestheda, Maryland, a suburban enclave outside Washington, D.C, exemplifies the kind of automobile-centric density that perpetuates traffic snarls, chain stores, and characterless buildings.

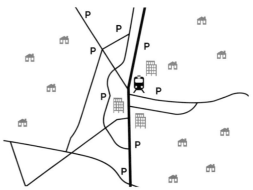

in 2012 launched an initiative to "upzone," or increase development capacity, in the Grand Central area in an effort to spark new development, create more transit-oriented density, and rejuvenate New York's main central business district.[10]

But even in vibrant older urban neighborhoods that have attracted a new mix of uses, towers of varying sizes are being developed to accommodate entrepreneurs, residents, and hotels. Adaptive reuse of truly historic buildings is a must, but existing building stock alone can never accommodate all of the needs of the evolving business or home, particularly in light of rapid technological and social shifts. Surgical new development remains critical to the rebirth of neighborhoods and the vitality of urban economies. Furthermore, many central business districts nationwide are anachronisms, with substandard office space constructed after World War II. Characterized by low ceilings, byzantine structural grids, and wasteful mechanical systems, such places are energy inefficient and often induce "sick building" syndrome among inhabitants. Public policy that strongly encourages the redevelopment of this building stock is critically important if American cities are to remain competitive.

The design of new buildings has tremendous significance for cities. While sustainability and functionality are undoubtedly important metrics, innovative architecture has proven to be a highly significant economic and social driver because of its ability to engender new forms for dwelling, work, and repose. Be it Boston's Macallen housing block by NADAAA, Cleveland's mixed-use Uptown project by Stanley Saitowitz, D.C.'s World Bank Headquarters by KPF, or New York's Atlantic Yards transit-based development by SHoP Architects, brilliant design generates civic excitement and attractiveness, and increases both land and social value. The best of these projects serve their cities as magnificent new structures accomplished within the constraints of local budgetary realities. Smart architecture is as smart about money as it is about design. Yet at its heart, urban architecture is about far more than satisfying a series of pragmatic concerns. Our best buildings conjure civic delight.

Truly great architecture invites, uplifts, and advances its city. A great building invites the public through physical or phenomenological transparency; it reveals itself to the city even while veiling surprises within. A great building inspires people through its beauty and material qualities, while enhancing the coherence and contradictions of the street. A great building can reveal a city by exposing its urban structure in new and unfamiliar ways, creating a better collective understanding of its past—and future.

Private real-estate development has much to answer for in terms of its inability to deliver even adequate, much less great, design. Most private

WHAT DENSITIES ARE CURRENTLY PERMITTED?

Planners in America's 50 largest metropolitan regions are not allowing enough density. Only 12% of our zoned land is permitted to contain hyperdense development.

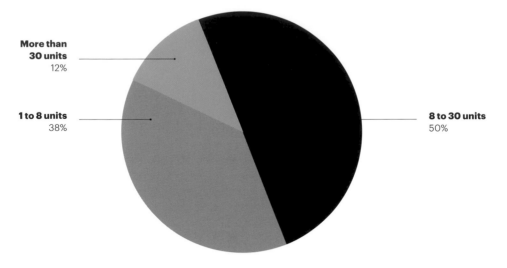

More than 30 units
12%

1 to 8 units
38%

8 to 30 units
50%

DENSIFICATION AROUND RAIL-BASED TRANSIT

Municipalities can allow for hyperdensity around existing or new transit stops.

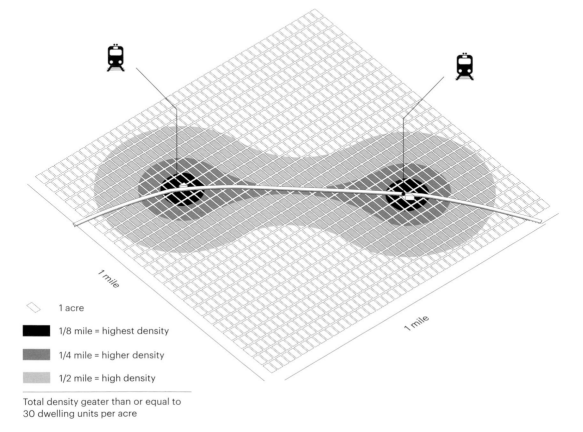

1 mile

1 mile

◇ 1 acre

■ 1/8 mile = highest density

■ 1/4 mile = higher density

■ 1/2 mile = high density

Total density geater than or equal to 30 dwelling units per acre

development generates horrible architecture for its inhabitants and its city. Even leading American developers are well behind their global counterparts in Asia, Europe, South America, and the Middle East in terms of embracing contemporary design. Domestic developers claim that this is a result of cost. Yet a quick survey of developer-driven projects worldwide reveals that it is more a consequence of their own conservatism and control. That even our high-quality developers tend to favor historicist architecture, which is meant to look old by borrowing stylistic elements from historic buildings but in reality is brand new, only obfuscates our shared understanding of the contemporary metropolis. However, a new generation of developers that places far more emphasis on progressive architecture is emerging today.

Often, people think historicist architecture will help preserve culture and the urban fabric. In reality it does neither; culture advances far too quickly to be frozen in historicist styles, and truly historic architecture is only denigrated by the false nature of historicism. Historic preservation of real landmarks is of paramount importance, but it is often abused. Our major cities have, for the most part, recognized and designated most historic buildings, leaving little for landmarks commissions to do but recognize and preserve unworthy buildings and districts. For many building owners, a historic designation can be more curse than blessing because of the regulatory implications. Furthermore, historic designations, particularly of entire districts, have increasingly become a backdoor method for preventing new development. A clear perversion of the nation's landmarks laws, such methods can have devastating economic, social, and environmental impacts because of the degree to which they prevent necessary densification and development. Preservation of truly historic urban areas and landmarks is

Private real-
developmer
to answer fo
of its inabilit
even adequa
less great, d

estate
t has much
r in terms
y to deliver
te, much
esign.

Downtown Dallas is already transit rich but does not feature heavy-gauge subway service.

A hyperdense downtown Dallas could support rapid mass-transit service and a host of new neighborhood amenities.

essential to the culture, life, and economy of any great city. Preservation as an antidevelopment cudgel suffocates the necessary growth of cities and dilutes the status of true landmarks.

Overzealous historic designations also reveal the degree to which urban residents fear change. In some cases, such fear is warranted—a beautiful old warehouse district in Toronto or a brownstone neighborhood in Washington, D.C., should not be besieged with towers. But across the United States, our urban centers contain low-density areas within their limits, areas with parking lots, gas stations, driveways, and lawns. These areas disproportionately draw upon scarce urban resources, resulting in expensive infrastructure costs per capita, nonproductive use of valuable urban land, and intensely negative environmental impacts. Municipalities have every right to intensify the land use of such areas, especially if they are near mass transit, without false claims of historic merit. And if residents are unwilling to allow denser, mixed-use development, they should be made to pay for the real and opportunity costs they place on a city's limited coffers.

This very drama is playing out in Los Angeles today. Mayor Antonio Villaraigosa and other enlightened city officials are fighting impassioned community members over a plan to rezone Hollywood for denser, mixed-use development in conjunction with the construction of a new subway line. As the *New York Times* reported, neighborhood associations are claiming preservationist grounds with an almost total disregard for the environmental and economic impacts of their parochialism.[11] Meanwhile, on the city's West Side, fear of Carmageddon II made headlines ahead of the shutdown of the 405 Freeway to allow for the demolition of a bridge, but this proved to be a non-event. Evidently, Los Angeles is changing from the automobile-oriented, smog-belching, ever-congested metropolis we have come to know into the dense, sustainable, thriving city it is destined to become.[12]

In addition to questions of design, preservation, and neighborhood character are, of course, the challenging concerns of properly planning for new hyperdensity. These include the ability to build skyscrapers when justified by transit, and the capacity of the surrounding blocks to accept bigger buildings. Zoning tools are critical for determining building density, massing, and land use, but most were created when we needed to segregate noxious activities. As the United States transitioned to a service economy, the need to separate where people work from where they live and play became unnecessary and, for the most part, counterproductive. Service workers today want jobs located near their homes and recreation; in some cases, they want to be able to do everything in the same building.[13] Zoning too often artificially separates uses and over-regulates market forces in ways that prevent them from responding to escalating and evolving urban demand.

CENTRAL BUSINESS DISTRICT
The traditional "hub-and-spoke" central business district

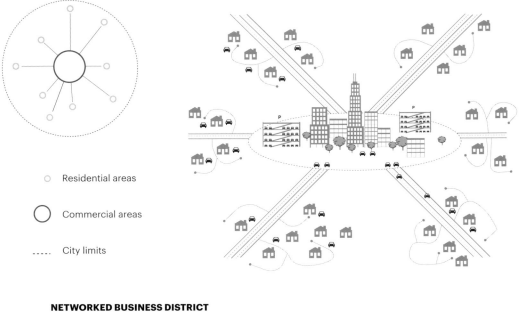

○ Residential areas

◯ Commercial areas

. . . . . City limits

NETWORKED BUSINESS DISTRICT
Multiple mixed-use business districts linked together

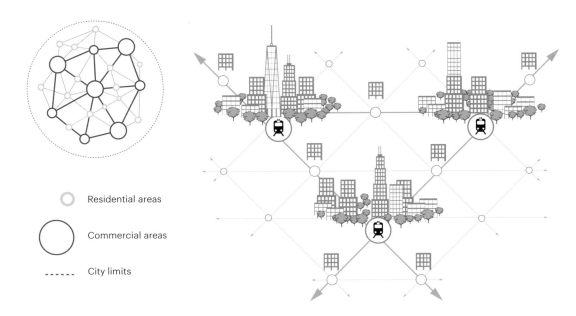

○ Residential areas

◯ Commercial areas

- - - - - - City limits

Good planning should be guided by desired objectives rather than prescribed physical outcomes; it should allow for flexible uses, densities and building form in response to changes in market conditions, architectural expression, and availability of infrastructure such as mass transit. Cities should unleash this performance-focused role of municipal planning regulations to create public policy and investments that spur private-market reaction, which, in turn, generates invaluable tax revenues to fund public needs. This is precisely the story behind some of the most successful recent policy-driven urban development, such as the preservation of New York's High Line and its role as a catalyst for the burgeoning mixed-use neighborhood that surrounds it.

Density, particularly vertical density, should obviously be planned at the locus of transportation. It is also possible to do the reverse, by funding new transportation in conjunction with new development. Similarly, public open space, schools, and other critical infrastructure can and should be planned in tandem with hyperdense development. Such multifaceted infrastructure forms the prerequisites for making hyperdensity not just livable but highly enjoyable. Yet even with the appropriate relationship of public infrastructure to private development, questions remain about the *morphology*, or formal characteristics, of a hyperdense city. This is a relatively new arena, and we can draw great lessons from international cities such as London and Vancouver as well as emerging urban areas like New Songdo City, outside of Seoul, and Beirut's new waterfront, which is being constructed in a public-private partnership with Solidere. New York, San Francisco, and Chicago provide fine examples of clustering hyperdense towers on grids of streets, but this is by no means the only way that hyperdensity can or should be planned. With rapid urbanization worldwide, experiments in hyperdense morphology will continue, and questions about the best formal qualities of intense, vertically dense, transit-based cities remain open-ended.

My advocacy for hyperdense, vertical cities should by no means be misconstrued as a prescription for everyone to live in an unyielding forest of skyscrapers. It is interesting to note that even Hong Kong, the city most criticized for its relentless tower slabs, is taking steps to enable greater diversity in the size and shape of buildings in the future. Variety in building heights is critical for city dwellers to

PLANNING FOR HYPERDENSITY

Beirut's new waterfront developments embrace hyperdensity.

DOCTOROFF'S VIRTUOUS CYCLE OF ECONOMIC DEVELOPMENT

As a city gains new residents, it gains tax revenue. This in turn increases the city's capacity to invest in civic amenities, which attract more residents, perpetuating the virtuous cycle of development.

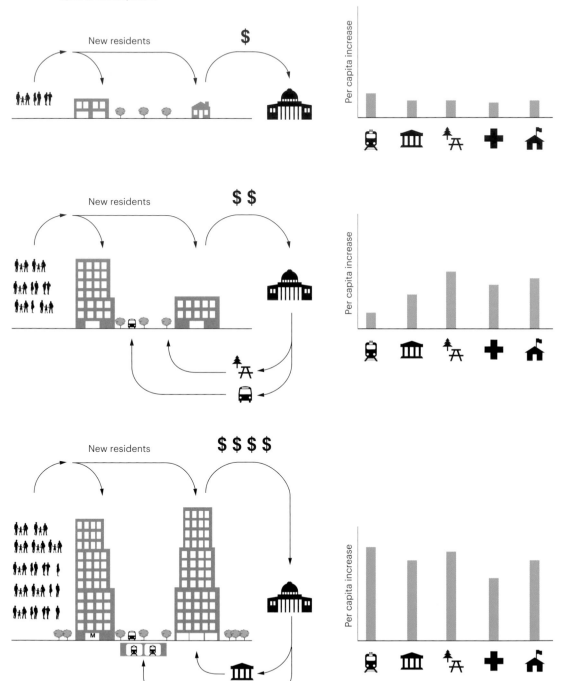

experience both sunlight and delight, with modulation in architecture and scale a must-have for urban joy. Low civic buildings featuring exuberant design, including museums, schools, and libraries, are essential building blocks in this regard. At Columbia University, my students and I have been working on a concept I call "cap and trade zoning," which would allow the free flow of air rights within an urban district, with an understanding that the overall amount of developable area in the district would be capped in relation to its proximity to mass transit. This would result in hyperdensity, to be sure, but would also create a "high-low" city of diverse building heights, uses, and ages. This concept would strengthen small businesses by permitting owners to sell their air rights, while allowing development to occur on nearby lots. Critics may argue that this approach would result in unpredictable development with varying building scales, to which I would reply, "Hip hip hooray!" Much of what passes as good planning today is known as "contextual zoning," a mechanism through which new architecture is tamed into mediocrity by mimicking a false understanding of the scale and aesthetics of existing neighborhoods. Through this process, the instincts of most planners to bring new development to the lowest common denominator trump the wonders of the unpredictable city. Jane Jacobs relentlessly critiqued this planner's urge for control in *The Death and Life of Great American Cities*, and her critique is no less true of planning practice today.

While increasing density is exactly what planners and architects nation-wide should be encouraging, national and local policy should be promoting hyperdensity as well. Sound urban development projects planned in concert with private developers, policymakers, design professionals, and communities represent the path to prosperity for America's cities. Through hyperdensity, public officials and developers can partner to help cities meet growing infra-structure and service needs without overreliance on the federal government, which has proven far too limited in its ability to address our most pressing problems, from joblessness to global warming.

Permitting the construction of hyperdensity creates what former New York City deputy mayor Daniel Doctoroff has called a "virtuous cycle of economic development": New residents generate new taxes, which, in turn, equals better municipal services in the form of good schools, beautiful parks, and effective policing. This better quality of life brings more new residents and workers, which requires even denser development, which ultimately results in sound municipal budgets, vibrant cities, and round-the-clock ridership for public transportation. How to make the most of this virtuous cycle, and how to make its benefits accessible to people on all rungs of the economic ladder, are the subjects of the next two chapters.

HOW TO BUILD THE "HIGH-LOW" CITY

STANDARD DISTRICT ZONING

Density is specified at the level of the district, causing uniform concentrations of buildings that block each other's views.

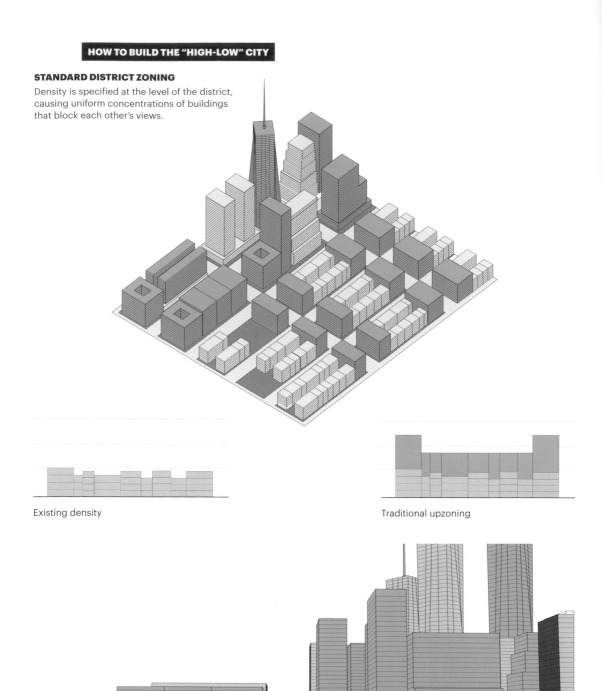

Existing density

Traditional upzoning

CAP AND TRADE ZONING

Each block can accommodate a range of building types, ages, and heights, resulting in a highly varied urban fabric that preserves access to views, natural air, and sunlight.

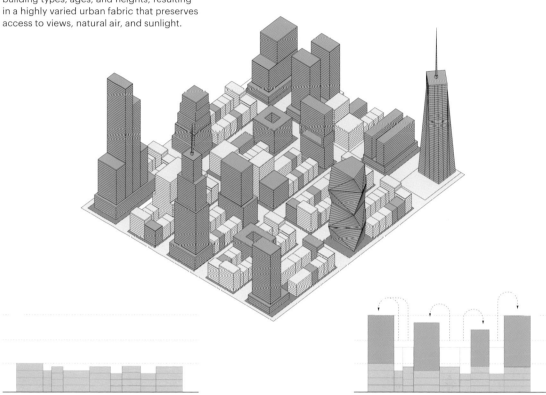

Existing density

Cap and trade upzoning

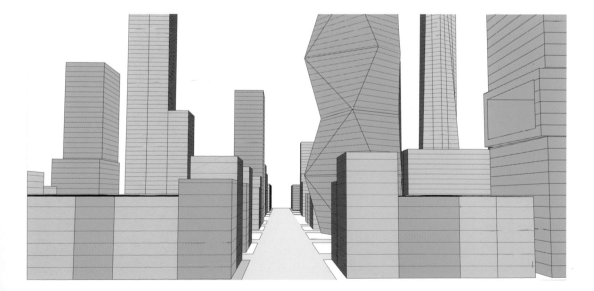

A municipality can sensitively increase the density of an area to help preserve historic structures while still achieving sustatinable growth.

1 Opportunity

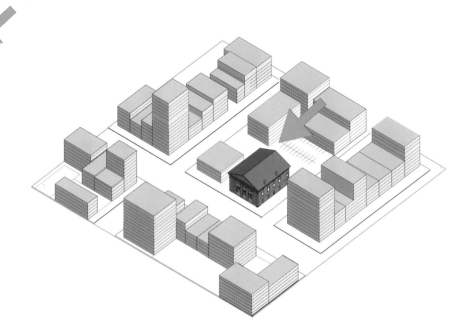

2 Local government upzones for potential new development.

Municipality

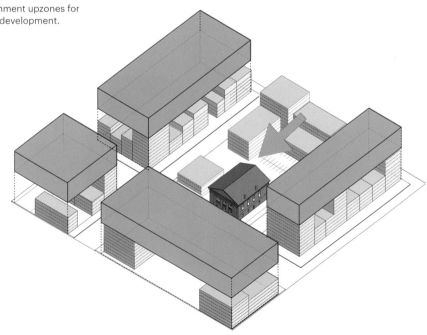

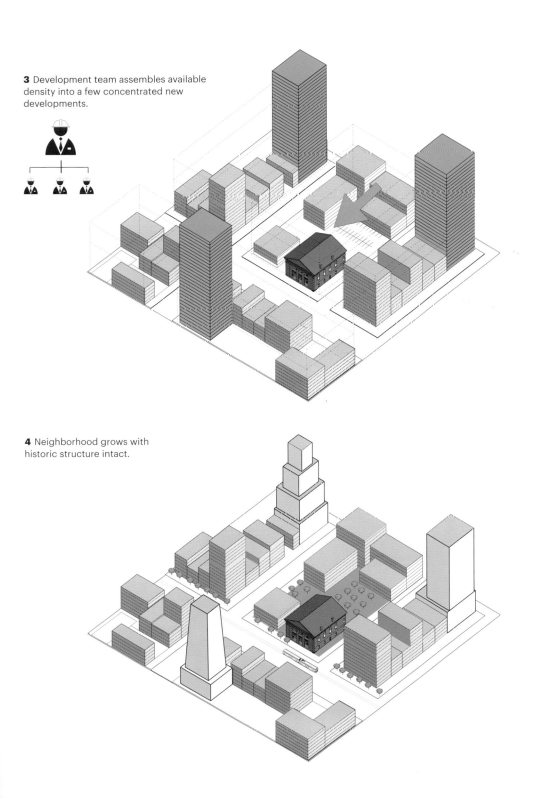

3 Development team assembles available density into a few concentrated new developments.

4 Neighborhood grows with historic structure intact.

Barclays Center, which opened in September 2012, is the first of several buildings SHoP Architects has designed for Atlantic Yards in Brooklyn, New York, where an open railyard has been decked over for new development.

Atlantic Yards will feature hyperdense, mixed-use development once three of the corners on the arena's block are built up with high-rise residential towers. These will be assembled on site with modular components made in a nearby quality-controlled factory.

Open space in the form of plazas, planted medians, and wider sidewalks is critical to the success of hyperdense development. SHoP's scheme includes a transit entry pavilion, a landscaped seating area, and a large plaza where crowds assemble and dissipate before and after events.

DENSITY FOR DENSITY'S SAKE

A worker walks in Dubai.

BUILDING AN INFRASTRUCTURE OF OPPORTUNITY

Hyperdensity should not be built without the infrastructure to support it. Few of the economic or environmental benefits of hyperdensity can be realized without essential infrastructure. Density alone is not a panacea and, in many cases, can be counterproductive without the systems that enable it to function well.

For instance, skyscrapers in the desert, often constructed along freeways and broad arterial roads, can represent the worst form of density one can build because of the resulting economic and environmental burdens of vehicular traffic and climate control. An archipelago of skyscrapers separated by freeways offers none of the social interaction needed to spark the economic productivity that dense urban environments can generate. Many such "cities" are being built worldwide, but they do not offer us a role model. The key metrics for whether a city should be emulated include not only its density but also the infrastructure and affordability that support that density. Together, these constituent parts form the urban design of a successful city, with infrastructure as its key underpinning.

Infrastructure is typically defined as transport systems for people, communications, water, sewage, electricity, and data. I use the term more broadly to include fundamental social systems, such as schools, cultural centers, health-care facilities, and parks. This expanded definition represents an "Infrastructure of Opportunity"—the means by which people can attain their aspirations with increased access to employment, education, recreation, enjoyment, and health.

A society that wisely invests in an Infrastructure of Opportunity arguably holds the best promise for a productive and joyful populace. This is particularly true for service economies, in which people trade goods and services, as they require the means for the social interaction enabled by reliable infrastructure. But infrastructure is extraordinarily expensive. Where do cities find the financing for such investments?

Density and the infrastructure that supports it must be built together.

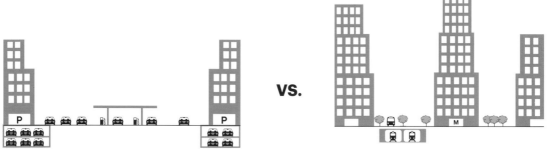

**MINDLESS DENSITY ONLY PROVIDES
AN INFRASTRUCTURE FOR CARS AND COMMUTING**

VS.

**HYPERDENSITY PROVIDES
AN INFRASTRUCTURE OF OPPORTUNITY**

DEFINING AN INFRASTRUCTURE OF OPPORTUNITY

An expanded definition of infrastructure includes other vital systems of the city.

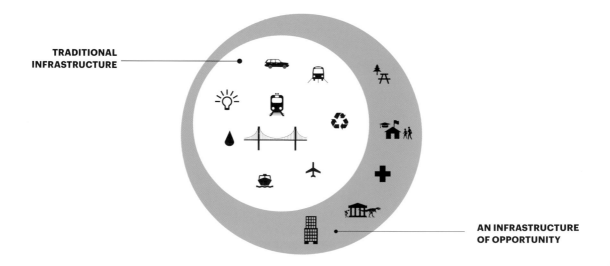

**TRADITIONAL
INFRASTRUCTURE**

**AN INFRASTRUCTURE
OF OPPORTUNITY**

Hyperdensity can be a critical contributor of such funds. It generates economic activity, which in turn increases land value. Cities have demonstrated that upzoning causes land values and tax revenues to rise; the same is true of building parks, museums, or mass transit. These increased revenues, however, must be put to public purpose. Without question, the development of hyperdensity entails significant risk, and private investors are entitled to profit from these risks. But developers should not receive an undue windfall from such governmental action.

Tax-increment financing (TIF) allows municipalities to finance infrastructure improvements by borrowing against the future tax revenues of planned development. As urban development pressure builds nationwide, cities have more opportunities to use this kind of public-sector action to spur private-sector reactions, funding important infrastructure along the way. Numerous examples of TIF projects, domestically and globally, demonstrate how this powerful method can fund the infrastructure needed for hyperdense development without draining municipal resources. Notable examples include the successful redevelopment of brownfield sites near downtown Dallas, which resulted in a new arena and substantially increased land values from surrounding commercial and residential development.[1] Chicago used TIF to partly fund its first new elevated-train station in 15 years; it opened in 2012.[2] In New York City, an entire district—Hudson Yards—is being built with a modified version of TIF, which is paying for the extension of a subway line and a park system. The strategy does carry risk—the development may not occur or may occur more slowly than anticipated—but most successful cities have strong track records of realizing development when the public sector pairs new infrastructure with well-considered upzonings.

Similarly, a number of public-private partnerships are attempting to advance transportation projects by connecting the future value of development with infrastructure investment, a strategy playing out at Union Station in Washington, D.C., and at San Francisco's Trans-Bay terminal, for example.[3] In Georgia, where a 2012 ballot referendum on a statewide comprehensive transit program (T-SPLOT) failed to pass, an alternate plan is moving forward to use tax-increment financing to fund the creation of a multimodal transit complex including bus, light rail, and train, much like similar developments in cities like Denver.[4] While less direct in terms of cause and effect, well-known open space investments are upping the value of surrounding hyperdense development in projects such as Chicago's Millennium Park and St. Louis's Citygarden.

It is critical to note that most forms of infrastructure cost much less per capita in dense environments. Transit, power, water, and sewer systems have far less distance to traverse in cities than in sprawling areas; this means

PUBLIC/PRIVATE PARTNERSHIPS

Expensive infrastructural projects require so much upfront capital that they often face funding gaps.

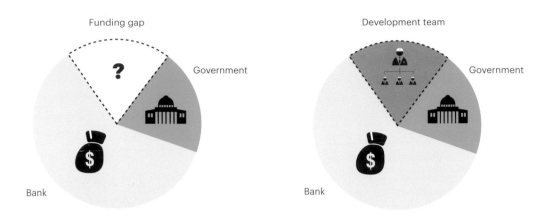

TAX-INCREMENT FINANCING (TIF)

Local governments usually cannot afford to fund expensive infrastructure. Instead, they can finance projects by selling bonds that are repaid through future tax revenues.

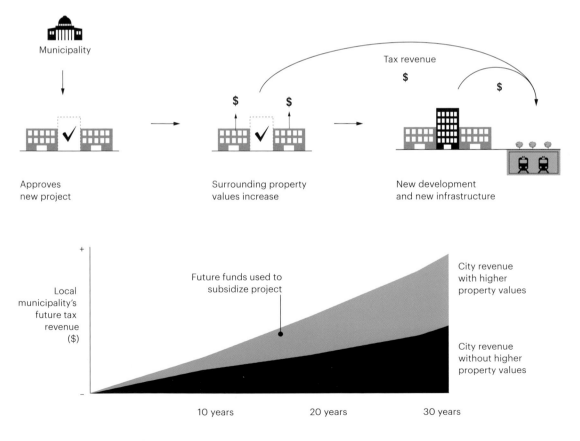

Japanese farming villages exemplify the advantages of compact communities.

cities can concentrate precious infrastructure dollars for maximum impact. One only need to look to traditional Japanese farming communities, in which most farmers live in compact villages with the farmland dispersed at the outskirts, to understand the advantages of lower infrastructure costs in more compact communities. This is a model that could help guide development of our own rural areas.

TIF structures and public-private partnerships can help fund infrastructure, and such infrastructure does cost less per person in hyperdense environments. But a true Infrastructure of Opportunity will require significant government investment. Along with national defense and protection against climate change, our infrastructure is critical to our economic security, arguably more so than the exorbitant amounts our government is increasingly allocating to entitlement spending. A recent report by a major centrist group pointed out this shift, particularly in relationship to the retirement of the baby boomer generation and the subsequent expansion of entitlement costs: "Today, there is a $1 trillion gulf between what we are spending on major entitlement programs and the money we devote to public investments. In ten years, the gap will be $2.6 trillion."[5]

Many rightfully argue that we can fund both entitlements and infrastructure if we just raise taxes, stop oil wars, or some combination thereof. Without question, the income tax rates under President Bill Clinton, combined with a more urban, less oil-dependent economy, would further our ability to fund legitimate social needs. But even in this framework, one worries that with entitlements the province of Democrats and tax cuts that of Republicans, infrastructure has become a political orphan.

Given our system of governance, the widespread political neglect of infrastructure is not entirely a surprise. Infrastructure investments require a long-term view, often stretching the patience of our four-year political cycle. In addition, representatives on both sides of the aisle increasingly view infrastructure investments with skepticism because of skyrocketing costs and the inefficiencies embedded in their procurement, issues that both large-scale builders and labor unions must address.

But the problem of high construction costs must be weighed against the lasting dividends that well-planned, merit-based infrastructure delivers, dividends that expand our tax base and support social services while keeping individual tax rates low. Historically, infrastructure investment enjoyed

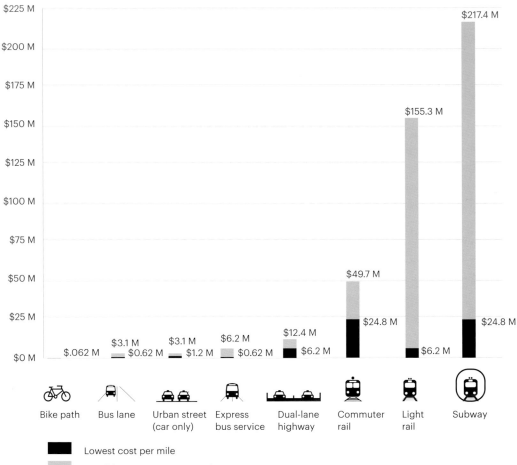

The cost of building infrastructure rises with the complexity of the system based on location and labor, for example.

$225 M

$200 M

$175 M

$150 M

$125 M

$100 M

$75 M

$50 M

$25 M

$0 M

$217.4 M

$155.3 M

$49.7 M

$24.8 M

$24.8 M

$12.4 M

$6.2 M

$6.2 M

$3.1 M

$3.1 M

$6.2 M

$.062 M

$0.62 M

$1.2 M

$0.62 M

$6.2 M

Bike path | Bus lane | Urban street (car only) | Express bus service | Dual-lane highway | Commuter rail | Light rail | Subway

■ Lowest cost per mile

▨ Variable range in cost per mile

some bipartisan congressional support, mainly because politicians of all stripes wanted to deliver projects for their constituents. Today, citizens often view such investments as political "pork," and when spending is not based on the merits, they may be right.

But in debating the benefits of infrastructure investment, today's political right too easily raises the specter of "bridges to nowhere" (even when they sometimes support said bridges). Simultaneously, some progressive groups increasingly favor bike lanes and express bus lines known as bus rapid transit (BRT) over the cost of building metros, despite the overwhelmingly superior capacity and environmental advantages of subways in big cities. It is interesting to note that in Bogotá, Colombia, the government is planning to augment the heralded BRT system known as the TransMilenio with a true

underground metro. In the United States, some activists even adopt the tactics of Jane Jacobs to fight necessary infrastructure improvements, all a vestige of the planning battles of the last century.

When it comes to infrastructure in the United States, the left and right at least agree about their respective versions of antiauthoritarianism. Most Americans today, for good or bad, don't trust big entities. This is the land of "do it yourself," or DIY, but societies by necessity require collective action, particularly in a service economy that relies on functioning physical and virtual networks. The creation of an Infrastructure of Opportunity, whether built through the public sector or through public-private partnerships, requires some faith in big entities—big government, big builders, or, in most cases, both. Most Americans view these entities not with faith but with intense skepticism. Unless we can resolve the fundamental philosophical question of whether we can muster at least a limited, vigilant trust in authority, we will be stuck with traffic congestion, unsafe roads and bridges, crumbling schools, and derelict public spaces.

But America, conceived as an egalitarian nation, is no stranger to infrastructure investment by and for the people. From the Transcontinental Railroad to the Tennessee Valley Authority, we have an extraordinary tradition of infrastructure investment, which has waned only in recent decades. The construction of the National Highway System occurred under the aegis of Republican president Eisenhower; the National Park System was initiated by Republican president Teddy Roosevelt. Today, both live on as just two examples of our ability to build a world larger than ourselves, in pursuit of the common rights of access and opportunity.

Individual cities, too, have flourished because of sound infrastructure investments. An economic powerhouse like Chicago would have been inconceivable without the construction of the Erie Canal, which allowed passage

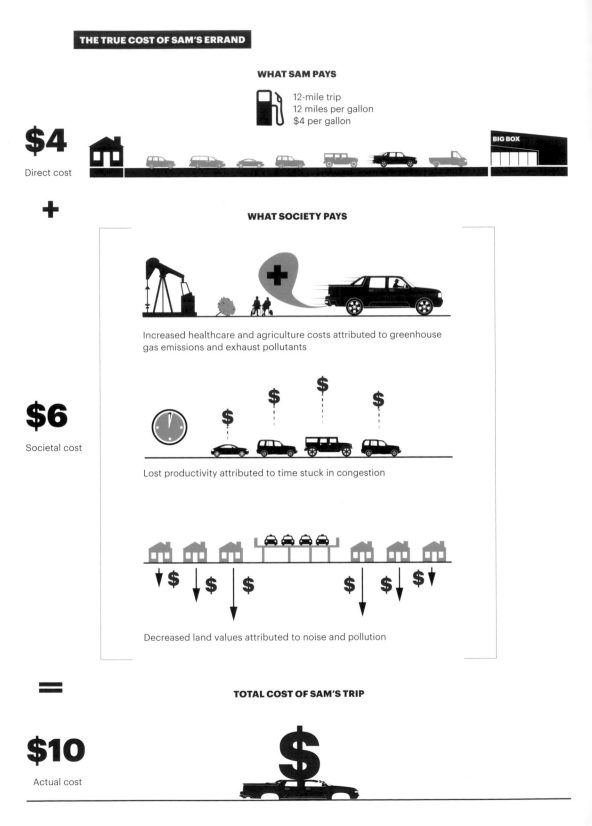

THE TRUE COST OF SAM'S ERRAND

WHAT SAM PAYS

12-mile trip
12 miles per gallon
$4 per gallon

$4
Direct cost

BIG BOX

+

WHAT SOCIETY PAYS

Increased healthcare and agriculture costs attributed to greenhouse gas emissions and exhaust pollutants

$6
Societal cost

Lost productivity attributed to time stuck in congestion

Decreased land values attributed to noise and pollution

=

TOTAL COST OF SAM'S TRIP

$10
Actual cost

of goods and commodities to the Atlantic. Light rail was critical to the development of Los Angeles, Boston, and many other cities across the United States until its downfall, due primarily to the National City Lines conspiracy. The New York City subway system originated through private investment but was later taken over by the public sector. Cities rely on layers of transit investments: Buses and sidewalks lead to subway stations and ferry stops. Subways connect with inner-city rail hubs. And in East Asia and Europe today, high-speed rail links these downtown hubs to other cities and international airports.

The dominance of passenger rail across our country, once the charge of corporate titans like Cornelius Vanderbilt, has atrophied due to the vastly disproportionate government subsidization of air and vehicular traffic, despite the proven economic and environmental efficiencies of rail. Even in corridors where demand for rail exceeds demand for air and car travel, persistent infrastructure problems plague the system.[6] Yet rail advocates are continually challenged to prove profitability, while few question whether airlines or auto companies would be profitable without the massive subsidies that enable runways, highways, SUVs, and bailouts. Similarly, critics of mass transit say it should be self-sufficient when, in fact, every mode of transportation, whether driving on a government-funded highway or walking on a public sidewalk, requires some form of subsidy. And because we do not properly price the cost of carbon emissions or the loss of productivity due to congestion, we do not charge car and airline passengers for the negative externalities of their behavior, a concept that dates back to Adam Smith and lies at the heart of any truly functioning capitalist marketplace.

Consider this simple example: Sam buys a $4-gallon of gasoline for his Cadillac Escalade and uses it all driving 12 miles round trip to buy a laptop case. His neighbor Luisa takes a recently built trolley to run the same errand, spending $3 for the round-trip fare. Luisa spends 25 percent less than Sam, but for the rest of us the more significant issue is what their respective trips cost society, and whether society is able to recoup these costs.

In Luisa's case, she used a mass-transit system that, in all likelihood, required subsidization beyond fare revenues to build and maintain. The trolley used electricity that probably came from a coal-fired power plant, so Luisa has, at some minor level, contributed to pollution, for which society incurs costs. Arguably, though, the trolley would have run regardless of Luisa's decision to ride it that day, so one can question whether Luisa's societal cost would exceed her $3-fare by much if the trolley is well used.[7] Luisa probably paid too little for her trolley trip if she were charged for all of the negative externalities of her behavior, but, at most, her fare should only have been a bit higher.

WHAT LUISA PAYS

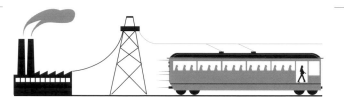

M MetroPass ◄◄◄

12-mile trip
$3 round-trip ticket

$3
Direct cost

+

WHAT SOCIETY PAYS

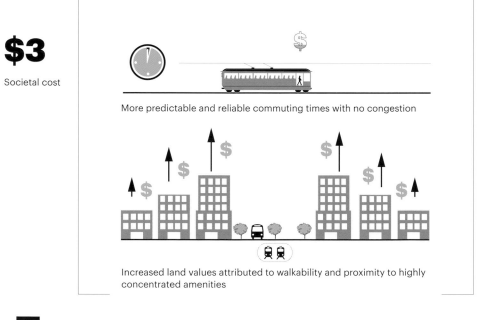

Greenhouse gas emissions and pollution controlled at source and yield lower emissions per capita

More predictable and reliable commuting times with no congestion

Increased land values attributed to walkability and proximity to highly concentrated amenities

$3
Societal cost

=

TOTAL COST OF LUISA'S TRIP

$6
Actual cost

By contrast, Sam's decision to drive his Escalade has demonstrably significant consequences because the cost of his behavior is a direct result of his choice to drive; and since only Sam occupies the vehicle, most of the societal costs of his errand are attributable only to him. His $4 of gasoline was likely taxed about 49 cents per gallon (the average joint federal and state rate), which is not nearly enough, according to most research, to cover his societal costs in terms of pollution, congestion, and highway use.[8] Many studies have shown that when these costs are included, the price of gasoline should approach $10 a gallon or more, simply to pay for one individual's decision to drive.[9] Based on this estimate, Sam should have paid $4 to the gas station and about $6 to the rest of us in order to compensate for his contribution to pollution and congestion. Chances are, if confronted with these expenses, Sam would probably trade his unprofitable relationship with his Escalade for a far more beautiful one with Luisa, since they could meet and fall in love on the trolley.

Both carbon and congestion pricing, therefore, could be key financing sources for new transportation infrastructure if we have the political will to assess the funds from drivers in the form of taxes and fees. If drivers paid the true costs of their actions, it would result in an enormous infrastructure investment fund that could build and maintain mass transit, which would offset the congestion and pollution that driving causes.

The *Wall Street Journal* has written about the billions of dollars of lost productivity associated with commuting in the past few decades.[10] In addition, according to the Texas Transportation Institute, "In 2010, congestion caused urban Americans to travel 4.8 billion hours more and to purchase an extra 1.9 billion gallons of fuel for a staggering annual congestion cost of $101 billion nationwide."[11] From London to Los Angeles, congestion pricing has helped societies recoup these soaring costs. But in most cities in the United States, we have gone in the reverse direction, with politicians unwilling to charge constituents for the social costs of their own behavior, even as these costs have shot up with the expansion of suburban regions and the legalization of light trucks, such as minivans and SUVs, as noncommercial passenger vehicles.

In cities across America, suburban residents commute into downtowns for economic opportunity, but they then expect the cities to fund the maintenance and functioning of their streets and subways without fair payment in return. To the surprise of most drivers, existing tolls and taxes represent a fraction of the actual costs of these systems, obscuring the enormous penalties borne by the rest of us when suburbanites drive. Collectively, we as a nation subsidize drivers, and as more of us move to cities and drive less, it is in our best interest to inform them that their free ride is over. In addition, the housing

RED-STATE SOCIALISM AND ITS IMPACT ON INFRASTRUCTURE, 2004

For every dollar it pays the federal government in taxes, each state receives a different amount of funding back. Below are the percentages per tax dollar paid in 2004. Most states with large cities give much more than they receive, while the less-urban states generally receive much more than they give.

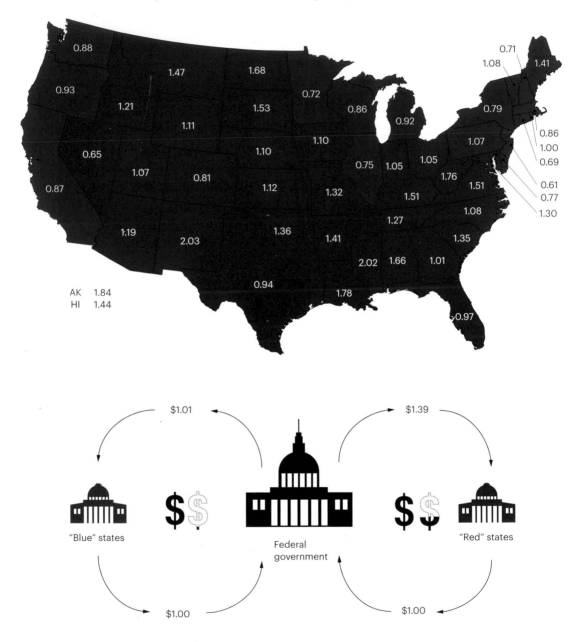

developers of exurbia and the automobile industry have both benefited tremendously from our lax conformance with Smith's free market principles. These industries, just like companies that illegally pollute the air or dump in waterways, owe us for the negative externalities of their work.

Pricing the negative externalities of behavior is critically important in a market-based society. But even if this were implemented, we still would not fully fund our infrastructure needs with such pricing alone. Infrastructure, when defined expansively, includes not just mass transit but schools, cultural facilities, parks, and other societal needs that drive opportunity. For major cities, this kind of essential infrastructure amounts to billions in both capital and operations expenditures, which nationwide would amount to trillions. Many will point to these trillions and decry the expenses as waste, blame unions for rising costs, and declare all spending as outrageous despite the public's clear need for and expectation of government services. Some waste and overspending exists in any large system, such as the defense budget, but is waste the real reason why we can't fund the infrastructure we require, or is it simply a lack of fairness?

Given that approximately 3 percent of the country—namely, its successful cities—generates approximately 90 percent of the nation's gross domestic product, this means that cities produce the vast majority of the tax dollars paid to state and federal coffers. Yet these cities receive a fraction of that money back in government funding. Ironically, the states that most vocally rally against government spending are the largest recipients of public-sector largesse. Most of the "blue" states are urban donors—that is, they contribute more to the federal government than they receive. Most of the "red" states are rural recipients, pulling in far more government subsidy than what they pay in taxes. Similarly, most cities contribute far more to state revenues than they receive back. These facts directly confront the beliefs of many Americans that their tax dollars disproportionately support urban welfare mothers and corrupt urban contractors, views that are demonstrably false.[12]

Imagine if this situation were simply made equitable. New York has a wish list of transportation projects that, combined, would cost about $32 billion—impossible to fund under current conditions. At the same time, the city sends approximately $18 billion more in taxes annually to Albany and Washington than it receives back in federal and state spending. If there were an equal balance of payments between the city and the state and federal governments for just two years, New York could fund all of its transportation projects, catalyzing an enormous boost to its economic and environmental performance—a gain that also would, no doubt, tremendously benefit Albany and Washington.

The federal government spends a disproportionate amount of money building and maintaining highways, nearly four times the amount allocated to all other transit modes.

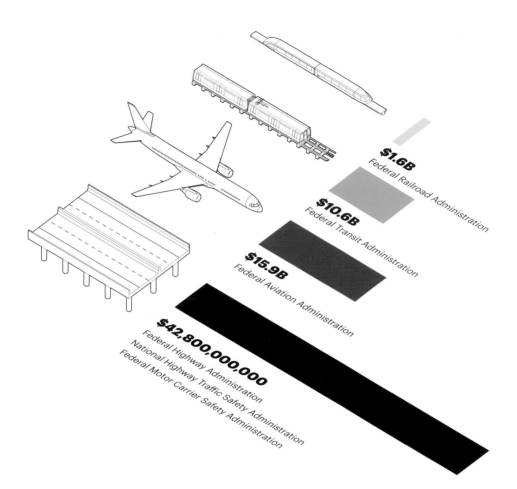

$1.6B
Federal Railroad Administration

$10.6B
Federal Transit Administration

$15.9B
Federal Aviation Administration

$42,800,000,000
Federal Highway Administration
National Highway Traffic Safety Administration
Federal Motor Carrier Safety Administration

If such a balance of payments were put into practice nationwide, cities, led by Democratic and Republican mayors alike, would suddenly move from debt to surplus, with replenished funds available not only for traditional infrastructure but also for schools, parks, cultural venues, and public-health facilities—the true Infrastructure of Opportunity. These improvements, in turn, would retain and attract more city dwellers, further expanding tax bases and creating a virtuous cycle of growth. The tired debate about government spending versus tax reduction could ultimately vanish due to the ability of infrastructure to fuel growth, expand the tax base, and lower individual tax liabilities.

As I write this book, in late 2012, this very debate is playing out furiously on the national stage. It started decades ago but is now fueled by unthinkable rancor and dysfunction. Witness the fiasco that now passes for a legislative process whenever Congress makes that special sausage known as the surface transportation bill, or ISTEA, the main funding mechanism for the nation's highways, bridges, and public transit. The last reauthorization was an embarrassment, with critical transit and inner-city rail needs unmet. President Obama's efforts to jump-start world-class infrastructure such as high-speed rail—in 2009, with ARRA (the American Recovery and Reinvestment Act, otherwise known as the stimulus bill), and with the more recent ISTEA reauthorization—have been whittled down to a series of half-measures that are struggling to have the desired transportation or other stimulus impacts.

Attempts to address the nation's ageing infrastructure have bubbled up at the regional and state levels from time to time but none has gained traction. Take, for example, Building America's Future, the laudable coalition co-chaired by former governors Arnold Schwarzenegger of California and Ed Rendell of Pennsylvania, and Mayor Michael Bloomberg of New York City. Despite such heavyweights in charge, the coalition has had little impact on the ground since it was founded in 2008. It has neither succeeded in galvanizing support for new infrastructure spending nor has it systematically lobbied Washington for the kinds of projects that constitute sound investments in our future, such as connecting our major cities via high-speed rail.

If infrastructure is a political orphan, in President Obama it may have a found an adoptive father, although a distant and understandably distracted one. In his January 2010 State of the Union address, he said: "We can put Americans to work today building the infrastructure of tomorrow. From the first railroads to the interstate highway system, our nation has always been built to compete. There's no reason Europe or China should have the fastest trains." It is a watershed moment when any U.S. president spares precious moments from a State of the Union address to utter such words. It is extraordinary that we have a president who regularly uses the word

HIGH-SPEED RAIL ACROSS THE GLOBE

High-speed rail is defined as a system that supports trains that go faster than 155 miles per hour.
Around the world today, there are over 15,000 miles of high-speed rail. Another 11,000 miles are planned.

Number of miles

China
6,649

Japan
3,776

Spain
2,389

France
1,323

Germany
1,039

Italy
577

Turkey
466

South Korea
374

Taiwan
216

Belgium
131

Netherlands
75

United Kingdom
71

Switzerland
67

United States
0

"infrastructure" in his speeches, or that our vice-president uses the word "density" with a palpable understanding of the concept as it relates to rail travel. Perhaps in the ever-maddening world of Washington, D.C.— the locus for the representatives of exurban America—such baby steps are the first moves toward a more urban America.

Yet it remains confounding that the best we got in 2010 toward high-speed rail was $8 billion, much of it targeted for a new line between Tampa and Orlando. Thanks to Rick Scott, Florida's then newly elected Tea Party governor, those funds were redirected to smaller projects nationwide. That left any hope for American high-speed rail in the hands of California governor Jerry Brown. But his plan to connect Los Angeles and San Francisco with a first-phase pilot project could unravel and threaten high-speed rail elsewhere in the United States. At inception, it will only connect low-density areas with minimal ridership potential because the connections to the big cities are not yet funded. Cities within 500 miles of each other provide the true ridership potential for high-speed rail.[13] Without significant federal cash to fund the expensive rights-of-way that must be created within the boundaries of large cities nationwide, high-speed rail will never succeed in America.

We need at least $150 billion to properly connect the major urban corridors within our megaregions, including Dallas-Houston, Chicago–St. Paul, Charlotte-Atlanta ("Char-Lanta"), the Cascadia region, the Northeast, and, yes, areas in California and Florida. Rail advocates, however, should fight any politicized effort to build high-speed rail in low-density areas where ridership would be minimal; this would only create white-elephant projects that would doom the future of American high-speed rail. To some degree, this has happened with Spain's vaunted new system, which attempted to bring together the nation's cultural mosaic but disregarded the ridership potential that rests only with big cities. (Some economists believe that overspending on the rail system helped to fuel Spain's current debt crisis.[14]) High-speed rail is expensive and should not be deployed for cultural, social,

Proponents o
rail are contir
to prove profi
few ask whetl
or auto compa
profitable wit
government s
and bailouts.

f passenger

ually pressed

tability, while

ner airlines

nies would be

hout massive

ubsidies

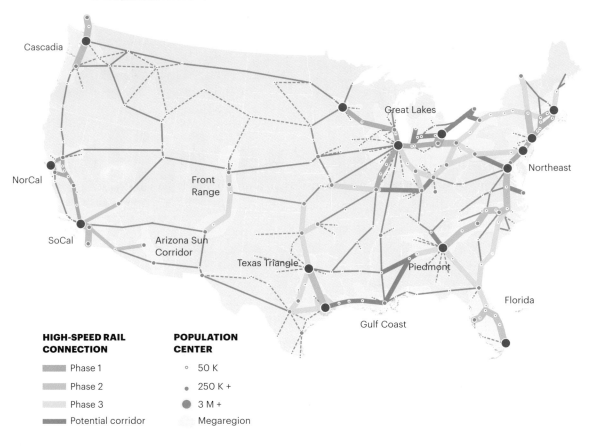

HIGH-SPEED RAIL FOR AMERICA

The organization America 2050 has proposed a high-speed rail network for the U.S. that can be phased in over time.

Cascadia

NorCal

SoCal

Front Range

Arizona Sun Corridor

Texas Triangle

Great Lakes

Northeast

Piedmont

Florida

Gulf Coast

HIGH-SPEED RAIL CONNECTION

- Phase 1
- Phase 2
- Phase 3
- Potential corridor

POPULATION CENTER

- ○ 50 K
- • 250 K +
- ⬤ 3 M +
- Megaregion

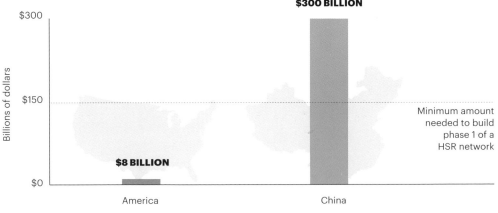

HIGH-SPEED RAIL FUNDING: CHINA VS. AMERICA

China has comitted nearly 40 times as much money toward its high-speed rail network as the U.S. has.

$300 BILLION

$300

$150

$0

Billions of dollars

$8 BILLION

Minimum amount needed to build phase 1 of a HSR network

America

China

or political reasons; it should be used to connect hyperdense cities to increase their economic output, which in turn increases GDP, lowers carbon footprints, and alleviates airport congestion nationwide.

When infrastructure investments are merit-based and urban, the stimulus effects can be tremendous. Consider that Vice President Joe Biden, speaking about the Florida high-speed rail proposal in 2010, stated that the $1.25-billion investment in the corridor would have generated more than 23,000 jobs over four years and that, by extension, 100 times that investment across the country could create over 2 million jobs nationally and connect our major cities. Now *that* would be stimulus.

So perhaps we should take solace in the fact that President Obama in 2010 referred to the overall $8-billion investment proposal as a "down payment." Maybe in the subtle use of the these words, in a presidency in which every word is said with discipline, Obama is signaling that he will get to it all in his second term.

Yet for the president to have stated, "There's no reason Europe or China should have the fastest trains," is, with all due respect, disingenuous. There are reasons. Those societies revel in their urban density, and they have the ability to allocate resources efficiently toward that end. China may soon overtake America in automobile production, but it also has unveiled the world's fastest passenger train to connect its thriving, hyperdense cities.

Beijing's new emphasis on high-speed rail is particularly relevant to the American context because China's land mass is similar in size to the continental United States. This means high-speed rail can be effective in connecting cities even in very large countries, contrary to critics who said it could only work in small nations, such as Japan. At a top speed of 217 miles per hour, China's Harmony Train, if operating in the United States, would propel us from Manhattan to downtown Charlotte via Washington in approximately three hours, eliminating an enormous amount of regional air traffic, freeing up runway slots for profitable long-haul flights, and resulting in far fewer delays for air travelers nationwide. This is not just a blue-state problem for the Northeast Corridor: Each year 1 million passengers fly between Atlanta and D.C., and similar numbers travel between Charlotte and New York City. The New South is in the house, and it has many of the same urban infrastructure needs that our older cities have—needs that perhaps should be fulfilled first in red and purple states if we are to be politically savvy about making our infrastructure investments appealing, successful, and merit-based.

HIGH-SPEED RAIL CAN WORK IN LARGE COUNTRIES

America and China are roughly equal in land area, yet China has over 6,600 miles of high-speed rail connecting some of the densest cities in the world, whereas the U.S. has no high-speed rail.

**UNITED STATES
0 miles of HSR**

3.79 million
square miles
of land

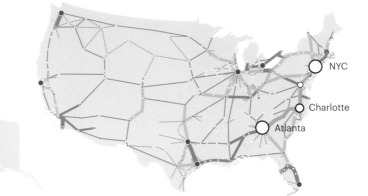

**CHINA
6,649 miles of HSR**

3.7 million
square miles
of land

TRAVEL TIMES: CAR VS. AIR VS. HIGH-SPEED RAIL

A national high-speed rail network gives consumers more choices; speeds trips; alleviates congestion in airports and on roads; brings riders directly to downtowns; and is more energy efficient.

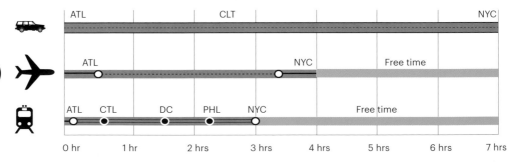

Going forward, one could imagine a very different approach to our governance and our economic malaise based on the premise that large-scale urban infrastructure investment would be both economically and environmentally beneficial. After the bailouts of the past few years, when banks were considered too big to fail, we could be told that we as a nation are, in fact, too big to fail. After preventing the global financial system and the auto industry from falling off the cliff, the White House could finally say, "OK, folks, you really are next!"

Imagine that early in President Obama's second term, four terrifying, push-me-pull-you facts, hopefully, become clear to his team:

1 Significant unemployment and middle-class wage stagnation will likely continue due to outsourcing, automation, and the ongoing transition to a service economy.

2 Spiraling entitlement costs, particularly health care for baby-boomer retirees, will continue to threaten the deficit and the dollar, suggesting limited federal spending.

3 Domestic energy supplies will continue to require controversial extraction processes like hydraulic fracturing, while Middle Eastern oil supplies will remain highly volatile.

4 Polar bears will continue to perfect the doggy paddle.

Faced with such facts, perhaps we might hear our leaders promote time-tested ideas of density and mass transportation, of cities using far less energy per capita than their suburban counterparts, of cities understood as being the solution to a vast swath of our problems, given the right emphasis on infrastructure. Imagine if the president said:

America, we have a silver bullet. We are going to rebuild this nation. We are going to create an Infrastructure of Opportunity for all Americans, and while we're at it, we're going to create the jobs of the future, build an innovation economy, rein in health-care costs, lower our dependence on foreign oil, and lead the planet to sustainability. We are going to do this in one fell swoop, with one big idea, called the American Smart Infrastructure Act (ASIA).

Imagine that Mr. Obama proposed to merge the federal transportation appropriations process with a revised version of cap-and-trade legislation on emissions into a consolidated bill called ASIA. Its premise would be as follows:

1 We will build and rebuild infrastructure that lowers greenhouse gas emissions and encourages urban density, with an emphasis on high-speed rail; urban mass transit; transmission grids from alternative energy sources; national broadband Internet; and critical roadway maintenance. We will deemphasize all infrastructure that exacerbates emissions, particularly roadway and airport expansion projects.

2 To expedite infrastructure construction, lower costs, accelerate job creation, and bring both political sides to the table, the government will streamline the National Environmental Protection Act (NEPA) and negotiate project labor agreements with unions. Millions will be employed quickly, pouring liquidity into Main Street.

3 Health-care costs will decrease as people rely less on driving and more on lifestyles that encourage walking. As people urbanize in response to new infrastructure and tax reform, rates of diabetes and chronic heart disease will decline, reducing the most costly sources of health care spending.

4 To pay for ASIA and help create an Infrastructure of Opportunity fund, we will recoup the hundreds of billions of dollars lost annually to traffic congestion by charging people for the costs of their pollution, particularly coal emissions, creating a market for cap-and-trade exchange. To do this fairly, we will a) pass a national $1-per-gallon gas tax whose revenues are committed only to smart infrastructure as defined above; b) override state legislatures that block cities from passing congestion-pricing plans at the municipal level, and offer matching federal ASIA grants to cities that enact congestion pricing; c) encourage public-private partnerships that build smart infrastructure by offering tax abatements, matching grants, and low-interest TIF bonds; and d) level the balance of payments between cities, states, and the federal government, allowing cities to keep more of the tax dollars they generate so long as they use these funds for smart infrastructure.

It is this bill—this silver bullet—that demands the fierce urgency of now. Perhaps we can imagine ASIA in America, with the hope of generating a new landscape for a new millennium, one in which anonymous sprawl would give way to a green, healthy, prosperous urbanity. Perhaps we can build a Country of Cities, with this new Infrastructure of Opportunity as its primary vehicle.

But a Country of Cities requires the creation of new bridges, both physical and social. We need bridges that lead the population out of the dependency of the suburbs and into the productivity and sustainability of our cities. When people cross this bridge, they must be able to find, on the other side, an urban life of true opportunity. And that demands not only a functional infrastructure with accessible transit and good schools, but also housing that is affordable to the widest possible economic spectrum. We now turn to the challenge of building more equitable cities.

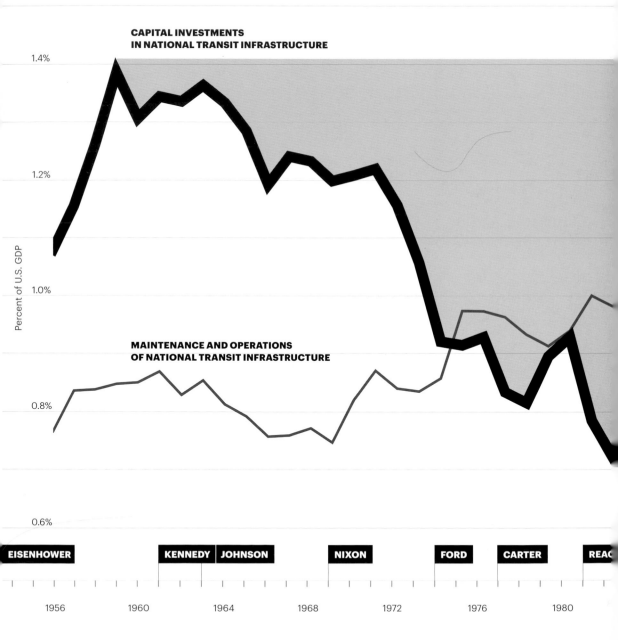

PUBLIC INVESTMENT IN INFRASTRUCTURE AS A PERCENT OF GROSS DOMESTIC PRODUCT

If we had kept our investment in transit infrastructure at 1959 levels, we would have invested $2.2 trillion more in our national infrastructure, which now finds itself in the worst state of decline and disrepair in its history. We would have had an additional $92 billion to put toward transit in 2007 alone. That year, we spent $114 billion on capital investments and $124 billion on maintenance and operations.

1.6%

1.4%

**CAPITAL INVESTMENTS
IN NATIONAL TRANSIT INFRASTRUCTURE**

1.2%

1.0%

**MAINTENANCE AND OPERATIONS
OF NATIONAL TRANSIT INFRASTRUCTURE**

0.8%

Percent of U.S. GDP

0.6%

EISENHOWER   **KENNEDY** | **JOHNSON**   **NIXON**   **FORD**   **CARTER**   **REAG**

1956   1960   1964   1968   1972   1976   1980

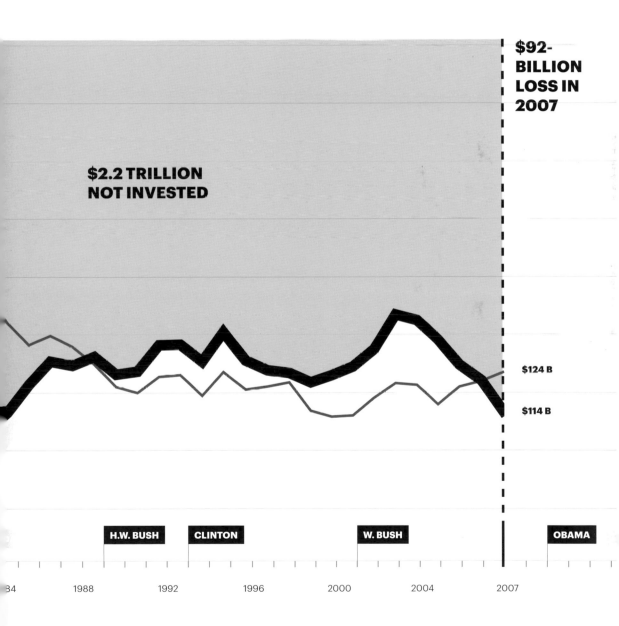

$92-BILLION LOSS IN 2007

$2.2 TRILLION NOT INVESTED

$124 B

$114 B

| H.W. BUSH | CLINTON | W. BUSH | OBAMA |

84   1988   1992   1996   2000   2004   2007

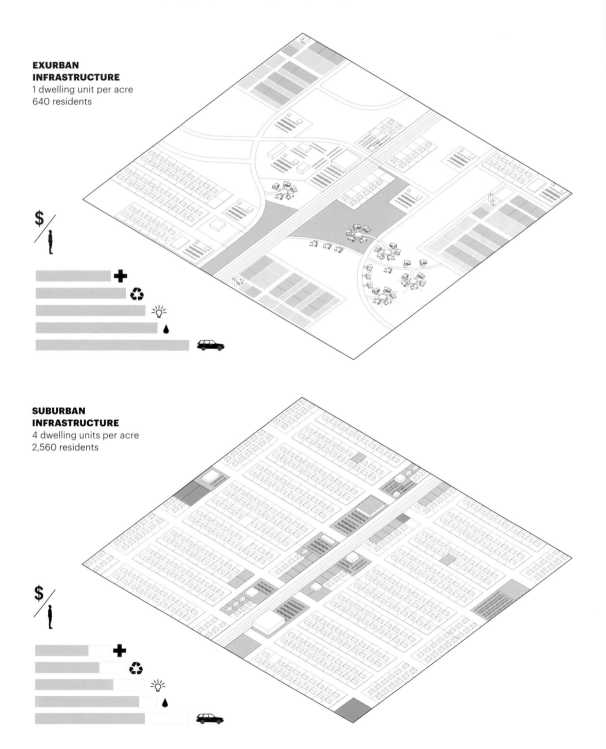

PER CAPITA COST OF INFRASTRUCTURE DECREASES AS DENSITY INCREASES

The cost and complexity of building mass transit and providing basic services, such as water and power, are offset by larger populations living in complex, hyperdense communities.

EXURBAN INFRASTRUCTURE
1 dwelling unit per acre
640 residents

$ /

SUBURBAN INFRASTRUCTURE
4 dwelling units per acre
2,560 residents

$ /

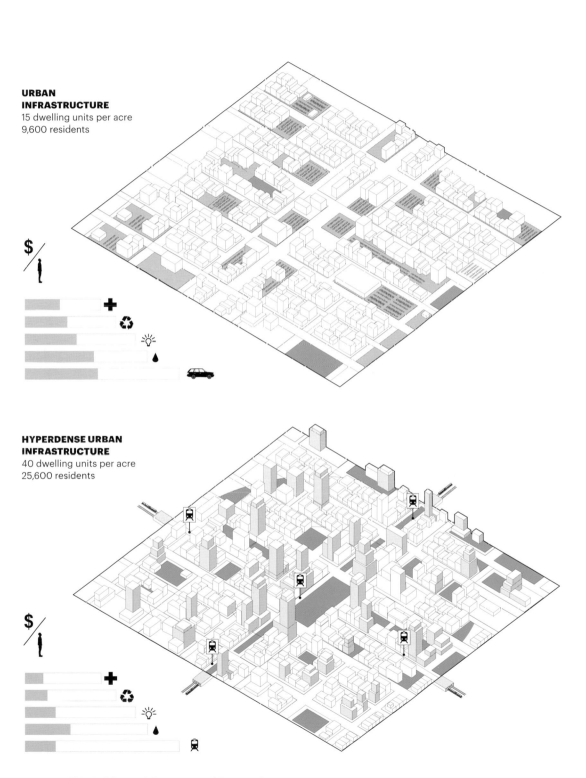

URBAN INFRASTRUCTURE
15 dwelling units per acre
9,600 residents

HYPERDENSE URBAN INFRASTRUCTURE
40 dwelling units per acre
25,600 residents

UPZONING CATALYZES DEVELOPMENT, INCREASING LAND VALUES AND CITY REVENUE

A municipality can increase the allowed density of an area to increase both property values and tax revenue.

1 Opportunity

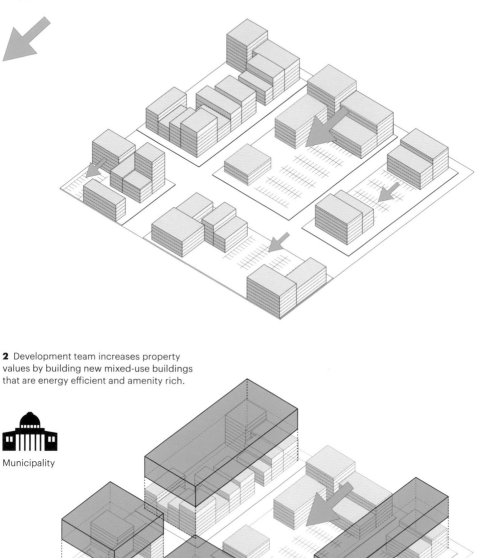

2 Development team increases property values by building new mixed-use buildings that are energy efficient and amenity rich.

Municipality

3 Local government upzones for potential new development.

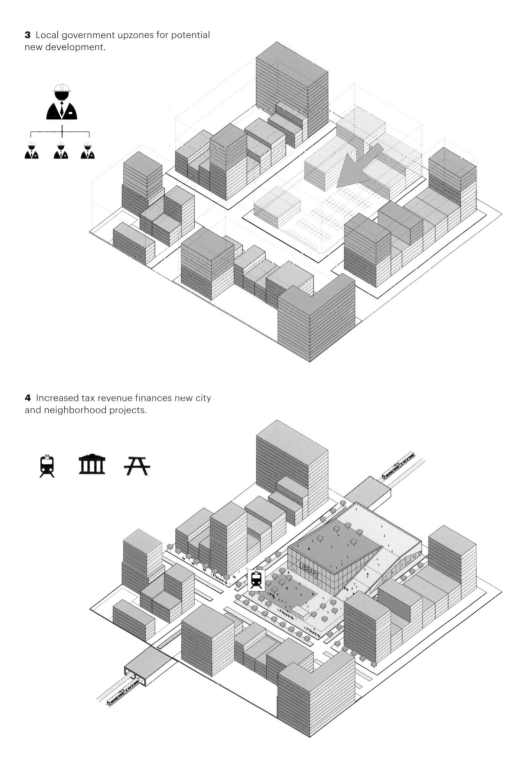

4 Increased tax revenue finances new city and neighborhood projects.

SUCCESSFUL PUBLIC HOUSING

Corine Vermeulen, *Lafayette Park Towers,
Detroit,* 2009

BUILDING THE EQUITABLE CITY

All of the merits of cities laid out in the preceding chapters can be undone by a lack of affordability. If cities do not provide affordable choices for housing, schools, transportation, health care, and food, people will not choose to live in them, and all of the economic and environmental benefits that are within our reach will pass us by. Affordability is a threshold issue.

America went through an extraordinary period of actually building urban public housing. During the Industrial Revolution, housing advocates grew concerned about the squalor in which many workers were housed, concerns that reached their apex a century later, in the 1960s, with the efforts of President Johnson and his Great Society. Under the auspices of Johnson Administration programs, visionaries such as Edward Logue built thousands of units of low- and mixed-income housing in cities across the country, often adopting the tower-in-the-park typology espoused by modernist architects such as Le Corbusier, Bruno Taut, and Peter and Alison Smithson (albeit with different underlying philosophies). While most decry this as a failed model, there's been little attention paid to housing of this type worldwide that continues to be successful, like Lafayette Park in Detroit, designed by Mies van der Rohe. Instead, projects such as Pruitt-Igoe in St. Louis and Cabrini-Green in Chicago—both now demolished—have become common punching bags for today's design professionals with total disregard for the noble motivations that fueled tower-in-the-park housing.[1] While the architecture is often the scapegoat for the failure of such complexes, the real problems are poor management and maintenance; a lack of sufficient density and mix of uses; and an orientation to the automobile such that the "park" is actually a parking lot.[2]

In the Reagan Administration, during which Johnson's War on Poverty drew to a close, public-housing construction was transformed into a voucher system, and ultimately into the byzantine tax-credit system we use today to help finance housing for lower-income people. As funds dedicated to these programs steadily dwindled, the nation moved away from "public housing" toward the concept of "affordable housing," in which the government partnered with developers to build mixed-income housing in return for various subsidies. This occurred concurrently with the stigmatization of public

Average residential rental costs per month as a percentage of New York City costs (NYC = 100)

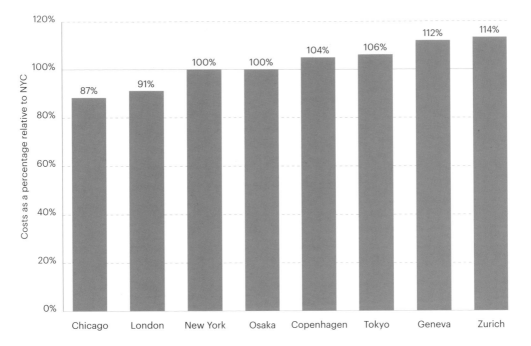

Affordable housing is based on household income. Typically, the proportion of its income a household pays toward housing should not exceed 30%, leaving enough money for other essentials.

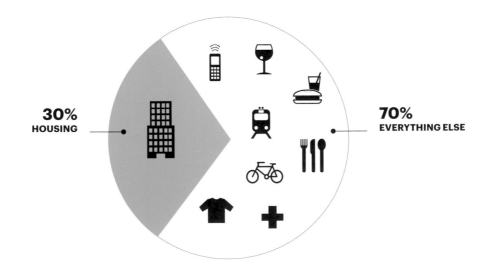

30%
HOUSING

70%
EVERYTHING ELSE

housing and its residents, due to a new political mindset that government support of low-income housing was inappropriate, despite the massive housing subsidies that middle- and upper-middle-class Americans continue to enjoy.

Yet there are many benefits to the system of developer-built affordable housing, primarily in terms of the mixing of incomes within buildings and neighborhoods as opposed to "warehousing the poor"—a criticism often waged by progressives concerned that public housing concentrates low-income residents in a single community. Studies show that poor urban families fare better in mixed-income environments, which typically feature better schools and less crime.[3] Furthermore, the private sector typically incurs lower construction costs and manages housing far better than the public sector.

The central problem with the current system, however, is the low amount of affordable housing it produces, despite the high amount of subsidies required. Often ranging in hundreds of thousands of dollars per unit produced, the subsidy levels used in current affordable-housing production are unsustainable without decreasing costs, increasing overall government funding for affordable housing, or both. But it is extremely difficult to achieve either one, given the expensive nature of urban markets and the competition for public funds, conditions that pose an enormous threat to the overall health of cities should they become enclaves for the wealthy, like many European capitals today. The demand for affordable housing in American cities, particularly in light of the growing desire among many of our citizens to urbanize, is a massive challenge, but not an insurmountable one.

It is no secret that successful cities are expensive. To some degree, they are victims of their own success. The combination of thriving urban economies, increased desire for urban lifestyles, and decreased urban crime has intensified the demand for urban housing and services. This demand now outstrips supply, making successful cities increasingly unattainable for families, workers, immigrants, and students, among others.

To a small extent, this is not entirely negative: Expensive urban cores encourage people to spread throughout a large city, inhabiting and stabilizing areas that otherwise would be homogenously poor. Over the last decade, in city after city, from Minneapolis to Memphis, urban fringes once characterized by crime and other dysfunctions have been transformed into vibrant, diverse, culturally thriving neighborhoods. While this naturally has raised fears about the potential problems associated with gentrification, studies indicate that such transformation can actually bring benefits to poor urban neighborhoods and the majority of their original residents, particularly in the form of more street life, lower crime, healthier food choices, and

The median income in the United States has not kept up with the cost of housing.

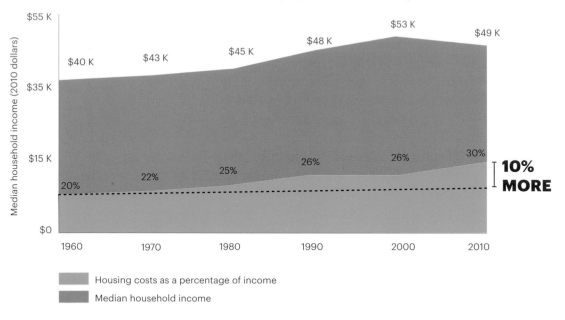

Median household income (2010 dollars)

$55 K
$35 K
$15 K
$0

$40 K $43 K $45 K $48 K $53 K $49 K

20% 22% 25% 26% 26% 30%

10% MORE

1960 1970 1980 1990 2000 2010

Housing costs as a percentage of income
Median household income

While the total amount of housing units in the United States has increased, the proportion of housing units that meet the "affordable" threshold has decreased by nearly half.

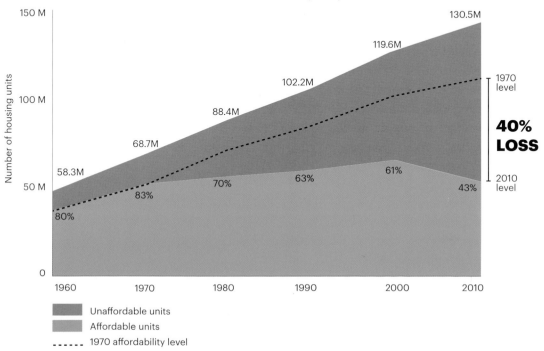

Number of housing units

150 M
100 M
50 M
0

58.3M 68.7M 88.4M 102.2M 119.6M 130.5M

80% 83% 70% 63% 61% 43%

1970 level

40% LOSS

2010 level

1960 1970 1980 1990 2000 2010

Unaffordable units
Affordable units
- - - - 1970 affordability level

enhanced schools. Gentrification need not represent displacement and loss of community.[4]

Moreover, affordability is relative. For instance, New York is very expensive compared to Baltimore or Detroit; but it is less expensive, even accounting for income and other factors, than the global cities it competes with, such as Tokyo. Manhattan and Chicago today remain far more socioeconomically diverse than central London or inner-city Paris. On the world stage, successful American cities are, surprisingly, "a deal."

However, the *New York Times* has reported that inequity in New York City rivals that of sub-Saharan Africa, with alarming income disparities growing between the rich and poor.[5] Obviously, we are not doing enough to address this abysmal state, but we must also consider what such inequity indicates. As economist Edward Glaeser points out, cities that are successful attract impoverished strivers who seek a better lot in life.[6] In that sense, most inequity metrics give us only a snapshot in time. Our true measure of success should be the opportunity we provide for strivers to succeed, encouraging more people to follow in their footsteps.

Nonetheless, most urban residents in the United States struggle to make ends meet. This is of paramount concern for not only those troubled by our lack of social equity but also those wanting to promote the general health and welfare of the city. Affordability, therefore, isn't just about delivering housing across a broader economic spectrum; it is about ensuring the diversity of our cities and their cultures. An unaffordable city makes it impossible for workers who provide critical services to live there and threatens the cultural production of creative industries, which is increasingly understood to be vital to urban economies.

The social ecology of a city is extraordinarily fragile. Once all the poor have been forced out, as has happened in most European capitals, the city becomes more cultural artifact than cultural hotbed, more museum than metropolis. It is precisely this European fate that American cities must avoid at all costs.

So what are the factors that impact the affordability of cities? For most people, the single largest expense is housing. Affordable housing, by definition, costs no more than one-third of a household's income.[7] But other factors must be considered to understand whether an individual's or a family's life is truly affordable. The cost of commuting is of increasing concern, with gasoline prices on the rise, not to mention the overall cost of vehicle ownership if one commutes by car. By contrast, mass transit almost always costs less, but if the transit system is unreliable, inconvenient, or unsafe, people will opt to drive or, worse, will be unable to either drive or walk to work.

Once all the p
been forced o
happened in
European cap
becomes mo
artifact than
hotbed, more
than metropo

oor have

ut, as has

host

itals, the city

e cultural

ultural

museum

is.

LAND VALUES INCREASE WITH INCREASED DEVELOPMENT CAPACITY

Higher allowable densities increase both the value of land and the value of the potential new development.

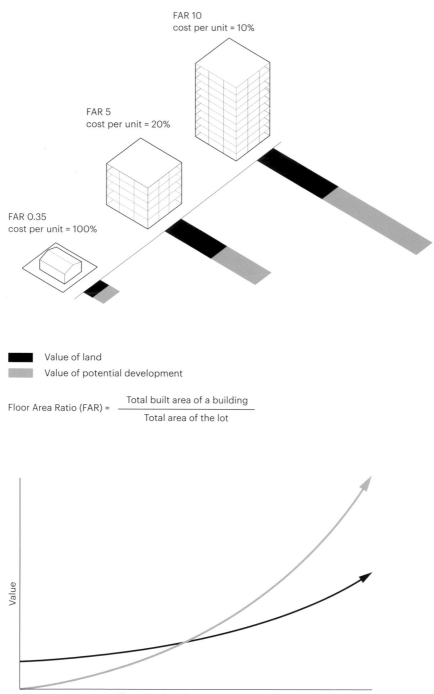

FAR 10
cost per unit = 10%

FAR 5
cost per unit = 20%

FAR 0.35
cost per unit = 100%

■ Value of land
▨ Value of potential development

Floor Area Ratio (FAR) = $\dfrac{\text{Total built area of a building}}{\text{Total area of the lot}}$

Value

Allowable density

Similarly, and as we examined in chapter two, heating and cooling costs per person in single-family suburban homes are far greater than those in apartment buildings, largely because houses are highly inefficient thermal envelopes that allow heat and air-conditioning to escape through roofs, windows, and foundations. By contrast, apartments heat and cool each other; and since apartments tend to be smaller than houses, they lend themselves to far more efficiency and therefore lower cost per person. Also, infrastructure costs—less noticeable but no less impactful—are more expensive in suburbs than in cities. Services including water, sewer, oil, gas, police, ambulance, fire protection, and garbage collection must traverse greater distances to reach customers in dispersed communities than in compact urban districts. Suburban residents incur these additional costs in the form of higher taxes and fees.

As journalist Alan Ehrenhalt describes in his book *The Great Inversion*, we are living in a period during which poverty is moving to suburbia. In a fully unanticipated twist of fate, and despite government incentives to the contrary, the city's economic opportunities and lifestyle have intensified the demand for urban real estate, pushing prices up and pushing people out. Poverty in suburban America has skyrocketed as a consequence, resulting in a triple whammy for this new disadvantaged population.[8] For most in this group, homeownership is out of the question, particularly in a post-subprime mortgage environment that requires high credit scores and low debt-to-income ratios. Second, for all the reasons mentioned above, the costs of gasoline, automobiles, heating, and cooling are rising rapidly, as are municipal taxes. Finally, and most ominously, the wealthier suburban enclaves with good public schools are out of reach of the new poor residents, who are left clustered in suburban ghettoes with faltering school systems and increased crime, a frightening harbinger of racially segregated, riot-torn suburban Europe.

For our society to avoid such a fate and maintain its advantages, we must reverse this trend, and once again, cities hold the key. Most cities today feature low-density areas within their municipal boundaries that have the capacity to house far more residents in economically and environmentally sound, hyperdense apartment buildings. Such affordable rental housing, located near mass transit, has the potential to spare people the costs of suburbia and keep socioeconomic diversity in our cities.

At the same time, the per-unit price tag on building an urban high-rise is typically higher than the cost of building a single-family home, despite the fact that the per-unit operating costs of apartment living are lower. We must deploy the full variety of available methods to lower the initial costs of apartment construction.

CONSTRUCTION COSTS PER UNIT DECREASE AS DENSITY INCREASES

While the cost of land increases where higher-density buildings are allowed, the cost to construct each unit goes down.

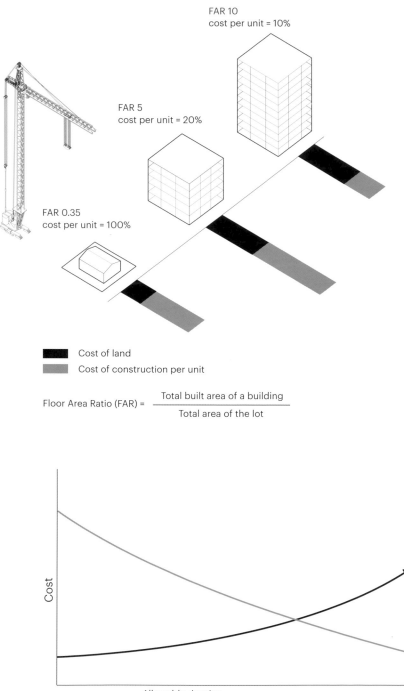

FAR 10
cost per unit = 10%

FAR 5
cost per unit = 20%

FAR 0.35
cost per unit = 100%

■ Cost of land
■ Cost of construction per unit

Floor Area Ratio (FAR) = $\dfrac{\text{Total built area of a building}}{\text{Total area of the lot}}$

Cost

Allowable density

Three factors determine housing prices:

1 The cost of land

2 The cost of construction, including the infrastructure that serves it

3 The cost of capital (that is, the interest on the loans needed to finance the project)

The market determines the price of land, but government plays a heavy role in influencing the market. This is because the price of land is not typically based on the size of its physical footprint but by its *development capacity*. For example, in a city, a parcel of land 100 feet by 100 feet is not priced by the fact that it is 10,000 square feet but by what and how much one can build on that parcel, a factor usually dictated by municipal zoning and other regulations. If zoning allows this parcel to contain 10 floors of housing, the land becomes far more valuable than if zoning allows only a five-story factory for, say, garment manufacturing. Nothing lowers urban value faster than overly restrictive zoning, which often results from "not in my backyard" or other special interest politics.

The greater the density permitted by zoning, the more the cost of land can be spread over a greater number of units. This is true despite the increases in land value that such an upzoning creates, because of the ability to amortize the higher land cost over a much larger building. Communities may choose to be parochial, fighting such densities in the cloak of Jane Jacobs when in fact it may be Jim Crow that they are channeling. Historically, there are far too many examples of communities fighting urbanization out of fear of racial and social integration, a fear to which our nation cannot afford to succumb.

Hyperdensity is affordable housing's best friend. The single greatest action municipalities can take to create urban affordable housing at a large scale is to increase density near transit stops, parks, and schools, potentially in return for affordable housing mandates. For years, municipalities avoided mandating developers to build mixed-income affordable housing because they didn't want to dampen urban housing production across the board. But demand has been so solid and sustained in most successful cities that this concern should be rethought: In economically strong cities, we should be mandating between 20 and 30 percent affordable housing in exchange for zoning that significantly increases allowable densities.

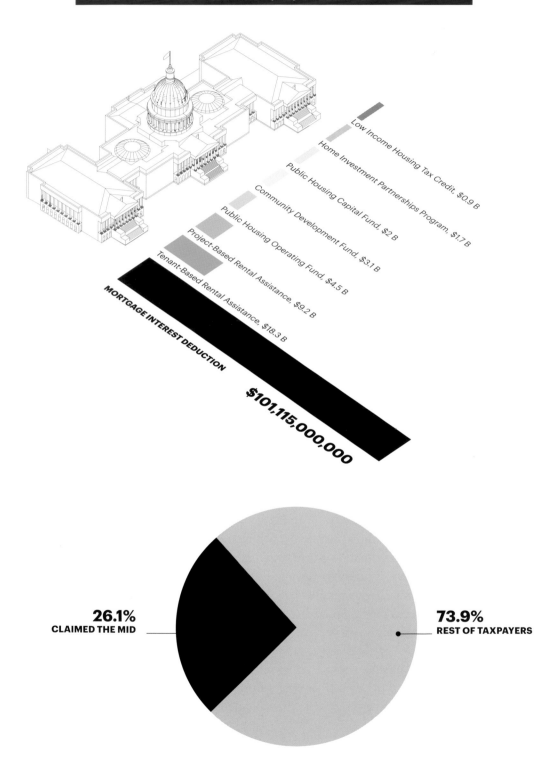

Low Income Housing Tax Credit, $0.9 B

Home Investment Partnerships Program, $1.7 B

Public Housing Capital Fund, $2 B

Community Development Fund, $3.1 B

Public Housing Operating Fund, $4.5 B

Project-Based Rental Assistance, $9.2 B

Tenant-Based Rental Assistance, $18.3 B

MORTGAGE INTEREST DEDUCTION

$101,115,000,000

26.1%
CLAIMED THE MID

73.9%
REST OF TAXPAYERS

The second factor in the expense of housing is the price of construction. Apartment-building construction costs are soaring; they diminished very little during the Great Recession. This is partially due to the fact that raw materials such as concrete are in heavy demand as the planet urbanizes. In addition, construction labor is typically much costlier for apartment buildings than for houses, because the skills required for high-rise construction are more complex, more specialized, and often involve union labor. For years, developers and labor have been at odds over costs in a seemingly zero-sum game.

But a breakthrough could be at hand with the advent of modular construction, in which union-built components are fabricated in controlled conditions and then stacked on-site like so many Lego pieces. This vast experiment is under way in New York City's Atlantic Yards, one of the most significant redevelopment projects occurring in the country today. Developed by Forest City Ratner and designed by SHoP Architects, Atlantic Yards features a new sports arena surrounded by millions of square feet of affordable housing, all at Brooklyn's main transit hub, where subway and commuter rail lines converge. Beyond its sheer scale, what makes the project unique is that its first phase will be built using modular construction in a high-rise configuration, promising the tallest modular building in the world. Featuring a projected construction-cost savings of 20 percent or more compared to conventional methods, and markedly higher architectural quality as a consequence of the controlled factory conditions under which the modules are being made, the project stands to revolutionize the way affordable urban housing can be built, all while delivering union jobs and a new manufacturing industry for our cities.[9]

Finally, in terms of capital, urban housing typically requires higher construction and development financing costs than its suburban counterparts. Banks tend to view high-rise construction and development as riskier than single-family house construction, a dubious assumption given the catastrophic state of large-scale subdivision projects whose values have plummeted. But this financing bias is in large-measure due to the extraordinary backing of mortgages by Washington, which, for the most part, incentivizes suburban development. While the federal mortgage interest deduction (MID) also supports urban condominium development, the scale of these projects pales in comparison to the amount of owner-occupied suburban housing being subsidized nationwide.

At well over $100 billion per year, the MID is the largest housing subsidy that our government grants—in fact, it is the largest federal subsidy of any type. The most galling aspect of this subsidy is the degree to which it helps the wealthy: The cap on the tax deduction for a married couple is over $1 million.

Communities
to be parochi
density in the
Jane Jacobs v
it may be Jim
they are chan

may choose
ıl, fighting
cloak of
hen in fact
Crow that
heling.

Other wealthy countries that do not allow the MID have similar homeownership rates as the United States.

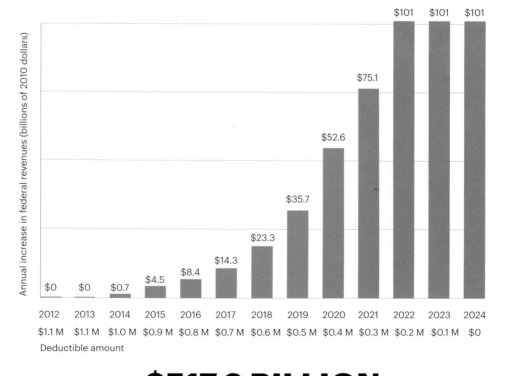

| | U.S. | Netherlands | Canada | U.K. | Australia |

- With MID
- Without MID

GRADUALLY ELIMINATE THE MORTGAGE INTEREST DEDUCTION

The Congressional Budget Office modeled a gradual phaseout of the MID by reducing the maximum mortgage amount eligible for the interest deduction from $1.1 million in 2013 to zero in 2024. The annual increment reduction of $100,000 would boost revenues by $517 billion over the course of the phaseout.

Annual increase in federal revenues (billions of 2010 dollars)

Year	2012	2013	2014	2015	2016	2017	2018	2019	2020	2021	2022	2023	2024
Value	$0	$0	$0.7	$4.5	$8.4	$14.3	$23.3	$35.7	$52.6	$75.1	$101	$101	$101
Deductible amount	$1.1 M	$1.1 M	$1.0 M	$0.9 M	$0.8 M	$0.7 M	$0.6 M	$0.5 M	$0.4 M	$0.3 M	$0.2 M	$0.1 M	$0

$517.6 BILLION

TOTAL REVENUE STREAM FROM ELIMINATING THE MID OVER A 12-YEAR PERIOD

Does our society really need to lower the cost of million-dollar mortgages and second homes?

Proponents argue that the MID has been central to American wealth creation. But as we witnessed during the Great Recession, the prospect of Americans being allowed to use their homes as ATM machines, based on false value suppositions, led to the worst housing crisis in our history. Some experts believe that American home prices in real dollar terms will not return to pre-crash values for two decades or more. Underwater housing—or housing worth less than the debt it carries—is an impediment to workforce mobility, in which renting rather than buying gives workers the ability to move where employment is strong rather than being chained to a mortgage that's not worth the paper it's printed on.[10]

Canada, the United Kingdom, and the Netherlands are among the many developed countries that do not offer an MID, and yet wealth creation continues in all three places with negligible impact on overall homeownership rates. And despite Canada's geographical and cultural similarities to the United States, it suffers from far less urban sprawl. In a post-crash American landscape, our northern neighbor is a glaring reminder that housing is not a roulette wheel for bankers or homeowners.

In our third category, then, reform of the cost of capital could—and should—happen at a federal level. Yes, through changes to municipal zoning that allow densification and through innovation in construction technologies, we can reduce the impact of the first two cost variables, land and construction, associated with urban housing. But no city, and no society, can deliver the housing needs of a broad socioeconomic spectrum without subsidies; the risks and costs are simply too great. A hodgepodge system of affordable-housing tax credits has replaced the federal system of directly building public housing units. Yet these tax credits and other subsidies for low-income Americans shamefully pale in comparison to the housing subsidies given to the middle and upper class.

Today, the average cost of a new house in the United States hovers around $270,000, while the median cost of a new house is closer to $220,000.[11] Yet the MID is disproportionately used by wealthier Americans who buy far more expensive homes. It is clear that the MID encourages the purchase of larger houses than otherwise might be bought if home investment were taxed on par with other investments. We should phase out the MID over time just as the nonpartisan Congressional Budget Office advocated in its 2011 report "Reducing the Deficit: Spending and Revenue Options."[12] The office recommended that the MID cap be reduced at a rate of $100,000 per year until it disappears. Such a gradual phasing out would prevent a shock to the housing market. It also would allow Americans to

THE MORTGAGE INTEREST DEDUCTION SUBSIDY BENEFITS THE WEALTHY

As a result of the MID, which is claimed by only a quarter of taxpayers, the federal government forgoes collecting revenue that would otherwise help build schools or pay for much-needed infrastructure. Furthermore, the total amount of mortgage interest the federal government subsidizes gives the ultra-wealthy a subsidy that is nearly five times that received by people who make less than the national median household income.

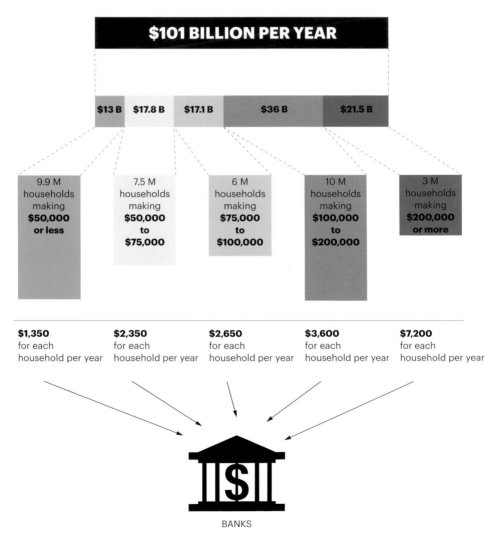

$101 BILLION PER YEAR

| $13 B | $17.8 B | $17.1 B | $36 B | $21.5 B |

| 9.9 M households making **$50,000 or less** | 7.5 M households making **$50,000 to $75,000** | 6 M households making **$75,000 to $100,000** | 10 M households making **$100,000 to $200,000** | 3 M households making **$200,000 or more** |

| **$1,350** for each household per year | **$2,350** for each household per year | **$2,650** for each household per year | **$3,600** for each household per year | **$7,200** for each household per year |

BANKS

adjust their consumer patterns away from the mindless consumption of larger and larger houses and toward savings and investment, a shift that economists from across the political spectrum support.

As the MID sunsets, we should use half of the money saved for much-needed deficit reduction and the rest to help finance the construction of affordable rental housing in our cities.[13] New, dense urban development would house people of a wide range of incomes, from the homeless and very poor, to the working poor, to the teachers, nurses, firefighters, and service-economy workers who deserve at least as much attention from the federal government as the residents of, say, Greenwich, Shaker Heights, Grosse Point Park, Bethesda, or Sausalito. Ironically, like wealthy Medicare recipients, few of the wealthy residents of these enclaves think they are receiving federal subsidies of any kind; they have come to believe in the MID as their God-given right. But the Book of Job tells us, "What the Lord giveth, the Lord taketh away," and it is high time for the good Lord, or at least good government, to act.

An annual redirection of approximately $258 billion from the MID toward urban affordable housing would generate tens of millions of apartments for lower- and middle-class Americans. Many will argue that this would represent redistributionist policy. So be it, but it is by no means economically unwise or socialist. To the contrary, the socialist nations of Europe allowed suburban ghettoes to grow unchecked, and we, in our capitalist nation, should not repeat this vile mistake. Thriving urban neighborhoods, accessible to strivers from the U.S. and abroad would fuel a new era of economic prosperity in our cities and, in turn, our nation.

We must get serious about urban affordability because without it, our nation will not find its way out of its present economic and environmental morass. Without it, we will continue to push our population outward rather than upward, lowering our productivity, expanding our carbon footprint, and decreasing our public health. We can take the needed measures to address the cost of land, construction, and financing with a combination of market-oriented tools and the admission that today we subsidize middle- and upper-class housing, but tomorrow we can level the playing field for all Americans without stigmatizing those with lower incomes as "victims" dependent on government assistance. As President Obama has stated, this is about giving people a "hand up, not a handout." Without these reforms, we will continue to be a country of countries, divided across the very lines along which we must unite.

With these strategic and achievable reforms, we would bring urban housing within the reach of millions nationwide. Developer-built affordable housing, coupled with access to good, diverse public school systems and convenient transit infrastructure, would unleash a new era of productivity that would help all Americans. This new era would be centered on the basic precept of "life, liberty, and the pursuit of happiness" by creating opportunities for everyone. Opportunity is the most American of values, and providing it fairly is the true meaning of social equity. We all understand that we will be born unequal and die unequal; the fundamental question for society is not whether we are equal, but whether we have an equal shot.

No environment can better yield equal opportunity, with greater access to economic productivity and lower costs to achieve it, than the American city. We can build prosperous, sustainable, joyous cities for all Americans. We can do it with the tools and the funds at hand. And we should do it, because it is the right thing to do—and the smart thing to do. We must build, for all of us, a Country of Cities.

1937–74: DIRECT CONSTRUCTION OF GOVERNMENT-SUBSIDIZED PUBLIC HOUSING

From the Great Depression through the Nixon era, the federal government directly
funded construction of large-scale public housing projects across the country.

Mortgage Interest Deduction,
Federal Housing Administration
loan backing

Federal
goverment

Local public
housing authority

New construction

PROS

Apartments enjoy ample natural light and air

Potential for open space immediately
adjacent to the high-rises

CONS

Parking instead of parks

Not dense enough

Removed from streetscape

Warehousing the poor

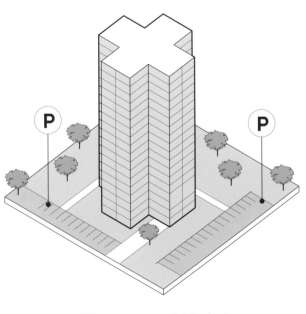

████ Government-subsidized units

Declining interest in large-scale public housing led the federal goverment to implement a new voucher-based system that supplemented rents primarily in suburban environments.

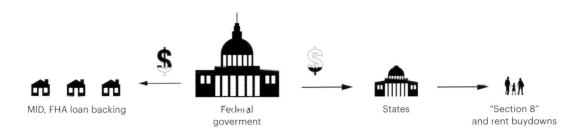

MID, FHA loan backing

Federal goverment

States

"Section 8" and rent buydowns

PROS

Tenants have relative flexibility in choosing the neighborhood in which they would like to live

Units look the same as market-rate dwellings; the stigma associated with public housing is removed

CONS

More sprawling and automobile-centric

More expensive to build per unit

Not dense enough to support transit

Many cities do not have Section 8 housing programs available

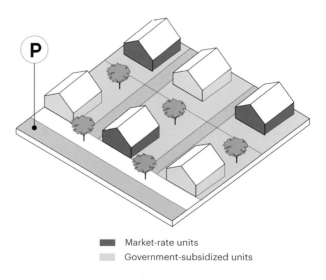

■ Market-rate units
▫ Government-subsidized units

With President Reagan's Tax Reform Act of 1986, a complex system of tax credits was created to involve private developers in the building of affordable housing within market-rate developments.

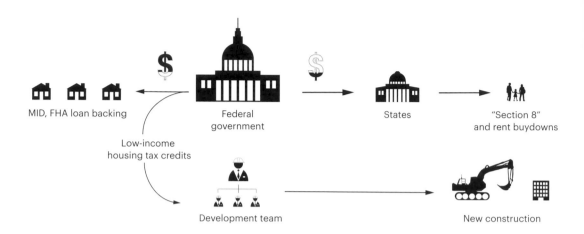

MID, FHA loan backing

Federal government

States

"Section 8" and rent buydowns

Low-income housing tax credits

Development team

New construction

PROS

Dense enough to support transit

Units look the same as market-rate dwellings; the stigma associated with public housing is removed

Private sector works with public sector

CONS

Too little funds available for tax credits

Too expensive to construct

With increased densities, the neighborhood has difficulty improving critical infrastructure, as money that could be diverted to mass transit is poured into parking facilities instead

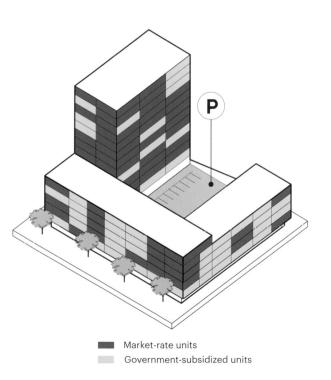

■ Market-rate units
□ Government-subsidized units

With funds redirected from suburban subsidies, new affordable urban housing can be built along with the amenities and infrastructure needed to support dense development.

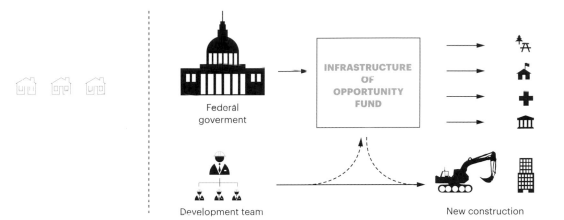

Federal goverment

Development team

INFRASTRUCTURE OF OPPORTUNITY FUND

New construction

PROS

Dense enough to support transit

Private sector works with public sector

Mixed-use

In lieu of an on-site parking requirement, developers pay into a mass transit fund or other neighborhood amenities

CONS

High cost of urban construction (see next page)

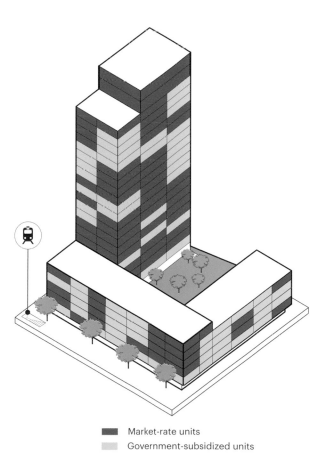

■ Market-rate units
□ Government-subsidized units

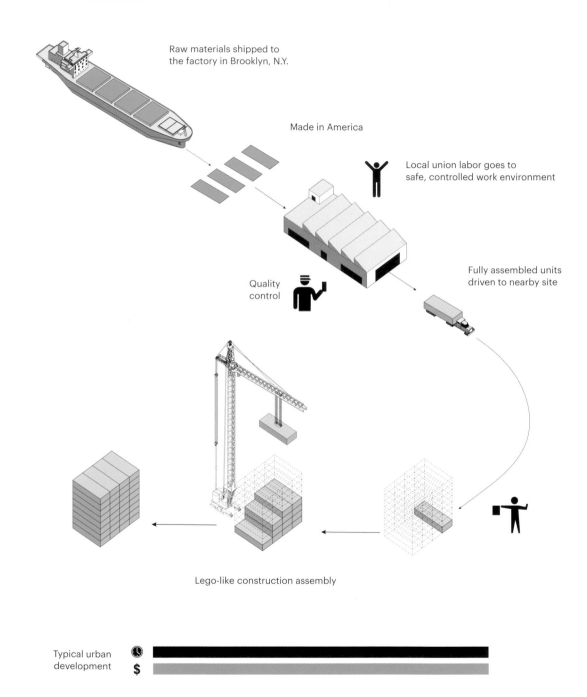

Raw materials shipped to
the factory in Brooklyn, N.Y.

Made in America

Local union labor goes to
safe, controlled work environment

Quality
control

Fully assembled units
driven to nearby site

Lego-like construction assembly

Typical urban
development

Modular
construction

Designed for modular construction, three new towers surrounding Barclays Center will create a hyperdense, mixed-use neighborhood at the nexus of various historic Brooklyn neighborhoods.

Continuous retail frontage will add to the mix of retail already present along the arena's perimeter, further contributing to the vitality and street life of the area.

A COUNTRY OF CITIES

A COUNTRY OF CITIES: OF TRAINS, TOWERS, AND TREES

Imagine a Country of Cities.

Imagine a new countryside dotted with large cities and small towns, dominated by trains, towers, and trees, with little but agriculture and nature in between. Imagine this transformation occurring in a matter of decades, just as it took only a few quick decades in the twentieth century to transform the beauty of America into anonymous sprawl. Imagine this new landscape, this Country of Cities, resulting not from new regulations or burdensome mandates but from the agency of ordinary Americans exercising market-based choices, free from the suburbanizing manipulations of the federal government.

Imagine a country in which government policies would support the real desires of its citizens, not the desires that supposedly existed six decades ago, during the postwar era. Americans today are urbanizing, with the demand for high-rise multifamily rental housing increasing dramatically in the wake of the economic crisis. Young people, immigrants, and seniors alike want to live near mass transit, near shops and restaurants, and near each other. Economic opportunities, environmentalism, public health, diversity, and the inherent joy of cities are together creating a profound and lasting transformation of the lifestyle sought by everyday Americans. Many of us are flocking to cities without government assistance, unlike our suburban counterparts who continue, however unknowingly, to enjoy enormous subsidies in terms of highway funding, mortgage deductions, relaxed standards for the emission levels of SUVs and minivans, and undertaxed pollution and congestion.

The growing urbanization of America represents a rising tide against the pernicious undertow of federal suburban subsidies, subsidies that swelled the current housing crisis and left so many Americans adrift and underwater. This tide can now lift all boats and, guided by a new national imagination, carry us to a more prosperous and sustainable land.

Imagine citizens who fully understood what most leading economists already know and what Jane Jacobs asserted when she wrote *Cities and the Wealth of Nations*: Cities wield overwhelming economic advantages in a global economy, advantages that, if unharnessed, would lead us out of our current malaise and establish a lasting, widespread American prosperity.

Imagine environmentalists who truly embraced cities as the only sustainable means of creating a lasting future for a planet of many billions, a future in which the realities of climate change could be mitigated by the inherent resilience and resource efficiencies of urbanity.

Imagine a culture that viewed cities as the central means of establishing a healthy and happy citizenry, a culture that not only walked more and reveled in the wonders of our vast urban parks but also interacted more across social and cultural boundaries to truly realize the thriving, vital, diverse nation that is our manifest destiny.

Imagine a nation that embraced the indisputable facts about the economic, ecological, and health benefits of cities and, as a consequence, directed its intellectual energies toward the development of hyperdensity at the local level, defying NIMBYism and an outdated national-planning apparatus that attempts but fails to work for the public good.

Imagine we could summon the will to build an Infrastructure of Opportunity by enacting ASIA, the American Smart Infrastructure Act, which would focus our resources on high-speed rail and mass transit, recapture the loss of hundreds of billions of dollars of societal pollution and congestion costs, and equalize the balance of payments cities make to state and federal governments.

Imagine America returning to a country of open roads and clear skies, in which a trip to a summer cottage, a cross-country drive, or a family vacation abroad were free from the mind-numbing congestion that bogs us down, preventing us from enjoying the most precious asset of a service economy, time.[1]

Imagine we could call upon our fundamental beliefs as a nation to then build cities that offered equal opportunities for all Americans through the construction of extensive and accessible urban affordable housing, development in which costs could be brought down through greater density, public-private partnerships, efficient construction technologies, and a redirection of the billions in mortgage interest deductions currently pocketed by the wealthy.

Is it folly to imagine this Country of Cities? To imagine our population and our political system acknowledging the countless urban advantages laid out in section one of this book and, as a consequence, enacting the policies described in section two? No doubt, to any wise reader, this might seem like wishful, potentially delusional thinking. Even if convinced by the overwhelming data regarding the advantages of cities, who among us believes we could successfully act on it? Who, for instance, believes we could convince localities to embrace hyperdensity or persuade the federal government to pass smart infrastructure legislation, or phase out the MID and use the proceeds to fund affordable housing? Is a Country of Cities a far-off land in an urban fairy tale?

But political sacred cows can be slain, and social third rails crossed, if we can just listen to each other regardless of political affiliation. Consider a recent editorial in the conservative *Wall Street Journal*, which stated in unambiguous terms:

> As an economic matter, the mortgage deduction has long done more harm than good, misallocating capital to housing at the expense of other industries that might create more national wealth. The economy would be stronger, and might have avoided the trauma of the last five years, if housing demand hadn't been artificially inflated by years of policy favoritism.[2]

Similarly, an expansive 2011 article in the liberal *New York Times* on the same topic noted that most economists decry the MID and agree that it does not increase the rate of homeownership because it so disproportionately favors wealthy consumers who would purchase homes regardless. Furthermore, one economist cited in the article went on to clarify the relationship between the deduction and suburbanization by noting that the deduction "hasn't helped to expand homeownership, but it's helped to support purchases of larger homes."[3]

Most significant, even the bipartisan Simpson-Bowles deficit-reduction commission suggested extraordinary reductions to the MID, including lowering the eligibility cap and eliminating the shocking ability for the wealthy to use the deduction for second homes. To be sure, none of these entities suggested using recaptured funds from the MID to support urban affordable housing—most have talked about it mainly in terms of deficit reduction—but the point remains: At a moment of national crisis and transformation, everything should be on the table.

In this book, I have challenged many sacred beliefs by proposing to charge for the negative externalities of personal behavior and redirect subsidies for the wealthy to invest in an Infrastructure of Opportunity. These investments are critical for unlocking the widespread social opportunities embedded in any new hyperdense neighborhood enabled through municipal policies. And in order to be beneficial, new hyperdensity will require support systems that cannot be borne by new development alone. Building infrastructure is a core responsibility of any good government, and only the public sector can fill the substantial gap between the contributions of private partnerships and the actual costs of these necessary projects.

To be clear: Fulfilling these needs through the redirection of existing subsidies will not incur new debt obligations for a nation already in deficit. On the contrary, these investments, unlike our currently unproductive subsidies, would have enormous potential to increase our GDP and ultimately transform our deficit into a surplus.

Investments in urban infrastructure and affordability will result in the kind of shared prosperity that has eluded us, not only during this economic downturn but also through the previous decade, during which most Americans saw their wages freeze. The causes of that stagnation are supposedly well known—among them, the ongoing transition from a manufacturing to a service economy; a significant shift in our tax code to favor the wealthy; and a staggering decline in our national education standards, which caused the United States to drop to fourteenth place in international rankings of reading skills.[4]

Yet few point to our car-oriented landscape as a culprit in our national morass, despite the dramatically increasing costs Americans are incurring to commute, raise children, buy homes, climate control environments, and stay healthy. And in the big picture, the diminishing wealth of the average American is leading to the collapse of municipal budgets, which still must fund everything from school systems to mass transit with only crumbs from the federal government.

THE FALL OF MAJESTIC

The suburbs of Majestic burn from within and without at the end of the third season of *Weeds*.

Americans may not consider our suburban landscape as the cause of our inertia, but perhaps we sense that we are trapped in a vicious cycle in which two-hour traffic jams might, in fact, be playing a role. Our physical environment is crumbling along with our social fabric. From *Weeds* to *The Wire*, we know in our hearts that we have a predicament embedded in the very way we live. Most of us feel the decline and together we sense that, as Roy Scheider's police chief in *Jaws* famously stated, we're "gonna need a bigger boat."

Our nation may be politically divided, but at least we share in the knowledge that something is deeply wrong in terms of our economic, environmental, and global security. Much of the housing in sprawling places like Phoenix, Las Vegas, and Atlanta is in foreclosure, with concomitant increases in unemployment several points higher than in our functioning service-economy cities.[5] Our young men and women are dying in mountains and deserts around the world, struggling against enemies funded by an Arabian peninsula that we have enriched because of a profligate lifestyle we have endorsed. And to paraphrase former Vice President Gore's quip on *Saturday Night Live* regarding our looming climate crisis: "There are guys in flip-flops hanging around the Christmas tree at Rockefeller Center."

Confronted with this seemingly intractable knot of challenges, we arrive at the final and most important set of questions: Do we matter to ourselves? Do we protect our kids or do we act like children? Do we have the will to make investments that would break our cycles of debt and decline? Do we have the introspection to protect our coastlines, our cities, and our citizens? Do we have the strength to reject the threat that is fossil fuel, both foreign and domestic? Do we have the vision to recognize that we have seen the enemy, and it is the subsidization of suburbia? Do we have the will to embrace high-density, transit-based living as the only solution, the only land use that reverses our economic stagnation, our rising seas, our spiraling health-care costs, our vulnerability to petro-dictators, and our free fall into a sprawling national deficit?

These challenges are not intractable; they are solvable through a national call to action. That call must focus on a different way of existing physically as a nation—a transformation as radical as the one that created the synthetic landscape of the twentieth-century United States. This is why we need a far more coherent public voice for true urbanity and the robust infrastructure it needs to prosper, a voice that speaks outside of the politics of both major parties until at least one comes to its senses.

The right tends to decry public spending. The left tends to favor entitlements over investments. The right fights regulations that curb sprawl and prices carbon. The left fights for environmental regulations, bureaucracies, and unwarranted community control that can imperil infrastructure.

All this to bicker, while Rome burns.

THE FALL OF ROME

Thomas Cole, *Destruction*, 1836.
Oil on canvas, 39½ x 63½ in.
Collection of The New-York Historical
Society, 1858

A COUNTRY OF HIGHWAYS, HOUSES, AND HEDGES: DENVER TODAY

A COUNTRY OF TRAINS, TOWERS, AND TREES: DENVER TOMORROW

TODAY: A COUNTRY OF HIGHWAYS, HOUSES, AND HEDGES

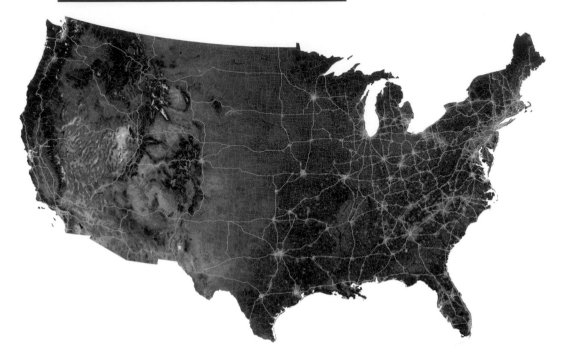

TOMORROW: A COUNTRY OF TRAINS, TOWERS, AND TREES

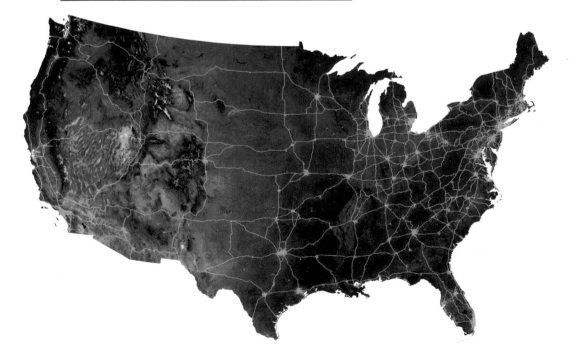

A COUNTRY OF CITIES: THE MANIFESTO

Let us form a truly urban coalition, one that binds the need for economic prosperity, environmental stewardship, and social mobility with the one-stop shopping of transit-rich hyperdensity. One that can rightfully claim that through smart urbanization, we can attack most of the major problems we see in the news media every day. One that can rally public sentiment to equally and credibly slay our demons, from foreclosures, to terrorism, to unfunded schools, to devastating oil spills, to ever more powerful storms.

Let us cry over natural and manmade disasters, towers destroyed by radicals, and Great Recessions, but let us then find some introspection in such tragedies. Let us rebuild this nation by being the America that constructed the Transcontinental Railroad and the Erie Canal; by being the America that welcomed striving immigrants to the shores of its cities; by being the America that envisioned vast national parks and the dignified wonders of the New Deal; by being the America that has always reveled in the majesty of its pristine landscape; by being the America that invented the Internet; by being the America that once believed we are all created equal.

Let us together rebuild an America that embraces cities and rejects traffic jams. Let us be a nation of fair choice, in which the government's subsidizing fingers have been taken off the scales; a nation where the best of market forces, driven by the desires of all of its people, allow cities to flourish. Let this new United States be a place where we heal our differences, pay our debts, and leave a replenished planet for generations to come.

We can build hyperdensity, along with an Infrastructure of Opportunity to nurture it. We can forge a nation where every one of us has a fair shot. We can provide more prosperous, more sustainable, and more joyful lives for all of our people. We can create a superior version of our most significant global export: the American city. We can and should construct not just a bigger boat but a better boat—an urban ark that delivers us to the safe harbor of prosperous shores.

We can, we should, we must, build a Country of Cities.

Imagine a cou
which our pol
actually supp
current desir
citizens, not t
that suppose
six decades a
the postwar e

ntry in
cies would
rt the
s of our
e desires
lly existed
go, during
ra.

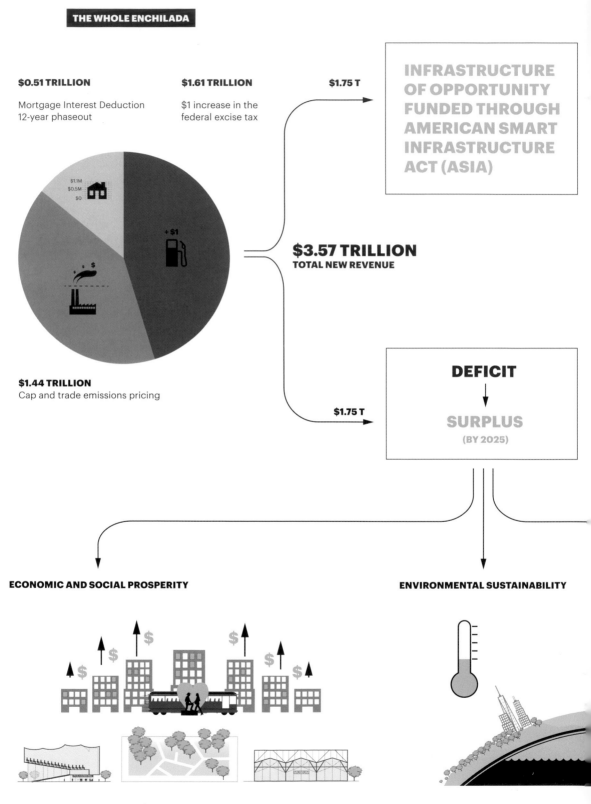

THE WHOLE ENCHILADA

$0.51 TRILLION

Mortgage Interest Deduction
12-year phaseout

$1.61 TRILLION

$1 increase in the
federal excise tax

$1.75 T

**INFRASTRUCTURE
OF OPPORTUNITY
FUNDED THROUGH
AMERICAN SMART
INFRASTRUCTURE
ACT (ASIA)**

$1.1M
$0.5M
$0

+ $1

$3.57 TRILLION
TOTAL NEW REVENUE

$1.44 TRILLION
Cap and trade emissions pricing

$1.75 T

DEFICIT

↓

SURPLUS
(BY 2025)

ECONOMIC AND SOCIAL PROSPERITY

ENVIRONMENTAL SUSTAINABILITY

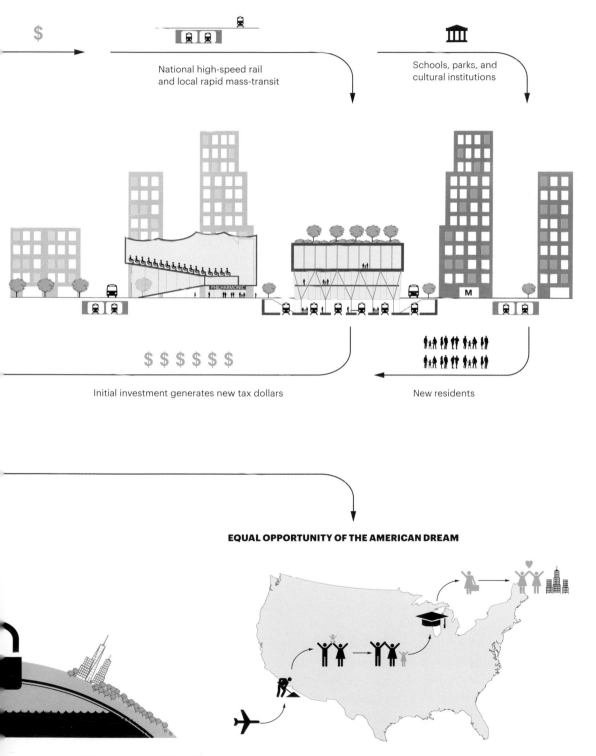

National high-speed rail
and local rapid mass-transit

Schools, parks, and
cultural institutions

$ $ $ $ $

Initial investment generates new tax dollars

New residents

EQUAL OPPORTUNITY OF THE AMERICAN DREAM

VISHAAN AND HIS FAMILY, 1969

In 1968, my parents—with two small children, $32, and graduate degrees in hand—made their way from the intellectual hotbed of Calcutta to the cultural upheaval of late-1960s America. A byproduct of President Johnson's liberalizing of the nation's immigration laws, my family's journey mirrored those made by thousands of others—including my wife, Maria Alataris, who with her parents and sister braved the trip from Greece the same year as our clan.

My parents crossed the Pacific for prosperity, adventure, intellectual freedom, and a more open education for their children. Suddenly freed by the advent of commercial air travel, little did they grasp their impending immersion into the world's cities. We, en route from Calcutta to Los Angeles, stopped overnight in Tokyo and, to my later amazement, spent the evening in town, far from the airport, to experience the city. I have always suspected that night transformed two young adults from villagers into urbanites, forever transfixed by the wonders of the metropolis, forever seeking to expose us to cities worldwide as we grew up on a shoestring budget and tooled around in a Dodge Dart that lasted over a dozen years.

My parents' struggles, in many ways, reflect the struggles of the contemporary metropolis. City building is invariably about ever changing forces seeking to innovate, discover, construct, reconstruct, and begin anew. It is to some degree this freedom from history that attracts us to cities, the sense that the sins of our predecessors can be cleansed by the reinvention and redemption available on every sidewalk.

Blessed with this great privilege of traveling across oceans and across the United States (I had the good fortune to traverse the country three times in my old Honda Civic), I have come to realize that all cities share this

VISHAAN AND HIS FAMILY, 2010

thread of progress through reinvention—of goods and services, art and architecture, technology and religion, personal identities and relationships, and professional definitions and collaborations. Luckily for me, the eclecticism of my education—erratically spanning art history, engineering, urban planning, and architecture—and my multiheaded profession as an architect, planner, and urban development academic all unwittingly reflect the fluid spirit of the contemporary city and its constant demands of both left brain and right. My experiences bringing these professional threads together as the Holliday Professor at Columbia University and a partner at SHoP Architects, and raising a family in New York City (enriched by train trips to our weekend cottage in the village of Bellport, with its smart planning, small houses, and preserved barrier island), continually reinforce, in my mind, the need in our epoch to work horizontally across disciplines to meet the hybrid economic, environmental, aesthetic, and social demands of city building today.

Little did I realize that hybrid call of the city is personal but also pertinent—pertinent to the global challenges we now confront as a society. It is one thing to have a private passion for a painting or a technology or a concerto, but it is something altogether different and humbling to realize the potential significance of one's calling to a larger world beset with challenges. It is with this passionate humility in mind, and with a deep and abiding love for this unique nation, that I offer this manifesto for an urban America. It is my naïve but enduring hope that we can build a Country of Cities in the lifetime of our children, and for them set the stage for an economically, environmentally, and socially better world.

NOTES AND ILLUSTRATION SOURCES

A COUNTRY OF COUNTRIES: OF HIGHWAYS, HOUSES, AND HEDGES

NOTES

1 President Barack Obama's *Executive Order 13503—Establishment of the White House Office of Urban Affairs* took a bold step in the right direction, but since the office was created, in 2009, it has failed to gain traction because of a lack of internal leadership compounded by waning public support from the president.

2 See, for instance, Michael Porter and Jan Rivkin, "Prosperity at Risk: Findings of Harvard Business School's Survey on U.S. Competitiveness," Jan. 2012, Harvard Business School, http://www.hbs.edu/competitiveness/pdf/hbscompsurvey.pdf.

3 B. S. Pushkarev and Jeffrey Zupan, *Urban Rail in America: An Exploration of Criteria for Fixed-Guideway Transit* (Bloomington: Indiana University Press, 1982).

4 The drive to make America less dependent on imports also pushed the country to innovate after the War of 1812. The inventions of this early wave of industrialization spurred the need for proximity that resulted in the densification of early cities. See Maury Klein, *The Genesis of Industrial America, 1870–1920* (Cambridge: Cambridge University Press, 2007).

5 Jim Walker, *Los Angeles Railway Yellow Cars* (Mount Pleasant: Arcadia, 2007), 175.

6 Mike Davis, *City of Quartz: Excavating the Future in Los Angeles* (London: Verso, 2006), 122.

7 See Dolores Hayden, *Building Suburbia: Green Fields and Urban Growth, 1820–2000* (New York: Vintage, 2004), ch. 11.

8 Richard W. Gable, "The Politics and Economics of the 1957–1958 Recession," *Western Political Quarterly* 12, no. 2 (June 1959), 557–59.

9 Ester R. Fuchs, *Mayors and Money: Fiscal Policy in New York and Chicago* (Chicago: University of Chicago Press, 1992).

10 Sam Roberts, "Infamous 'Drop Dead' Was Never Said by Ford," *New York Times*, Dec. 28, 2006, sec. New York Region, http://www.nytimes.com/2006/12/28/nyregion/28veto.html.

11 Fuchs, *Mayors and Money*.

12 On the collapse of the housing market, see Herman Schwartz, *Subprime Nation: American Power, Global Capital, and the Housing Bubble* (Ithaca: Cornell University Press, 2009); on the environment, see Al Gore, *An Inconvenient Truth: The Planetary Emergency of Global Warming and What We Can Do About It* (New York: Rodale, 2006); and on inequality, see Paul Krugman, *End This Depression Now!* (New York: W. W. Norton, 2012).

13 James Truslow Adams and Howard Schneiderman, *The Epic of America* (Piscataway: Transaction, 2012).

14 Jude 1:7. The biblical cities of Sodom and Gomorrah have become synonymous with impenitent sin, and their fall with a proverbial manifestation of God's wrath.

15 Saskia Sassen, *Cities in a World Economy* (Los Angeles: Pine Forge Press, 2006).

16 Paul E. Godek, "The Regulation of Fuel Economy and the Demand for 'Light Trucks,'" *Journal of Law and Economics* 40, no. 2 (Oct. 1, 1997), 495–510.

17 Conor Dougherty and Robbie Whelan, "Cities Outpace Suburbs in Growth," *Wall Street Journal*, June 28, 2012, sec. Economy, http://online.wsj.com/article/SB10001424052702304830704577493032619987956.html.

18 Associated Press, "Cities Grow More Than Suburbs, First Time in 100 Years," June 28, 2012, *TODAY.com*, http://today.msnbc.msn.com/id/47992439/ns/today-money/t/cities-grow-more-suburbs-first-time-years.

19 Alan Ehrenhalt, *The Great Inversion and the Future of the American City* (New York: Knopf, 2012).

20 Richard C. Porter, *Economics at the Wheel: The Costs of Cars and Drivers* (San Diego: Academic, 1999).

21 Antonio Estache and Danny Leipziger, eds., *Stuck in the Middle: Is Fiscal Policy Failing the Middle Class?* (Washington, D.C.: Brookings Institution Press, 2009).

22 Richard Florida, *The Great Reset: How the Post-Crash Economy Will Change the Way We Live and Work* (New York: Harper Business, 2011), 173.

23 For Arizona developments in opposition to Agenda 21, see "Agenda 21: Arizona Close to Passing Anti-UN-Sustainability Bill," *U.S. News on NBCNEWS.com*, Apr. 26, 2012, http://usnews.

msnbc.msn.com/_news/2012/04/26/11415282-agenda-21-arizona-close-to-passing-anti-unsustainability-bill. For opposition to Agenda 21 in places such as Iowa, Tennessee, and South Carolina, see, for instance, Reuters, "Tea Party Activists Fight Agenda 21, Seeing Threatening U.N. Plot," *Huffington Post*, Oct. 15, 2012, http://www.huffingtonpost.com/2012/10/15/agenda-21-tea-party_n_1965893.html.

24 Lisa Hymas, "Romney, Once an Anti-Sprawl Crusader, Created Model for Obama 'Smart Growth' Program," *Grist*, Apr. 23, 2012, http://grist.org/election-2012/romney-once-an-anti-sprawl-crusader-created-model-for-obama-smart-growth-program.

25 See Vishaan Chakrabarti, "This Land Is Our Land," Sept. 21, 2010, http://urbanomnibus.net/2010/07/this-is-our-land; Vanessa Baird, "Why Population Hysteria Is More Damaging Than It Seems," *Guardian*, sec. Environment, Oct. 24, 2011, http://www.guardian.co.uk/environment/2011/oct/24/population-hysteria-damaging?newsfeed=true; and Edward L. Glaeser, *Triumph of the City: How Our Greatest Invention Makes Us Richer, Smarter, Greener, Healthier, and Happier* (New York: Penguin, 2011), 1.

26 Fareed Zakaria, *The Post-American World* (New York: W. W. Norton, 2008).

ILLUSTRATIONS

P. 20 AMERICA TODAY

Voter turnout data: http://en.wikipedia.org/wiki/United_States_presidential_election,_2012. Based on 2012 population estimate of 312 million Americans.

Land consumption data: Allison Borchers, Fernando Carriazo, Robert Ebel, and Cynthia Nickerson, *Major Uses of Land in the United States, 2007*, EIB-89, U.S. Department of Agriculture, Economic Research Service, Dec. 2011.

Debt data: http://www.corelogic.com/about-us/researchtrends/asset_upload_file448_16434.pdf (accessed Nov. 28, 2012).

P. 22 DENSITY CAN TAKE MANY FORMS WITH VARYING QUALITIES

B. S. Pushkarev and Jeffrey Zupan, *Urban Rail in America: An Exploration of Criteria for*

Fixed-Guideway Transit (Bloomington: Indiana University Press, 1982).

P. 26 AT WHAT DENSITIES DO AMERICANS LIVE?

2006–2010 ACS 5 Year Estimates Data, http://www.census.gov/acs/www (National Dataset 2011; accessed Dec. 14, 2012); and 2012 TIGER/Line Shapefiles, prepared by the U.S. Census Bureau, 2012, http://www.census.gov/cgi-bin/geo/shapefiles2012/main (accessed Dec. 14, 2012).

P. 26 DENSITIES UNABLE TO SUPPORT RAPID MASS TRANSIT

Pushkarev and Zupan, *Urban Rail in America*.

P. 28 DENSITIES ABLE TO SUPPORT RAPID MASS TRANSIT

Ibid.

P. 29 RAPID RAIL TRANSIT NOW!

"Rail Rapid Transit Now!" Rapid Transit Action Group, Los Angeles Chamber of Commerce, Feb. 1948, http://libraryarchives.metro.net/DPGTL/trafficplans/1948_rail_rapid_transit_now.pdf.

P. 30 THE MAJORITY OF AMERICANS LIVE IN SUBURBS

Theodore Caplow, Louis Hicks, and Ben J. Wattenberg, *The First Measured Century: An Illustrated Guide to Trends in America, 1900–2000* (Washington, D.C.: Aei, 2000).

P. 30 AMERICANS LIVING IN SUBURBS, 1910–2010

For 1900–2000: Caplow et al., *The First Measured Century*. See also 2000 Census Redistricting Data, http://www.census.gov/census2000/sumfile1.html (National Dataset; accessed Dec. 14, 2012); and 2010 Census Redistricting Data, http://2010.census.gov/news/press-kits/summary-file-1.html (National Dataset 2011; accessed Dec. 14, 2012).

P. 36 BUSH'S "OWNERSHIP SOCIETY"

Rich Addicks/*Atlanta Journal-Constitution*.

P. 37 IDYLLIC SUBURBIA IN MOVIES

1 RKO/Photofest.

2 20th Century-Fox/Photofest.

3 Selznick Releasing Organization/Photofest.

P. 38 DYSTOPIC SUBURBIA IN MOVIES

1 Columbia Pictures/Photofest.

2 Sony Pictures/Photofest.

3 DreamWorks/Photofest.

P. 39 URBAN DYSTOPIA
Warner Bros./Photofest.
P. 40 SUBSIDY DENIAL
Image source: http://ajones1021.files.wordpress.
com/2012/08/keep-your-government-hands-off-
my-medicare1.jpg.
P. 41 THE JEFFERSONIAN GRID
Aerial images: Google Maps.
P. 42 BOB'S BIG PLAN
Nickelodeon Network/Photofest.
PP. 44–45 HOUSEHOLD SIZE VS. HOME SIZE
U.S. Census Bureau, *Characteristics of New
Housing, Housing and Household Economic
Statistics Division*, last revised Oct. 31, 2011,
http://www.census.gov/housing/ahs/; and 2012
TIGER/Line Shapefiles, prepared by the U.S.
Census Bureau, 2012, http://www.census.gov/
cgi-bin/geo/shapefiles2012/main.
**PP. 44–45 HOUSING STOCK AND
POPULATION GROWTH**
Ibid.
PP. 46–47 DEVELOPMENT ON PLANET EARTH
Global Human Footprint (Geographic), v2,
Center for International Earth Science Information
Network (CIESIN), Columbia University,
http://sedac.ciesin.columbia.edu/maps/gallery/
set/wildareas-V2-human-footprint-geographic,
(accessed July 12, 2012).
**PP. 48–49 THE WORLD'S POPULATION COULD
FIT IN TEXAS**
Calculation method: Seven billion people divided
by the land area of Texas (268,820 square
miles, or 172,000 acres) equals 40.6 people per
acre. This rough population density was then
modeled to account for a 7 percent loss factor
for roads, sidewalks, etc. It was assumed that
each household would contain 1.5 to 2.5 people,
thereby allowing the entire population of the
world to live at 25 dwelling units per acre within
Texas's borders.

**CHAPTER 1
CITIES, PROSPERITY, AND GLOBALIZATION**

NOTES

1 Bill Steigerwald, "City Views: Urban Studies
Legend Jane Jacobs on Gentrification, the New
Urbanism, and Her Legacy," *Reason* (June 2001),
http://reason.com/archives/2001/06/01/city-views.
2 IHS Global Insight, "U.S. Metro Economies:
Outlook—Gross Metropolitan Product, and
Critical Role of Transportation Infrastructure,"
prepared for The United States Conference of
Mayors and The Council on Metro Economies
and the New American City (Lexington, Ky.:
IHS, 2012), Table 1, http://usmayors.org/
metroeconomies/0712/FullReport.
3 Michael E. Porter, *Competitive Advantage:
Creating and Sustaining Superior Performance*
(New York: Simon and Schuster, 1998).
4 Edward L. Glaeser, *Triumph of the City: How
Our Greatest Invention Makes Us Richer, Smarter,
Greener, Healthier, and Happier* (New York:
Penguin, 2011).
5 Richard Florida, *The Great Reset: How the Post-
Crash Economy Will Change the Way We Live and
Work* (New York: Harper Business, 2011).
6 See Ryan Avent, *The Gated City* (Amazon,
2001), http://www.amazon.com/Gated-City-
Kindle-Single-ebook/dp/B005KGATLO.
7 Ibid.
8 Matthew Yglesias, *The Rent Is Too Damn High:
What to Do About It, and Why It Matters More
Than You Think* (New York: Simon and Schuster,
2012).
9 Wendell Cox, "What Is a Half-Urban World?"
Newgeography.com, Nov. 21, 2012, http://www.
newgeography.com/content/003249-what-a-half-
urban-world.
10 Saskia Sassen, *The Global City: New York,
London, Tokyo* (Princeton: Princeton University
Press, 2001).
11 Ibid., 5.
12 Garages, tractor sheds, and horse barns,
which are excluded from taxation, encourage
the ballooning of house sizes, with detached
structures often serving as additional living space
within a property.
13 On the global expansion of credit, see Richard
Duncan, *The New Depression: The Breakdown
of the Paper Money Economy* (New York: Wiley,
2012). "PIIGS" refers to Portugal, Ireland, Italy,
Greece, and Spain, which were lumped together
for their substantial economic insolvency
problems around the start of the 2008 global
recession.
14 Agustino Fontevecchia, "10 Million
Underwater Mortgages and Shadow Inventory
Worth $246B Mean Housing Trouble," *Forbes*,
June 26, 2012, http://www.forbes.com/sites/
afontevecchia/2012/06/26/10-million-underwater-
mortgages-and-shadow-inventory-worth-246b-
mean-housing-trouble.

15 Wolff reports that "the share of wealth owned by the bottom 80 percent of households fell from 19 to 16 percent between 1982 and 1992 and they received only 1 percent of the increase in wealth between 1983 and 1989." Edward N. Wolff, "Recent Trends in Household Wealth in the United States: Rising Debt and the Middle-Class Squeeze—An Update to 2007," *Levy Economics Institute of Bard College* (Mar. 2010), http://www.levyinstitute.org/pubs/wp_589.pdf.

16 The fastest growing metropolitan economies are those of rapidly urbanizing southern cities. See IHS Global Insight, "U.S. Metro Economics: Outlook."

17 Government Finance Research Center, *Building Prosperity: Financing Public Infrastructure for Economic Development* (Washington, D.C.: Government Finance Research Center of the Municipal Finance Officers Association, 1983), 2.

18 Jennifer S. Vey and Richard M. McGahey, eds., *Retooling for Growth: Building a 21st Century Economy in America's Older Industrial Areas* (Washington, D.C.: Brookings Institution, 2008).

19 Jane Jacobs, *Cities and the Wealth of Nations* (New York: Vintage, 1984), 58.

20 Glaeser, *Triumph of the City*, 49.

ILLUSTRATIONS

P. 52 JANE JACOBS, ECONOMIC EXPANSIONIST
Courtesy of the Estate of Jane Jacobs.

P. 54 JANE JACOBS'S THEORY OF IMPORT REPLACEMENT IN CITIES
See Jane Jacobs, *Cities and the Wealth of Nations* (New York: Vintage Books, 1984).

P. 56 WHERE AMERICAN PROSPERITY IS PRODUCED
Economic data: IHS Global Insight, "U.S. Metro Economies: Outlook—Gross Metropolitan Product, and Critical Role of Transportation Infrastructure," prepared for The United States Conference of Mayors and The Council on Metro Economies and the New American City (Lexington, Ky.: IHS, 2012), Table 1, http://usmayors.org/metroeconomies/0712/FullReport. Area data: Allison Borchers, Fernando Carriazo, Robert Ebel, and Cynthia Nickerson, *Major Uses of Land in the United States, 2007*, EIB-89, U.S. Department of Agriculture, Economic Research Service, Dec. 2011, http://www.ers.usda.gov/media/188404/eib89_2_.pdf.

P. 58 AMERICAN CITIES ARE MORE PRODUCTIVE THAN THE VAST MAJORITY OF STATES
See IHS Global Insight, "U.S. Metro Economies: Outlook."

P. 60 DENSITY AND PRODUCTIVITY
Ryan Avent, *The Gated City* (Amazon, 2011), http://www.amazon.com/Gated-City-Kindle-Single-ebook/dp/B005KGATLO.

P. 60 JOB DENSITY AND PER CAPITA INNOVATION RATE
Gerald Carlino, Satyajit Chatterjee, and Robert Hunt, "Urban Density and the Rate of Invention," report prepared for Federal Reserve Bank of Philadelphia, 2006, Figure 1. Data covers patents from 1975 to 1999.

P. 62 JOB DENSITY AND PROXIMITY TO OTHER ACTIVITIES
Todd Litman, "Economic Value of Walkability," paper presented at Transportation Research Board 82nd Annual Meeting, Washington, D.C., Jan. 2003, http://www.vtpi.org/walkability.pdf; and Center for Transit Oriented Development (CTOD) Database, http://toddata.cnt.org/db_tool.php#v=report&ts=Chicago&r=.5&y=41.885099999999994&x=-87.93120096000001&z=10 (accessed Dec. 12, 2012).

P. 64 AMERICA'S WORKFORCE HAS CHANGED OVER TIME
U.S. Department of Labor Database, Statistics, Historical Employment, Hours, and Earnings, Table B-1: Employees on nonfarm payrolls by industry sector and selected industry detail, http://www.bls.gov/webapps/legacy/cesbtab1.htm (parameters used: seasonally adjusted annualized totals; accessed Dec. 12, 2012).

P. 68 AMERICA'S MOST LETHAL EXPORT: THE SUBURB
Google Images.

P. 70 AMERICA'S OUTSTANDING MORTGAGE DEBT, 1960–2010
For GDP data 1963–97: U.S. Bureau of Economic Analysis, "Gross Domestic Product by State (Millions of Current Dollars)," http://www.bea.gov/iTable/iTableHtml.cfm?reqid=70&step=10&isuri=1&7007=-1&7093=Levels&7003=200&7035=-1&7036=-1&7001=1200&7002=1&7090=70&7004=NAICS&7005=-1&7006=00000 (accessed Dec. 21, 2012).

For GDP data 1997–current: U.S. Bureau of Economic Analysis, "Gross Domestic Product by State (Millions of Current Dollars)," http://www.bea.gov/iTable/iTableHtml.cfm?reqid

=70&step=10&isuri=1&7007=-1&7093=Leve
ls&7090=70&7035=-1&7036=-1&7001=1200&
7002=1&7003=200&7004=SIC&7005=-
1&7006=00000 (accessed Dec. 12, 2012).
For historical mortgage debt data: Federal
Reserve Bulletin, Statistical Supplement to
the Federal Reserve Bulletin, Mortgage Debt
Outstanding, http://www.federalreserve.gov/
pubs/supplement/2004/01/table1_54.htm
(accessed Dec. 12, 2012).
For current release mortgage debt data: Board
of Governors of the Federal Reserve System,
Economic Research & Data, Statistics & Historical
Data, Outstanding Mortgage Debt, http://www.
federalreserve.gov/econresdata/releases/
mortoutstand/current.htm (accessed Dec. 12, 2012).

**P. 70 NON-PERFORMING HOME MORTGAGE
LOANS, 2002–10**
International Monetary Fund, *World Economic
Outlook: Growth Resuming, Dangers Remain*, Apr.
2012, Figure 3.1.1, http://www.imf.org/external/
pubs/ft/weo/2012/01/pdf/text.pdf.

P. 71 REAL HOUSE PRICES
Ibid., Figure 3.1.2.

**P. 71 HOUSEHOLD DEBT-TO-INCOME RATIO
OF SELECTED COUNTRIES, 2002–10**
Ibid., Figure 3.1.3.

**PP. 72–73 AMERICAN MODEL VS. CITY-STATE
MODEL**
Photograph p. 72: http://www.flickr.com/photos/
gamutsedge/2801611606/sizes/l/in/photostream;
all rights reserved Gamut's Edge.
Photograph p. 73: "Victoria's Peak," courtesy of
Benjamin Rothenbuehler.

**CHAPTER 2
CITIES, SUSTAINABILITY, AND RESILIENCE**

NOTES

1 Jeffrey D. Sachs, *The End of Poverty: Economic
Possibilities for Our Time* (New York: Penguin, 2005).
2 See, for instance, David Owen, *Green
Metropolis: Why Living Smaller, Living Closer, and
Driving Less Are the Keys to Sustainability* (New
York: Riverhead Hardcover, 2009).
3 Http://www.chicagoclimateaction.org
(accessed Sept. 25, 2012).
4 Timothy Beatley, *Green Urbanism: Learning
from European Cities* (Washington, D.C.: Island
Press, 1999).
5 See Elisabeth Rosenthal, "Air-Conditioning Is
an Environmental Quandary," *New York Times*,
Aug. 18, 2012, sec. Sunday Review, http://www.
nytimes.com/2012/08/19/sunday-review/air-
conditioning-is-an-environmental-quandary.html;
and Rosenthal and Andrew W. Lehren, "Incentive
to Slow Climate Change Drives Output of Harmful
Gases," *New York Times*, Aug. 8, 2012, sec. World/
Asia Pacific, http://www.nytimes.com/2012/08/09/
world/asia/incentive-to-slow-climate-change-
drives-output-of-harmful-gases.html.
6 William McDonough and Michael Braungart,
*Cradle to Cradle: Remaking the Way We Make
Things* (New York: North Point, 2002), 16.
7 The author readily admits to his love of fast
cars. He simply avoids driving to work, and puts
about 2,000 miles per year on a car.
8 U.S. Energy Information Administration,
"Weekly U.S. All Grades All Formulations Retail
Gasoline Prices (Dollars Per Gallon)," http://
www.eia.gov/dnav/pet/hist/LeafHandler.
ashx?n=PET&s=EMM_EPM0_PTE_NUS_DPG&f=W
(accessed Aug. 18, 2012).
9 United Nations, *Agenda 21: Earth Summit,
The United Nations Programme of Action from
Rio* (United Nations: 1993), http://www.amazon.
com/Agenda-21-Summit-Nations-Programme/
dp/9211005094.
10 Jim Acosta, "What's with Newt Gingrich and
Agenda 21?" *CNN Politics*, Nov. 18, 2011, http://
politicalticker.blogs.cnn.com/2011/11/18/whats-
with-newt-gingrich-and-agenda-21.
11 See United Nations, *Agenda 21*.
12 Al Gore, *An Inconvenient Truth: The Planetary
Emergency of Global Warming and What We Can
Do About It* (New York: Rodale, 2006), 11.
13 Http://climaterealityproject.org (accessed
Aug. 10, 2012).
14 Peyton M. Craighill and Juliet Eilperin,
"Temperatures Climbing, Weather More Unstable,
a Majority Says in Poll," *Washington Post*, July 13,
2012, sec. National, http://www.washingtonpost.
com/national/health-science/post-stanford-poll-
finds-more-americans-believe-climate-change-is-
happening/2012/07/12/gJQAh92wgW_story.html.
15 Bill McKibben, "Global Warming's Terrifying
New Math," *Rolling Stone*, July 19, 2012, http://
www.rollingstone.com/politics/news/global-
warmings-terrifying-new-math-20120719.
16 Vishaan Chakrabarti, "When Silence Is
Betrayal," *Architects Newspaper*, Feb. 14, 2007.

17 For information on the LoLo proposal by Leigh D'Ambra, Scott Hayner, Muchan Park, and Luc Wilson from Columbia University design studio co-taught by Vishaan Chakrabarti and Laurie Hawkinson, see Julie Satow, "Visions of LoLo, a Neighborhood Rising from Landfill," *New York Times*, Nov. 22, 2011, sec. Real Estate/Commercial, http://www.nytimes.com/2011/11/23/realestate/commercial/visions-of-lolo-a-neighborhood-rising-from-landfill.html.

ILLUSTRATIONS

P. 74 THIS IS NOT SUSTAINABILITY
Courtesy of RhythmicQuietud.

P. 76 GLOBAL CONSUMPTION VS. AMERICAN CONSUMPTION RATES
World Wildlife Fund, *Living Planet Report 2012: Biodiversity, Biocapacity and Better Choices*, 2012, http://awsassets.panda.org/downloads/1_lpr_2012_online_full_size single_pages_final_120516.pdf.

P. 76 WORLD POPULATION, 1750 PROJECTED TO 2100
United Nations Department of Economic and Social Affairs, Population Division, *Seven Billion and Growing: The Role of Population Policy in Achieving Sustainability*, Technical Paper No. 2011/3. Figure 1: The world population according to different projection variants, 1750–2100, http://www.un.org/esa/population/publications/technicalpapers/TP2011-3_SevenBillionandGrowing.pdf.

P. 80 POPULATION DENSITY AND ENERGY CONSUMPTION IN SELECTED METROPOLITAN AREAS
Peter Newman and Jeffrey Kenworthy, *Sustainability and Cities: Overcoming Automobile Dependence* (New York: Island Press, 1999). Figures converted from hectares to acres.

P. 80 POPULATION DENSITY AND CO₂ EMISSIONS IN SELECTED METROPOLITAN AREAS
For American averages: Peter Haas, Gajus Miknaitis, Harley Cooper, Linda Young, and Albert Benedict, *Transit Oriented Development and the Potential for VMT-related Greenhouse Gas Emissions Growth Reduction*, Center for Neighborhood Technology, Table 1: National Transit Zone Types, Mar. 2010, http://www.cnt.org/repository/TOD-Potential-GHG-Emissions-Growth.FINAL.pdf.

For other cities: European Commission Joint Research Center, *EEA Report 10/2006: Urban Sprawl in Europe—The Ignored Challenge*, Figure 10, European Environment Agency, Office for Official Publications of the European Communities, Nov. 24, 2006, http://www.eea.europa.eu/publications/eea_report_2006_10.

P. 82 AVERAGE CARBON EMISSIONS PER HOUSEHOLD BY SELECTED NEIGHBORHOOD TYPES
Ibid.

P. 84 AVERAGE DISTANCES TRAVELED BY CAR FOR SELECTED ACTIVITIES
U.S. Department of Energy, *2009 National Household Travel Survey*, May 21, 2012, http://www1.eere.energy.gov/vehiclesandfuels/facts/2012_fotw728.html.

P. 85 DRIVING COULD BE FUN AGAIN
AMC/Photofest.

P. 88 AVERAGE ANNUAL RETAIL PRICE OF GASOLINE, 1929–2011
U.S. Department of Energy, Energy Information Administration, *Annual Energy Review 2011*, 1/3, Section 5, Table 24: Petroleum and Other Liquids, Retail Motor Gasoline and On-Highway Diesel Fuel Prices, Selected Years, 1929–2011, http://www1.eere.energy.gov/vehiclesandfuels/facts/2012_fotw741.html. Retail price includes federal and state taxes. Price is for regular leaded gasoline until 1990 and for regular unleaded gasoline thereafter. Dollars calculated using the Gross Domestic Product Inflation Index.

P. 88 TOTAL VEHICLE MILES TRAVELED BY ALL AMERICANS YEARLY, 1987–2011
U.S. Department of Transportation, Federal Highway Administration, "Annual Vehicle Distance Traveled in Miles and Related Data—2010 1/By Highway Category and Vehicle Type," *Highway Statistics Series*, Feb. 2012, http://www.fhwa.dot.gov/policyinformation/statistics/2010/vm1.cfm.

P. 89 THE TEA PARTY AND AGENDA 21
1 Top: http://www.theblaze.com/wp-content/uploads/2012/01/Jan-Feb-Final-cover- 147x200.jpg. **2** Bottom: http://1.bp.blogspot.com/-23GzU061ThQ/TaXVQz1LsBI/AAAAAAAAAUk/SdZluojmzG4/s400/UN+TANKS+copy.jpg.

P. 90 AMERICAN COMMUTER-FLOW TRENDS, SUBURBAN VS. PRINCIPAL CITIES
Brian McKenzie and Melanie Rapino, *Commuting in the United States: 2009—American Community Survey Reports*, U.S. Department of Commerce, Economics and Statistics Administration,

Sept. 2011, Table 2: Place of Work by Means of Transportation for Metropolitan Statistical Area Level, http://www.census.gov/prod/2011pubs/acs-15.pdf.

P. 90 AMERICAN COMMUTER MASS-TRANSIT RIDERSHIP

American Public Transportation Association, *2012 Public Transportation Fact Book*, Mar. 2012, http://www.apta.com/resources/statistics/Documents/FactBook/2012-Fact-Book-Appendix-A.pdf.

P. 92 ANNUAL FEDERAL ENERGY SUBSIDIES

Mark Clayton, "Budget Hawks: Does US Need to Give Gas and Oil Companies $41 Billion a Year?" *The Christian Science Monitor*, Mar. 9, 2011, http://www.csmonitor.com/USA/Politics/2011/0309/Budget-hawks-Does-US-need-to-give-gas-and-oil-companies-41-billion-a-year.

P. 92 GLOBAL OIL PRODUCTION, 1930–2010

For 1930–54, using projected Hubbert curve: W. B. Carlson, "The Modeling of World Oil Production Using Sigmoidal Functions Update 2010," *Energy Sources, Part B: Economics, Planning, and Policy* 6, no. 2, 2011.

For 1954–2011: U.S. Department of Energy, *Annual Energy Review 2011*, Table 2: Crude Oil Production and Crude Oil Well Productivity, 1954–2011; and "BP Statistical Review of World Energy," *Production and Consumption*, June 2012, http://www.bp.com/liveassets/bp_internet/globalbp/globalbp_uk_english/reports_and_publications/statistical_energy_review_2011/STAGING/local_assets/pdf/statistical_review_of_world_energy_full_report_2012.pdf.

P. 94 GLOBAL WARMING AND SEA LEVEL RISE

Bill McKibben, "Global Warming's Terrifying New Math," *Rolling Stone*, July 19, 2012, http://www.rollingstone.com/politics/news/global-warmings-terrifying-new-math-20120719.

PP. 98–99 ENERGY CONSUMPTION AVERAGES BY HOUSEHOLD TYPE

EnergyStar Household Energy Calculator, https://www.energystar.gov/index.cfm?fuseaction=home_energy_yardstick.showgetstarted.

Data for physical attributes of household types: D&R International, Ltd., under contract to Pacific Northwest National Laboratory, *2011 Buildings Energy Data Book*, prepared for the U.S. Department of Energy, Buildings Technologies Program, Energy Efficiency and Renewable Energy, U.S. Department of Energy, Mar. 2012, http://buildingsdatabook.eren.doe.gov/docs/DataBooks/2011_BEDB.pdf.

PP. 100–101 HYPERDENSITY LEAVES NATURE NATURAL

Ibid.

CHAPTER 3
CITIES, HEALTH, AND JOY

NOTES

1 Geoffrey Perret, "The 1956 Federal Highway Act," in *Triumphs and Tragedies of the Modern Presidency: Seventy-Six Case Studies in Presidential Leadership*, ed. David Abshire (Westport: Praeger, 2001).

2 Moses famously built his parkways with low bridge clearances to keep inner-city buses, and the minorities they carried, out of the suburbs. See Robert A. Caro, *The Power Broker: Robert Moses and the Fall of New York* (New York: Vintage, 1975).

3 Reid Ewing and Barbara A. McCann, *Measuring the Health Effects of Sprawl: A National Analysis of Physical Activity, Obesity and Chronic Disease*, Smart Growth America, Surface Transportation Policy Project, Sept. 2003, http://www.smartgrowthamerica.org/report/HealthSprawl8.03.pdf.

4 See, for instance, Christine M. Hoehner, "Commuting Distance, Cardiorespiratory Fitness, and Metabolic Risk," *American Journal of Preventive Medicine* 42, no. 6 (June 2012); and Matt McMillen, "Long Commute? Your Heart and Waistline May Suffer for It," *Time*, May 8, 2012, http://healthland.time.com/2012/05/08/long-commute-your-heart-and-waistline-may-suffer-for-it.

5 The American Lung Association, *State of the Air 2012*, http://www.stateoftheair.org/2012/key-findings/2008-2010/ozone-pollution.html (accessed Sept. 25, 2012).

6 Amy Biolchini, "Death Among Children: Traffic Fatalities Leading Cause Worldwide," *AnnArbor.com*, May 14, 2012, http://annarbor.com/news/death-among-children-traffic-fatalities-leading-cause-worldwide.

7 See Erika Sandow, *On the Road: Social Aspects of Commuting Long Distances to Work* (Umeå: Kulturgeografiska Institutionen, 2011), http://umu.diva-portal.org/smash/record.jsf?pid=diva2:415050; and Nicole C. Brambila, "Together Apart: Commuter Marriages on the Rise," *USATODAY.COM*, Feb. 20, 2012, http://yourlife.usatoday.com/sex-relationships/story/2012-02-20/Together-apart-Commuter-marriages-on-the-rise/53170648/1.

8 *Driver Distraction in Commercial Vehicle Operations: Final Report,* U.S. Department of Transportation, Federal Motor Carrier Safety Administration, Sept. 2009, http://www.distraction.gov/research/PDF-Files/Driver-Distraction-Commercial-Vehicle-Operations.pdf.

9 Conor Dougherty and Robbie Whelan, "Cities Outpace Suburbs in Growth," *Wall Street Journal,* June 28, 2012, sec. Economy, http://online.wsj.com/article/SB10001424052702304830704577493032619987956.html; and Alan Ehrenhalt, *The Great Inversion and the Future of the American City* (New York: Knopf, 2012).

10 Ibid. This particular trio of shows, which the author mentions in his lectures, is also cited in Ehrenhalt, *The Great Inversion*.

11 Adecco Group North America, *Adecco Graduation Survey 2012,* http://www.adeccousa.com/articles/Adecco-Graduation-Survey-2012.html?id=200&url=/pressroom/pressreleases/Pages/Forms/AllItems.aspx&templateurl=/adeccogroup/News/press-releases/Pages/press-release.aspx.

12 See Helen Bartlett and Nancy Peel, "Healthy Ageing in the Community," in *Ageing and Place,* Gavin J. Andrews and David R. Phillips, eds. (New York: Routledge, 2004).

13 See Chris Phillipson, "Urbanization and Ageing: Towards a New Environmental Gerontology," *Ageing and Society* 24, issue 6, Nov. 18, 2004, 963–72, http://dx.doi.org/10.1017/S0144686X04002405; and Constance Rosenblum, "Elderly-Friendly Manhattan," *New York Times,* Aug. 12, 2011, sec. Real Estate, http://www.nytimes.com/2011/08/14/realestate/elderly-friendly-manhattan.html.

14 Edward L. Glaeser, *Triumph of the City: How Our Greatest Invention Makes Us Richer, Smarter, Greener, Healthier, and Happier* (New York: Penguin, 2011), 7–8.

15 Jennifer Medina, "Los Angeles Envisions Grand Park as Draw for Downtown," *New York Times,* Aug. 18, 2012, sec. U.S., http://www.nytimes.com/2012/08/19/us/los-angeles-envisions-grand-park-as-draw-for-downtown.html; Ron Magers, "Bloomingdale Trail to Be World's Longest Elevated Park," Aug. 19, 2012, http://abclocal.go.com/wls/story?section=resources&id=8778834; and Tim Rogers, "Klyde Warren Park Announces Programming," July 30, 2012, http://frontburner.dmagazine.com/2012/07/30/klyde-warren-park-announces-programming.

ILLUSTRATIONS

P. 104 NATIONAL HIGHWAY SYSTEM
U.S. Department of Transportation, Federal Highway Administration, *The National Highway Planning Network* (NHPN), Sept. 20, 2012, http://www.fhwa.dot.gov/planning/processes/tools/nhpn.

P. 104 PRESIDENT EISENHOWER
Http://www.eisenhower.archives.gov/research/audiovisual/images/interstate_highway_system/80_28_4.jpg.

P. 106 COMMUTING DISTANCE AFFECTS LEVELS OF PHYSICAL ACTIVITY
Christine M. Hoehner, "Commuting Distance, Cardiorespiratory Fitness, and Metabolic Risk," *American Journal of Preventive Medicine* 42, no. 6, June 2012.

P. 106 COMMUTING DISTANCE AFFECTS PREVALANCE OF OBESITY
Ibid.

P. 108 ROMANCE AND COMMUTING TIME
Erika Sandow, *On the Road: Social Aspects of Commuting Long Distances to Work* (Umeå: Kulturgeografiska Institutionen, 2011), http://umu.divaportal.org/smash/record.jsf?pid=diva2:415050.

P. 109 A NEW BREED OF URBAN SITCOM
1, 2 NBC/Photofest.
3 HBO/Photofest.

P. 110 CITIES APPEAL TO YOUNG PROFESSIONALS
Adecco Group North America, *Adecco Graduation Survey 2012,* http://www.adeccousa.com/articles/Adecco-Graduation-Survey-2012.html?id=200&url=/pressroom/pressreleases/Pages/Forms/AllItems.aspx&templateurl=/adeccogroup/News/press-releases/Pages/press-release.aspx.

P. 114 CRIME IN AMERICA: CITIES VS. SUBURBS
U.S. Department of Justice, *National Homicide Reports,* Federal Bureau of Investigation, Uniform Crime Reporting Statistics, Table 6: Crime in the United States by Metropolitan Statistical Area, 2010, http://www.fbi.gov/about-us/cjis/ucr/crime-in-the.u.s/2010/crime-in-the-u.s.-2010/tables/table-6.

P. 114 NATIONAL HOMICIDE RATES PER 100,000 RESIDENTS
Data for 1960–2010: U.S. Department of Justice, *National Homicide Reports,* Federal Bureau of Investigation, Uniform Crime Reporting Statistics, Table 16: Crime in the United States

by Metropolitan Statistical Area, 2011, http://
www.ucrdatatool.gov/Search/Crime/State/
RunCrimeTrendsInOneVar.cfm (parameters
used: a. United States total, b. murder,
c. 1976–2010).
Data for 1900–1960: Homicides per 100,000
Population per Year, Theodore Caplow,
Louis Hicks, and Ben J. Wattenberg, *The First
Measured Century: An Illustrated Guide to Trends
in America, 1900–2000* (Washington, D.C.:
Aei, 2000).

P. 115 NEW URBAN PARKS

1 Courtesy of DDima.
2 Courtesy of Steve Hall and HedrichBlessing.
3 Courtesy of Aerial Photography, Inc., Dallas.

P. 116 EAST RIVER WATERFRONT, LOWER MANHATTAN

1 © Peter Mauss/Esto.
2 Courtesy of Dana Lynn Getman.
3 Rendering by SHoP.

P. 118 KNOWLEDGE AND CULTURE

1 Courtesy of Pragnesh Parikh Photography,
OMA/LMN Architects.
2 Courtesy of Nigel Young/Foster + Partners.
3 Courtesy of Morphosis and Mark Knight
Photography.

PP. 120–21 THE ADVANTAGES OF MASS TRANSIT AND WALKABILITY

Joseph Cortright, *Walking the Walk:
How Walkability Raises Housing Values in
U.S. Cities*, CEOs for Cities, Aug. 2009,
www.ceosforcities.org/files/WalkingTheWalk_
CEOsforCities1.pdf; Anastasia Loukaitou-Sideris
and Renia Ehrefeucht, *Vibrant Sidewalks in
the United States: Re-integrating Walking
and a Quintessential Social Realm*, 2010,
22–29, http://www.uctc.net/access/36/access-
36vibrantsidewalks.pdf; and Todd Litman,
"If Health Matters: Integrating Public Health
Objectives into Transportation Decision-Making,"
Victoria Transport Policy Institute, Dec. 6, 2012,
http://www.vtpi.org/health.pdf.

P. 120 ONE-WAY COMMUTE TIMES TO WORK

U.S. Department of Transportation, Research
and Innovative Technology Administration,
Transportation Statistics Annual Report 2010,
Table 4–20: Travel Time to Work, 2009, http://
www.bts.gov/publications/transportation_
statistics_annual_report/2010/html/chapter_02/
table_04_20.html.

P. 121 COST OF BOREDOM AND DISTRACTION WHILE DRIVING

U.S. Department of Transportation, National
Highway Traffic Safety Administration, *Traffic
Safety Facts Research Note*, Sept. 2010, http://
www.distraction.gov/download/research-pdf/
Distracted-Driving-2009.pdf; and Santokh
Singh, *Distracted Driving and Driver, Roadway,
and Environmental Factors*, U.S. Department of
Transportation, National Highway Traffic Safety
Administration, Sept. 2010, Table 1, http://
www.distraction.gov/download/research-pdf/
Distracted-Driving-and-Driver-Roadway-
Environmental-Factors.pdf.

CHAPTER 4
BUILDING HYPERDENSITY AND CIVIC DELIGHT

NOTES

1 Density that supports mass transit is
understood to be greater than or equal to
30 housing units per acre, as described
in the introduction.
2 Institute for Urban Strategies, *Global
Power Inner-City Index 2010* (Tokyo: Mori
Memorial Foundation, 2010). The density of
Paris is calculated using data from the *Global
Power-Inner City Index*, which indicates that
its population is 21,000 people per square
kilometer. The data has been converted to
people per acre; this has a closer relation to
dwelling units per acre, which governs many of
the diagrams in this book. There is no broadly
accepted measure of density, and published
estimates vary as much as methodologies
have varied over time. For examples of density
measures used throughout history, see Meta
Berghauser Pont and Per Haupt, *Spacematrix:
Space, Density and Urban Form* (Rotterdam: NAi
Publishers, 2010).
3 Institute for Urban Strategies, *Global Power
City Index Yearbook 2011* (Tokyo: Mori Memorial
Foundation, 2011).
4 Edward Keenan, "Is CityPlace Toronto's Next
Ghetto?" *The Grid*, sec. Real Estate, Nov. 10,
2011, http://www.thegridto.com/life/real-estate/
is-cityplace-torontos-next-ghetto.
5 Jacob A. Riis, *How the Other Half Lives:
Studies Among the Tenements of New York* (New
York: Penguin Classics, 1997).

6 In 1991, during a visit to Europe, the author interviewed "tower-in-the-park" residents who reported having no interest in living in the medieval city, though it is both beautiful and dense with the traditional mixed-uses of an urban core.

7 London continues to plan and build skyscrapers as do Frankfurt, Warsaw, Moscow, and Istanbul, all of which have urban-led economies. See, for instance, The Investor, "New London Skyscrapers," *Monevator*, Dec. 8, 2011, http://monevator.com/new-london-skyscrapers-a-big-bet-on-the-city-of-londons-future.

8 See Atlanta's Regional Transportation Referendum: "TIA Tsplost—One Percent Sales Tax Referendum to Fund Transportation Projects in the Atlanta Region," http://www.metroatlantatransportationvote.com/. For Cincinnati's efforts to increase mass-transit capacity and ridership, see Steven Vance, "Railvolution!" *Architect's Newspaper,* June 1, 2012, http://archpaper.com/news/articles.asp?id=6084.

9 According to the U.S. Green Building Council, "The LEED for Neighborhood Development Rating System integrates the principles of smart growth, urbanism and green building into the first national system for neighborhood design." For a full description of LEED neighborhood standards, see http://www.usgbc.org/DisplayPage.aspx?CMSPageID=148.

10 Laura Kusisto and Eliot Brown, "Midtown's New Look Unveiled," *Wall Street Journal,* July 11, 2012, sec. NY Real Estate Residential, http://online.wsj.com/article/SB10001424052702303919504577521411010664218.html.

11 Adam Nagourney, "Far-Reaching Rezoning Plan for Hollywood Gains Key Support," *New York Times*, Mar. 28, 2012, sec. U.S., http://www.nytimes.com/2012/03/29/us/far-reaching-rezoning-plan-for-hollywood-gains-key-support.html.

12 Alan Zarembo, Ari Bloomekatz, and Nicole Santa Cruz, "L.A. Downshifts and Takes It Easy," *Los Angeles Times,* July 17, 2011, http://articles.latimes.com/2011/jul/17/local/la-me-405-closure-20110717.

13 Catherine Saint Louis, "Running a Home Business in New York," *New York Times*, Aug. 24, 2012, sec. Real Estate, http://www.nytimes.com/2012/08/26/realestate/running-a-home-business-in-new-york.html.

ILLUSTRATIONS

P. 126 STEREOTYPES OF HYPERDENSITY
1 Courtesy of Baycrest.
2 Courtesy of Eduardo Londres Pinha.

P. 128 TOOLS OF URBAN PLANNING
For the legal origins of zoning, see U.S. Supreme Court case *Village of Euclid, Ohio v. Ambler Realty Co.*, 272 U.S. 365 (1926). The first significant case regarding the relatively new practice of zoning, it served to substantially bolster zoning ordinances in towns across the United States and in other countries, including Canada. For examples regarding bulk (building form) controls, see the 1916 and 1961 New York City zoning resolutions and the work of Hugh Ferris.

P. 129 UPWARD TO HOME!
Originally published in *The Literary Digest*, Mar. 12, 1932, 37.

P. 130 DENSITY BELOVED AND BEMOANED
3-D models based on publicly accessible GIS data and ESRI aerial imagery. Aerial images sourced from Google Maps.

P. 132 SKYSCRAPERS AND GDP IN EUROPE
GDP source: PricewaterhouseCoopers LLP, *Global City GDP Rankings, 2008–2025 Report*, Table 3.3, http://www.ukmediacentre.pwc.com/imagelibrary/downloadMedia.ashx?MediaDetailsID=1562.
Population source: Wendell Cox Consultancy, *Demographia World Urban Areas (World Agglomerations)*, 8th Annual Edition, Version 2, July 2012, Table 1: Largest Urban Areas in the World, http://www.demographia.com/db-worldua.pdf.

P. 133 HYPERDENSE LONDON
Courtesy of Paul Howes.

P. 134 LOSS OF DENSITY ACROSS METROPOLITAN REGIONS IN AMERICA, 1910–2000
Data source: Shlomo Angel, Jason Parent, Daniel L. Civco, and Alejandro M. Blei, "The Persistent Decline in Urban Densities: Global and Historical Evidence of 'Sprawl'" (working paper, Lincoln Institute of Land Policy, 2010), Figure 8.3: The Decline of the Share of the Population Living in Areas With Transit-Sustaining Densities, https://www.lincolninst.edu/pubs/dl/1834_1085_Angel%20Final%201.pdf (data converted from hectares to acres).

P. 136 DENSIFIED SUBURBIA: THE WORST OF BOTH WORLDS

Donald C. Shoup, "The Trouble with Minimum Parking Requirements," *Transportation Research Part A: Policy and Practice* 33 (Sept. 1999), 549–74.

P. 136 BETHESDA, MARYLAND

Diagram data: See Bethesda CBD Master Plan, Montgomery County Department of Planning, July 1994, http://www.montgomeryplanning.org/community/plan_areas/bethesda_chevy_chase/master_plans/bethesda_cc/ch1_bethcbd.pdf.

P. 138 WHAT DENSITIES ARE CURRENTLY PERMITTED?

Rolf Pendall, Robert Puentes, and Jonathan Martin, "From Traditional to Reformed: A Review of the Land Use Regulations in the Nation's 50 Largest Metropolitan Areas," The Brookings Institution, Metropolitan Policy Program, Aug. 2, 2006, http://www.brookings.edu/~/media/research/files/reports/2006/8/metropolitanpolicy%20pendall/20060802_pendall.pdf; and William A. Fishcel, "An Economic History of Zoning and a Cure for Its Exclusionary Effects," *Urban Studies* 41, no. 2 (Feb. 2004), 317–40.

P. 138 DENSIFICATION AROUND RAIL-BASED TRANSIT

William A. Fischel, "Do Growth Controls Matter? A Review of Empirical Evidence on the Effectiveness and Efficiency of Local Government Land Use Regulation" (working paper, Lincoln Institute of Land Policy, Jan. 1990).

P. 139 FORMS OF HYPERDENSITY

1 Courtesy of KPF, © Tim Hursley.

2 Photograph by John Horner.

3 Courtesy of Stanley Saitowitz/Natoma Architects.

P. 142 HYPERDENSIFICATION OF DALLAS, TEXAS

Model data source: 3-D LIDAR models and conceptual massing models.

P. 144 THE EMERGING NETWORKED BUSINESS DISTRICT

Jeffrey R. Brown and Gregory L. Thompson, "Should Transit Serve the CBD or a Diverse Array of Destinations? A Case Study Comparison of Two Transit Systems," *Journal of Public Transportation* 15, no. 1 (Apr. 2012); and Masahisa Fujita and Jacques-François Thisse, *Economies of Agglomeration: Cities, Industrial Location, and Regional Growth* (Cambridge: Cambridge University Press, 2002).

P. 145 PLANNING FOR HYPERDENSITY

Photograph by the author.

P. 146 DOCTOROFF'S VIRTUOUS CYCLE OF ECONOMIC DEVELOPMENT

Concept credited to Dan Doctoroff, New York City deputy mayor for economic development under Mayor Michael Bloomberg.

PP. 152–53 BUILDING THE "HIGH-LOW" CITY

Page 152: top, photograph © Bruce Damonte; bottom, SHoP.

Page 153: top and middle, photographs © Bruce Damonte; bottom, Omar Toro-Vaca.

**CHAPTER 5
BUILDING AN INFRASTRUCTURE
OF OPPORTUNITY**

NOTES

1 Rudolph Bush, "Victory Pays? City Hall Looks to Kick-Start West Dallas Development and Ease AAC Parking Woes with Victory Park Funds," *City Hall Blog*, Mar. 10, 2012, http://cityhallblog.dallasnews.com/2012/03/victory-pays-city-hall-looks-t.html.

2 John Kilkevitch, "After 15-Year Dry Spell, CTA Opens New Station in Chicago at Morgan and Lake," *Chicago Tribune*, May 25, 2012, http://articles.chicagotribune.com/2012-05-25/news/ct-met-cta-morgan-station-0525-20120525_1_l-station-yellow-line-morgan-and-lake.

3 For funding gaps in Amtrak's Union Station plans, see Jonathan O'Connell and Ashley Halsey III, "Amtrak to Propose $7 billion Overhaul at Union Station," *Washington Post*, sec. Local, July 24, 2012, http://www.washingtonpost.com/local/amtrak-to-propose-7-billion-overhaul-at-union-station/2012/07/24/gJQApGwi7W_story.html. For value capture and funding schemes related to San Francisco's Transbay Transit Center, see Chrissy Mancini Nichols, "Value Capture Case Studies: San Francisco's Transbay Transit Center," *Metropolitan Planning Council*, Jan. 27, 2012, http://www.metroplanning.org/news-events/article/6315.

4 Jim Richardson, "Atlanta Has Opportunity to Stand Out," *Atlanta Journal Constitution*, sec. Opinion, Apr. 17, 2012, http://www.ajc.com/opinion/atlanta-has-opportunity-to-1419702.html.

5 Jessica Perez, Gabe Horwitz, and David Kendall, "Collision Course: Why Democrats Must Back Entitlement Reform," *Third Way*, July 2012, http://content.thirdway.org/publications/564/

Third_Way_Report_-_Collision_Course_Why_
Democrats_Must_Back_Entitlement_Reform.pdf.

6 Ron Nixon, "Air Travel's Hassles Drive Riders
to Amtrak's Acela," *New York Times*, Aug. 16,
2012, sec. Business Day, http://www.nytimes.
com/2012/08/16/business/hassles-of-air-travel-
push-passengers-to-amtrak.html.

7 If Luisa's trolley was virtually empty due to
poor planning and insufficient surrounding
densities, critics are right to bemoan such
investments. While all transit systems experience fluctuations in use, a well-planned system
coupled with hyperdensity should incur little
incremental cost with an additional user.

8 American Petroleum Institute, "Motor Fuel
Taxes," http://www.api.org/Oil-and-Natural-Gas-
Overview/Industry-Economics/Fuel-Taxes.aspx
(accessed Dec. 12, 2012).

9 Richard C. Porter, *Economics at the Wheel:
The Costs of Cars and Drivers* (San Diego:
Academic, 1999).

10 Joseph White, "American Idle: On the Road,"
Wall Street Journal, Feb. 2, 2011, sec. Eyes on
the Road, http://online.wsj.com/article/SB1000
14240527487034459045761180822999960882.
html?KEYWORDS=joseph+white.

11 Texas Transportation Institute, "2011 Annual
Urban Mobility Report," http://mobility.tamu.edu/
ums (accessed Dec. 12, 2012).

12 PolitiFact, "'Red State Socialism' Graphic
Says GOP-Leaning States Get Lion's Share of
Federal Dollars," *Tampa Bay Times*, Jan. 26,
2012, http://www.politifact.com/truth-o-meter/
statements/2012/jan/26/blog-posting/red-state-
socialism-graphic-says-gop-leaning-state.

13 Petra Todorovich and Yoav Hagler, "High
Speed Rail in America—America 2050," Lincoln
Institute of Land Policy and The Rockefeller
Foundation, Jan. 2011, http://www.america2050.
org/pdf/HSR-in-America-Complete.pdf.

14 See, for instance, Phillip Inman, "Spain Must
Halt Rail Expansion, Says Expert," *Guardian*, May
3, 2012, sec. Economics, http://www.guardian.
co.uk/world/2012/may/03/spain-halt-rail-
expansion.

ILLUSTRATIONS

P. 154 DENSITY FOR DENSITY'S SAKE
Cécile Hartmann, "Worker," 2008, color
photograph from the *Dubai* series, courtesy of
the artist, all rights reserved.

P. 158 PUBLIC/PRIVATE PARTNERSHIPS
Tiffany Dovey, William D. Eggers, Michael
Flynn, Irene Walsh, and Jim Ziglar, "Partnering
for Value: Structuring Effective Public-Private
Partnerships for Infrastructure," Deloitte, 2010,
http://www.deloitte.com/assets/Dcom-Global/
Local%20Assets/Documents/Public%20Sector/
dtt_ps_partneringforvalue_090710.pdf; and K.
Kaufmann, "Public/Private Partnerships: Wide
Ranging Views and Successful Approaches,"
Urban Land, Oct. 31, 2011, http://urbanland.uli.
org/Articles/2011/Fall11/KaufmanPartnership.

P. 158 TAX-INCREMENT FINANCING (TIF)
Richard F. Dye and David F. Therriman, "The
Effects of Tax Increment Financing on Economic
Development," *Journal or Urban Economics*
47, issue 21, Mar. 2000, 306–28; and Joyce Y.
Man and Mark S. Rosentraub, "Tax Increment
Financing: Municipal Adoption and Effects on
Property Value Growth," *Public Finance Review*
26, issue 6, Nov. 1998, 523–47.

P. 159 COMPACTNESS IS EFFICIENT
Photograph by the author.

**P. 160 AVERAGE GLOBAL RANGE OF
TRANSPORTATION CONSTRUCTION
COSTS PER MILE**
United Nations Environment Programme,
"Cities: Investing in Energy and Resource
Efficiency," 2011, Table 2, http://www.unep.
org/greeneconomy/Portals/88/documents/
ger/GER_12_Cities.pdf; and Erick Guerra and
Robert Cervero, "Mass Transit and Mass:
Densities Needed to Make Transit Investments
Pay Off," UCTC Policy Brief 2011–12, University
of California, Berkeley, http://www.uctc.net/
research/briefs/UCTC PB 2011-02.pdf.

P. 161 LEGACY OF U.S. INFRASTRUCTURE
1 Courtesy of Frank E. Sadowski, Jr., webmaster,
http://www.eriecanal.org.

2 Http://explorepahistory.com/kora/files/1/2/1-2-
67F-25-ExplorePAHistory-a0c0n2-a_349.JPG.

3 Http://tva.com/75th/timeline.htm.

P. 162 THE TRUE COST OF SAM'S ERRAND
Calculated with methodology recommended
in "Transportation Cost and Benefit Analysis:
Techniques, Estimates and Implications,"
Victoria Transport Policy Institute, 2002,
www.vtpi.org/tca. Ian W. H. Parry, Margaret
Walls, and Winston Harrington, "Automobile
Externalities and Policies" (working paper,
Resources for the Future) Jan. 1. 2007, http://
papers.ssrn.com/sol3/papers.cfm?abstract_
id=927794##.

P. 164 THE TRUE COST OF LUISA'S ERRAND
Calculated with methodology recommended in "Transportation Cost and Benefit Analysis: Techniques, Estimates and Implications." Parry, Walls, and Harrington, "Automobile Externalities and Policies."

P. 166 RED-STATE SOCIALISM AND ITS IMPACT ON INFRASTRUCTURE, 2004
Based on chart produced by Jesse Erlbaum, http://www.flickr.com/photos/michaelpinto/2987025203; and Tax Foundation, "Federal Spending Received per Dollar of Taxes Paid by State, 2005," Oct. 9, 2007, http://taxfoundation.org/article/federal-spending-received-dollar-taxes-paid-state-2005.

P. 168 ANNUAL FEDERAL INFRASTRUCTURE BUDGET
U.S. Department of Transportation, Budget Report, Fiscal Year 2013 Estimates, http://www.dot.gov/mission/budget/fy2013-budget-estimates (data for Federal Aviation Administration, Federal Highway Administration, Federal Railroad Administration, and Federal Transit Authority; all figures reflect actual fiscal year 2011).

P. 170 HIGH-SPEED RAIL ACROSS THE GLOBE
Building America's Future, "Building America's Future: Falling Apart and Falling Behind," 2011, http://www.bafuture.com/sites/default/files/Report_0.pdf.

P. 171 ADVOCATING FOR INFRASTRUCTURE
1 Photograph © Ann Johansson.
2 United States Government Work, Pete Souza, White House, State of the Union Address, 2010.

P. 174 HIGH-SPEED RAIL FOR AMERICA
Petra Todorovich and Yoav Hagler, "High Speed Rail in America—America 2050," Lincoln Institute of Land Policy and The Rockefeller Foundation, Jan. 2011, http://www.america2050.org/pdf/HSR-in-America-Complete.pdf. America 2050's High-Speed Rail Phasing Map illustrates results from the described research, as well as taking into account the current state of rail planning across the country. It prioritizes the connection of major metropolitan centers within 500 miles with high levels of economic activity and integration.

P. 176 HIGH-SPEED RAIL FUNDING: CHINA VS. AMERICA
Petra Todorovich, Daniel Schned, and Robert Lane, "High-Speed Rail, International Lessons for U.S. Policy Makers," Lincoln Institute of Land Policy, Sept. 2011, https://www.lincolninst.edu/pubs/dl/1948_1268_High-Speed%20Rail%20PFR_Webster.pdf. Keith Bradsher, "China Sees Growth Engine in a Web of Fast Trains," *New York Times*, Feb. 13, 2012, sec. Global Business, http://www.nytimes.com/2010/02/13/business/global/13rail.html?_r=2&pagewanted=1.

P. 176 HIGH-SPEED RAIL CAN WORK IN LARGE COUNTRIES
Reg Harman, "High Speed Trains and the Development and Regeneration of Cities," *Greengauge 21*, June 2006, http://www.greengauge21.net/wp-content/uploads/hsr-regneration-of-cities.pdf; and B. S. Pushkarev and Jeffrey Zupan, *Urban Rail in America: An Exploration of Criteria for Fixed-Guideway Transit* (Bloomington: Indiana University Press, 1982).

P. 176 TRAVEL TIMES: CAR VS. AIR VS. HIGH-SPEED RAIL
Physical distances of routes calculated in ESRI ArcGIS 10.1. For high-speed-rail travel times, see Todorovich and Hagler, "High Speed Rail in America."

PP. 180–81 PUBLIC INVESTMENT IN INFRASTRUCTURE AS A PERCENT OF GROSS DOMESTIC PRODUCT
Congressional Budget Office, "Public Spending on Transportation and Water Infrastructure," Nov. 2010, http://www.cbo.gov/sites/default/files/cbofiles/ftpdocs/119xx/doc11940/11-17-infrastructure.pdf.

PP. 182–83 PER CAPITA COST OF INFRASTRUCTURE DECREASES AS DENSITY INCREASES
Jonathan Ford, "A Comparative Analysis of Infrastructure Costs in Smart Growth and Conventional Suburban Communities," Environmental Protection Agency, Jan. 13, 2010, http://www.morrisbeacon.com/media/portfolio-projects/research/MBD-EPA-infrastructure.pdf?v=2012-08-17; Eric Eidlin, "The Worst of All Worlds: Los Angeles, California, and the Emerging Reality of Dense Sprawl," *Journal of the Transportation Research Board* 1902, 2005, http://trb.metapress.com/content/el5w1471m0124134/?genre=article&id=doi%3a10.3141%2f1902-01; Todd Litman, "Understanding Smart Growth Savings," Victoria Transport Policy Institute, Dec. 10, 2012, http://www.vtpi.org/sg_save.pdf; and Steven E. Polzin, "Relationship Between Land Use, Urban Form, and Vehicle Miles of Travel: The State of Knowledge and Implications for Transportation Planning," U.S. Department of Transportation, Florida

Department of Transportation, University of South Florida, Center for Urban Transportation Research, Mar. 2004, http://www.cutr.usf.edu/pubs/Trans-LU%20White%20Paper%20Final.pdf.

PP. 184–85 UPZONING CATALYZES DEVELOPMENT, INCREASING LAND VALUES AND CITY REVENUE

Richard W. Bartke and John S. Lamb, "Upzoning, Public Policy, and Fairness—A Study and Proposal," *17 William & Mary Law Review* 701, 1976, http://scholarship.law.wm.edu/wmlr/vol17/iss4/4; and Laura Wolf-Powers, "Up-Zoning New York City's Mixed Use Neighborhoods: Property-Led Economic Development and the Anatomy of a Planning Dilemma," *University of Pennsylvania, Journal of Planning, Education and Research* 24, no. 4, June 2005, 379–93, http://repository.upenn.edu/cplan_papers/45.

CHAPTER 6
BUILDING THE EQUITABLE CITY

NOTES

1 Reinhold Martin, Raphael Sperry, Amit C. Price Patel, Liz Ogbu, and Tom Angotti, "A Roundtable Debate on 'Foreclosed: Rehousing the American Dream,'" *Places: Design Observer,* June 25, 2012, http://places.designobserver.com/feature/foreclosed-exhibition-roundtable/34578.
2 Richard Plunz, *A History of Housing in New York City* (New York: Columbia University Press, 1990).
3 See, for instance, Carolyn Y. Johnson, "Massive Housing Experiment Finds Those Who Moved to Less-Impoverished Neighborhoods Were Happier," *Boston Globe*, Sept. 20, 2012, http://www.bostonglobe.com/lifestyle/health-wellness/2012/09/20/massive-housing-experiment-finds-those-who-moved-less-impoverished-neighborhoods-were-happier/VJrJ04voNcQ895eA1v9C6I/story.html.
4 Lance Freeman, *There Goes the 'Hood: Views of Gentrification from the Ground Up* (Philadelphia: Temple University Press, 2006), 163.
5 Sam Roberts, "Income Data Shows Widening Gap Between New York City's Richest and Poorest," *New York Times*, Sept. 20, 2012, sec. N.Y./Region, http://www.nytimes.com/2012/09/20/nyregion/rich-got-richer-and-poor-poorer-in-nyc-2011-data-shows.html.
6 Edward L. Glaeser, *Triumph of the City: How Our Greatest Invention Makes Us Richer, Smarter,* *Greener, Healthier, and Happier* (New York: Penguin, 2011).

7 U.S. Department of Housing and Urban Development, "Affordable Housing," http://www.hud.gov/offices/cpd/affordablehousing (accessed July 30, 2012).
8 On increased levels of poverty in America, see Associated Press, "US Poverty on Track to Reach 46-Year High; Suburbs, Underemployed Workers, Children Hit Hard," *Washington Post*, July 23, 2012 sec. Business, http://www.washingtonpost.com/business/us-poverty-on-track-to-reach-46-year-high-suburbs-underemployed-workers-children-hit-hard/2012/07/22/gJQA3XaUIW_story.html. On suburban poverty, see Lisa McGirr, "The New Suburban Poverty," *Campaign Stops*, Mar. 19, 2012, http://campaignstops.blogs.nytimes.com/2012/03/19/the-new-suburban-poverty. Also see Brookings Institution report that states: "The population in extreme-poverty neighborhoods rose more than twice as fast in suburbs as in cities from 2000 to 2005. The same is true of poor residents in extreme-poverty tracts, who increased by 41 percent in suburbs, compared to 17 percent in cities." Alan Berube, Elizabeth Kneebone, and Carey Nadeau, "The Re-Emergence of Concentrated Poverty: Metropolitan Trends in the 2000s," The Brookings Institution, Nov. 3, 2011, http://www.brookings.edu/research/papers/2011/11/03-poverty-kneebone-nadeau-berube.
9 It is interesting to note that module construction is a difficult industry to outsource because of the massive shipping costs associated with bringing large, empty modules across vast expanses. Consequently, the modules for Atlantic Yards will be built nearby, in Brooklyn, bolstering what is a dwindling manufacturing base for New York City.
10 Richard Florida, *The Great Reset: How New Ways of Living and Working Drive Post-Crash Prosperity* (New York: Harper, 2010).
11 For U.S. housing costs, see U.S. Census Bureau, http://www.census.gov/const/uspriceann.pdf (accessed Sept. 26, 2012).
12 For existing proposals on eliminating the MID, see Congressional Budget Office, "Reducing the Deficit: Spending and Revenue Options," Mar. 2011, http://www.cbo.gov/sites/default/files/cbofiles/ftpdocs/120xx/doc12085/03-10-reducingthedeficit.pdf.
13 Ibid.

ILLUSTRATIONS

P. 186 SUCCESSFUL PUBLIC HOUSING
Courtesy of Corine Vermeulen.

P. 188 COST OF HOUSING IN SELECTED GLOBAL CITIES
Institute for Urban Strategies, *Global Power City Index Yearbook 2011* (Tokyo: Mori Memorial Foundation, 2011).

P. 188 DEFINING AFFORDABILITY
See U.S. Department of Housing and Urban Development, Community Planning and Development Office definition of affordability: http://portal.hud.gov/hudportal/HUD?src=/program_offices/comm_planning/affordablehousing (accessed Oct. 26, 2012).

P. 190 HOUSING COSTS ARE INCREASING
Joint Center for Housing Studies of Harvard University, "Rental Market Stresses: Impacts of the Great Recession on Affordability and Multifamily Lending," July 2011, http://www.aecf.org/~/media/Pubs/Other/R/RentalMarketStressesImpactsoftheGreatRecession/1001550RentalMarketStresses.pdf.

P. 190 AFFORDABLE HOUSING STOCK IS DECLINING
Ibid.

P. 194 LAND VALUES INCREASE WITH INCREASED DEVELOPMENT CAPACITY
Helen F. Ladd, "Population Growth, Density and Costs of Providing Public Services," *Urban Studies* 29, no. 2, 1992, 273–95; Steven C. Bourassa, "Land Value Taxation and New Housing Development in Pittsburgh," *Growth and Change* 18, 1987, 44–56; and A. Sancton and B. Montgomery, "Municipal Government and Residential Land Development," in *The Changing Canadian Metropolis: A Public Policy Perspective,* ed. Frances Frisken (Berkeley: Institute of Government Studies Press, University of California, 1994).

P. 196 CONSTRUCTION COSTS PER UNIT DECREASE AS DENSITY INCREASES
John G. Ellis, "Explaining Residential Density," *Places* 16, no. 2, 2004, 34, http://www.escholarship.org/uc/item/2np5t9ct. This rule of thumb assumes that there is no need to construct a parking podium, which significantly increases high-density construction costs.

P. 198 THE MORTGAGE INTEREST DEDUCTION (MID) IS OUR LARGEST FEDERAL SUBSIDY

U.S. Department of Housing and Urban Development, IRS Statistics of Income Division, Individual Master File System, Dec. 2010, http://www.whitehouse.gov/sites/default/files/omb/budget/fy2013/assets/housing.pdf (all figures from FY2013, except MID [FY2009] and TBRA [FY2008]).

P. 202 THE MORTGAGE INTEREST DEDUCTION IS NOT NECESSARY TO PROMOTE HOMEOWNERSHIP
Steven C. Bourassa, Donald R. Haurin, Patric H. Hendershott, and Martin Hoesli, "Mortgage Interest Deductions and Homeownership: An International Survey" (working paper, Swiss Finance Institute, Feb. 9, 2012), http://dx.doi.org/10.2139/ssrn.2002865.

P. 202 GRADUALLY ELIMINATE THE MORTGAGE INTEREST DEDUCTION
See Congressional Budget Office, "Reducing the Deficit: Spending and Revenue Options," Mar. 2011, Revenues Option 4, 146, http://www.cbo.gov/sites/default/files/cbofiles/ftpdocs/120xx/doc12085/03-10-reducingthedeficit.pdf; Eric Toder, Margery Austin Turner, Katherine Lim, and Liza Getsinger, "Reforming the Mortgage Interest Deduction," Tax Policy Center: A Joint Report by Brookings and The Urban Institute, Apr. 2010, Table 10a: Distributional Effects of Eliminating, Scaling Back, or Reforming the Mortgage Interest Deduction, http://www.urban.org/uploadedpdf/412099-mortgage-deduction-reform.pdf. The Urban Institute estimates employing 2007 American Community Survey Public use microdata applied to data generated by the Tax Policy Center Microsimulation Model.

P. 204 THE MORTGAGE INTEREST DEDUCTION SUBSIDY BENEFITS THE WEALTHY
U.S. Department of Housing and Urban Development, IRS Statistics of Income Division, Individual Master File System.

P. 208 1937–74: DIRECT CONSTRUCTION OF GOVERNMENT-SUBSIDIZED PUBLIC HOUSING
Housing Act of 1937; 75th Congr., 1st sess., *Chapter 896, 50 Stat. 888* (Sept. 1, 1937); *Housing Act of 1949;* S, 1070, 81st Congr., 1st sess., Pub. L. 81–171 (July 15, 1949); John F. McDonald, "Public Housing Construction and the Cities: 1937–1967," *Urban Studies Research,* 2011; Roger Biles, "Public Housing and the Postwar Urban Renaissance, 1949–1973," in *From Tenements to the Taylor Homes,* ed. John

F. Bauman, Roger Biles, and Kristin M. Szylvian (University Park: Pennsylvania State University Press, 2000), 143–62.

P. 209 1974–86: GOVERNMENT-SUBSIDIZED PUBLIC HOUSING

Peter Marcuse, "Interpreting 'Public Housing' History," *Journal of Architectural and Planning Research* 12, no. 3, 1995, 240–58.

P. 210 1986–TODAY: HOUSING TAX CREDIT SYSTEM

Karen Franck and Michael Mostoller, "From Courts to Open Space to Streets: Changes in the Site Design of U.S. Public Housing," *Journal of Architectural and Planning Research* 3, no. 12, fall 1995, 186–220; and Michael Stegman, "The Role of Public Housing in a Revitalized National Housing Policy," in *Building Foundations: Housing and Federal Policy,* ed. Denise DiPasquale and Langley Carleton Keyes (Philadelphia: University of Pennsylvania Press, 1990), 333–64.

P. 212 MODULAR CONSTRUCTION: A POTENTIAL NEW MODEL FOR AFFORDABLE HOUSING

Robert Koch, "An Overview of Manufactured and Modular Approaches to Multi-Family Construction" (report by Fugleberg Koch Architects, Winter Park, Fla., 2007); John R. Rydall, "Modular Construction: Innovation, Flexibility and Adaptability by Design," *BioPharm International*, Oct. 1, 2004, http://www.biopharminternational.com/biopharm/article/articleDetail.jsp?id=132783; and Anthony Downs, ed., *Growth Management and Affordable Housing: Do They Conflict?* (Washington, D.C.: Brookings Institution, 2004).

P. 213 ATLANTIC YARDS: A HYPERDENSE, MODULAR, AND AFFORDABLE FUTURE

Courtesy of SHoP.

A COUNTRY OF CITIES: OF TRAINS, TOWERS, AND TREES

NOTES

1 The author sees no harm in small weekend homes as long as the government subsidies enumerated throughout the book, such as the mortgage interest deduction and cheap gas, do not fuel their proliferation.

2 Editorial, "Tax Reform Skirmish," *Wall Street Journal*, Aug. 21, 2012, sec. Review and Outlook, http://online.wsj.com/article/SB10000872396390443855804577603640127069620.html.

3 See Celia Chen of Moody's Analytics quoted in, "Despite Critics, Mortgage Interest Deduction Persists," *New York Times*, sec. Business, Nov. 8, 2011, http://travel.nytimes.com/2011/11/09/your-money/despite-critics-mortgage-interest-deduction-persists.html?pagewanted=all.

4 See Organization for Security and Co-operation and Development Programme for International Student Assessment, http://www.oecd.org/pisa/pisaproductspisa2009keyfindings.htm (accessed Sept. 25, 2012).

5 Melinda Fulmer, "Foreclosure Rates: 20 Cities with Highest Filings and State-by-state Rankings," *MSN Real Estate*, http://realestate.msn.com/article.aspx?cp-documentid=28364347 (accessed Dec. 12, 2012; figures are for the first quarter of 2011).

ILLUSTRATIONS

P. 218 THE FALL OF MAJESTIC
© Showtime/Photofest.

P. 219 THE FALL OF ROME
© New York Historical Society.

A COUNTRY OF CITIES: THE MANIFESTO

ILLUSTRATION

PP. 226–27 THE WHOLE ENCHILADA: SOURCES FOR THE INFRASTRUCTURE OF OPPORTUNITY FUND

See chapters 4, 5, and 6 for source material on each initiative.

INDEX

Italic page numbers refer to illustrations.

Gore, Al, 91, 93, 219
Great Recession, *71*, *88*, 110, 199, 203, 223
gross domestic product (GDP): and cities, 55,
  56, 167, 175; and high-rise buildings, *132*; and
  outstanding mortgage debt, *70*; and public
  infrastructure investment, *180–81*; and public
  policy, 218
happiness. *See* joy
health: and auto-based transit, 77, 105, *106*, 107,
  108; and cities, 42, 103–5, 107, 111, 117–18,
  205, 216; commuting distance and obesity
  prevalence, *106*; commuting distance and
  physical activity levels, *106*; costs of, 105,
  177, 178; and hyperdensity, 107, 127; and
  infrastructure, 155, 169; stress, 103, 107, 108;
  and suburban development, 103, 104; and
  sustainability, 77; and technology, 131; and
  walkability, 107, 118, 178, 216
high-rise buildings: financing costs, 199;
  and hyperdensity stereotypes, *126*; and
  infrastructure, 155; and neighborhoods, 135;
  and open-space uses, *22*; per-unit costs of,
  195, *196*; skyscrapers and GDP in Europe, *132*;
  and urbanism, 129, *130*, 131, 133; and urban
  planning, 143, 145
highway construction: funding for, 31, 91, 104,
  104, 161, 165, *168*, 169, 178, 215; and public
  policy, 38, 163
Hoehner, Christine, *106*
homeownership: and globalization, 61, 63;
  and mortgage interest deduction, *202*, 203,
  217; and public policy, 31, 33; and suburban
  development, 63, 195
home size vs. household size, *44–45*
Hong Kong, 69, *73*, *126*, 129, 131, 145
households: debt-to-income ratio of selected
  countries, *71*; household size vs. home size,
  44–45
housing market: affordable housing, 55, 57, 81,
  155, 187, *188*, 189, *190*, 191, 195, 197, 199, 203,
  205–6, *210*, *211*, *212*, *213*, 216, 217, 218; in
  cities, 57, 189, 195; collapse of, 33, 203, 216,
  219; and construction prices, 195, *196*, 197,
  199; and gentrification, 61, 189, 191; in global
  cities, *188*, 191; housing stock and population
  growth, *44–45*; increasing costs, *190*; and
  modular construction, 199, *212*, *213*; and
  mortgage interest deduction, 38, 39, *198*, 199,
  202, 203, *204*, 205; public housing, *186*, 187,
  189, 203, *208*, *209*; and public policy, 31, 55,
  57, 61, 63, 118, 165, 167, 203, *208*, 215, 216; real
  house prices, *71*; rental market, 39, 57; and

single-family homes, 27, 31, 33, 41, *70*, 109,
  199. *See also* mortgages
Howard, Ebenezer, Garden City, 27, *102*, 103
human capital theory, 55, 57, 61, 63
Hunt, Robert, *60*
hyperdensity: and construction costs per unit,
  195, *196*, 197; definition of, 21, 127; forms of,
  22, *130*; and health, 107, 127; and historic
  preservation, *150–51*; and infrastructure,
  77, 118, 127, 143, 147, *154*, 155, *156*, 157, 159,
  171, 175, 178, *183*; morphology of, 145, 147;
  and neighborhoods, 133, 135, *136*, 137, 143,
  147; and public policy, 118, 133, 135, *138*,
  143, 145, 147, 218; stereotypes of, *126*; and
  sustainability, 27, 42, 43, *100–101*, 117, 127; and
  transit, 21, 23, *28*, 41, 129, 135, *138*, 143, 145,
  147, 223; and urban development, 127, 137, 147,
  211, *213*, 216, 223; and urban planning, 127,
  130, 132–33, *138*, *142*, 143, *144*, 145, 147. *See
  also* cities
immigrants, 55, 215, 223
import replacement, 53, *54*
India, 41, 59, 61, 115
Indonesia, 59
Industrial Revolution, 29, 103, 187
infrastructure: and cities, 38, 39, 42, 61, 65, 77,
  95, 167, 169, *183*, 195, 216; direct and societal
  costs, *162*, 163, *164*, 165; financing for, 155,
  157, 159–60, 161, *166*, 167, *168*, 169, 171, *174*,
  177–78, *180–81*, 218, 219; and hyperdensity, 77,
  118, 127, 143, 147, *154*, 155, *156*, 157, 159, 171,
  175, 178, *183*; infrastructure of opportunity,
  155, *156*, 159, 161, 167, 169, 177, 178, 179, 216,
  218, 223, *226*; legacy of, *161*; per capita costs,
  182–83; and public-private partnerships,
  157, *158*, 159, 161, 178, 216, 218; and urban
  development, 42, 61, 65, 77, 117, 143, 157, 168
innovation, 55, *60*, 69
Internet, 59, 178, 223
ISTEA, 169
Jacobs, Jane: and activists fighting density, 133,
  161, 197; on economic advantages of cities, 53,
  55, 118, 216; on economic expansionism, *52*,
  53; on import replacement, 53, *54*; on urban
  planning, 147; on urban renewal, 65, 133
Japan, 129, *130*, 159, *159*, 175, 191
Jeffersonian grid, 40, *41*
Johnson, Lyndon B., 31, 187
joy: in automobile driving, 85, *85*; commuting
  and romance, 107–8, *108*; and commuting to
  work, *120–21*; and culture, 37, 111, 117, *122–23*;
  and images of urban living, 103, 105, 109;

Project directors: Diana Murphy and Vishaan Chakrabarti
Research: Omar Toro-Vaca
Diagrams: Ryan Lovett, SHoP Architects
Copy-editor: Anne Thompson
Design and production: Michael Bierut and Britt Cobb, Pentagram
Separations and printing: Oceanic Graphic International, Hong Kong

Library of Congress Cataloging-in-Publication Data is available upon request.
ISBN 978-1-935202-17-2

BOOKS

Metropolis Books
ARTBOOK | D.A.P.
155 Sixth Avenue, 2nd floor
New York, NY 10013
tel 212 627 1999
fax 212 627 9484
www.artbook.com
www.metropolisbooks.com